ADOPTION FANTASIES

FORMATIONS: ADOPTION, KINSHIP, AND CULTURE
Emily Hipchen and John McLeod, Series Editors

ADOPTION FANTASIES

THE FETISHIZATION OF ASIAN ADOPTEES
FROM GIRLHOOD TO WOMANHOOD

Kimberly D. McKee

THE OHIO STATE UNIVERSITY PRESS

COLUMBUS

Publication of this book was supported by Grand Valley State University.

Library of Congress Cataloging-in-Publication Data
Names: McKee, Kimberly (Kimberly D.), author.
Title: Adoption fantasies : the fetishization of Asian adoptees from girlhood to womanhood / Kimberly D. McKee.
Description: Columbus : The Ohio State University Press, 2023. | Series: Formations : adoption, kinship, and culture | Includes bibliographical references and index. | Summary: "Analyzes the media, cultural, and interpersonal mechanisms that contribute to the fetishization and commodification of adopted Asian American women's and girls' bodies through an examination of the 'nexus of objectification' at which they are situated in order to understand their racialized experiences and how they negotiate competing expectations of them as adoptees and hypersexualized Asian women"— Provided by publisher.
Identifiers: LCCN 2023028405 | ISBN 9780814215579 (hardback) | ISBN 9780814283318 (ebook)
Subjects: LCSH: Adoption in motion pictures. | Asian American women in motion pictures. | Objectification (Social psychology) in motion pictures. | LCGFT: Film criticism.
Classification: LCC PN1995.9.A28 M25 2023 | DDC 791.43/652208995—dc23/eng/20230824
LC record available at https://lccn.loc.gov/2023028405

Other identifiers: ISBN 9780814258927 (paperback)

Cover design by adam bohannon
Text composition by Stuart Rodriguez
Type set in Minion Pro

To Omma, if it were not for you and countless women like you, we would not be here today.

To Parker, you're always in my heart and my head. I love you.

CONTENTS

ACKNOWLEDGMENTS

To my fellow Asian adopted women and girls reading this book, I wrote this for us. I hope you can recognize parts of yourselves in my experiences shared within these pages and my analysis of how popular culture implicitly and explicitly played a role in our navigation of the world. I wrote this book for those adopted Asian women and girls who continue to confront their racialized identities as Asian Americans and seek opportunities to learn what it means to operate the world as an Asian American woman and girl when our adoptions were not designed to provide us those tools. I owe a debt of gratitude to those adoptees whom I have gotten to know since I first entered the adoptee community as an adult in 2007. Yet, I would be remiss if I did not acknowledge the ways negotiating my identity as an Asian adopted young woman came to the fore while an undergraduate and during time spent with Susan Seutter and others, including those I met through Sigma Psi Zeta Sorority, Inc.

This book began as a small nugget of conversations in graduate school, sparked by a conversation with bell hooks on one of her visits to the Women's, Gender, and Sexuality Studies Department at The Ohio State University. Conversations afterward with Denise A. Delgado, Kate Livingston, and Krista L. Benson alongside my postdoctoral fellowship at Grinnell College offered the opportunity for the initial kernel of this project to grow. Over the last decade, my explorations of the tenuous bonds of adoptive kinship in the case of Soon-Yi Previn, Woody Allen, and Mia Farrow resulted in a monograph that explores representations of Asian adopted women and girls from 1992 to 2015. I hold deep appreciation for the friendship of Adrienne A. Winans, who has seen my work in various stages since we were in graduate school. Krupal Amin, Douglas S. Ishii, Anne Mai Yee Jansen, Emily K. Yoon, and Laura A. Wright, thank you for keeping my spirits up as I wrote during my sabbatical in our virtual happy hours.

Many thanks to Emily Hipchen and John McLeod for their work with the Formations series and their feedback on the manuscript. To this end, thank you to Kristen Elias Rowley. Your support as an editor and belief in this project and my work has been incredible. Thank you to The Ohio State University Press team and to the manuscript readers. Their reports supported the manuscript's refinement. Thank you to David Martinez for indexing the book. I am appreciative of the keen editing eyes and assistance from anna genoese and Sai Isoke. Thank you to Annie Yi, whose attention to detail helped clarify and refine the manuscript. A special thanks to Jenn Kocsmiersky, whose digital illustration, *Rocket,* graces the cover of this book. When I first saw the image, I knew in my heart that it captures the complexities of identity and who we are as Asian adoptees.

The manuscript benefited from the support of colleagues at Grand Valley State University. Thank you to the Center for Scholarly and Creative Excellence for supporting this project with monies from the Book Publication Subvention Fund and funding from a Catalyst Grant for Research and Creative Activity and the mini-grant program. I am thankful for the support from Mark Schaub, Melanie Shell-Weiss, and Lynnette Keen. Thank you also to Amber Dierking and Mary Williford. I appreciate my friendships with Meghan Cai and Sarah Clark. Additional thanks to the Pew Faculty Teaching and Learning Center for organizing the pilot writing group program, where my writing benefited from feedback from Fred Antzcak and Julia Snider.

Parts of this book were published previously. Earlier versions of chapter 3 appeared in "'Let's Not Get Hysterical': Was He Even Her Father?," *Feminist Formations* 30, no. 2 (2018): 147–74, and "From Adoptee to Trespasser: The Asian Adoptee Woman as Oriental Fantasy," in *Adoption & Discourses of Multiculturalism: Europe, the Americas and the Pacific,* edited by Jenny Heijun Wills, Tobias Hübinette, and Indigo Willing, 150–73 (Ann Arbor: University of Michigan Press, 2020). An earlier version of chapter 5 appeared in "The Consumption of Adoption and Adoptees in American Middlebrow Culture," *Biography: An Interdisciplinary Quarterly* 42, no. 3 (2019): 669–92. I am appreciative of the editors' and external reviewers' comments on these essays.

I am thankful for the support of my Asian American studies colleagues and the Association for Asian American Studies. Participating in the first two iterations of the Asian American Feminist Writing Group that Judy Tzu-Chun Wu, Patricia P. Chu, and I helped organize in the beginning of the pandemic offered structure as I developed manuscript chapters. Feedback from Jonathan Hsy, Lynn Itagaki, and Erin O'Malley informed chapter 2. Thank you to Patricia P. Chu, Kavita Daiya, Tamara C. Ho, and Judy Tzu-Chun Wu, whose feedback on a grant proposal supported refining the manuscript's overall interventions. Conversations with those attending the American Studies Association Korea conference over the years have informed this project: Joseph Jeon, Eun Joo Kim, Daniel Y. Kim, Robert Ji-Song Ku, James Kyung-Jin Lee, and David Roh. Gratitude to Kyung-Sook Boo, Jinah Kim, Nadia Kim, S. Heijin Lee, Anita Mannur, and Valerie Soe, as ASAK served as an opportunity to make deeper connections. Many thanks to Yaejoon Kwon for organizing the writing group during my sabbatical year, bringing together Asian American studies colleagues. Writing with Catherine H. Nguyen during my sabbatical offered opportunities to hone my manuscript. Conversations with Mai-Linh Hong over the years also are so valued. Much gratitude to James Kyung-Jin Lee and Jennifer A. Ho for your invaluable feedback as readers for my book manuscript workshop. And thank you to Grace Gerloff for your work transcribing notes from that workshop and to those who offered additional comments: Kelly Condit-Shrestha, Erica Kanesaka, Jieun Lee, Krista Benson, Adrienne A. Winans, and Douglas S. Ishii.

To the critical adoption studies community, thank you to those who have come before and alongside who continue to do the work of interrogating adoption. This includes the scholarship of and conversations with Marianne Novy, Margaret Homans, Lori Askeland, Cynthia Callahan, Emily Hipchen, John McLeod, Marina Fedosik, Hosu Kim, and Eleana J. Kim. Thank you to the Alliance for the Study of Adoption and Culture and the International Korean Adoptee Associations' (IKAA) International Symposium on Korean Adoption Studies. I remain appreciative of the community of adoptee scholars of Korean and Asian adoption—Kim Park Nelson, Tobias Hübinette, JaeRan Kim, Lene Myong, Kimberly Langrehr, Elizabeth Raleigh, Sara Docan-Morgan, Kit Myers, Kelly Condit-Shrestha, Jenny Heijun Wills, Aeriel A. Ashlee, Kira A. Donnell, Boon Young Han, Ryan Gustafsson, Emily Bartz, and Ayla McCullough. The interdisciplinary collaboration with Jade H. Wexler, Jieyi Cai, Amelia Blankenau, Heewon Lee, Oh Myo Kim, Adam Y. J. Kim, and Richard M. Lee over the last year demonstrated how fruitful and rich the study of adoption is across (inter)disciplines. Dedicated writing time with Kit Myers and Kelly Condit-Shrestha offered opportunities to connect with friends, write, and discuss adoption while I plugged away at the manuscript during my sabbatical. Sun Yung Shin, Shannon Gibney, and Sarah Park Dahlen, thank you for being there as I finished the manuscript while on sabbatical and afterward. I say this with a teeny bit of irony; I am so grateful for this adoptee/ally community we've forged. Let's forever be adoptee killjoys.

Finally, this book has been informed and shaped by my family. Whether he realized it or not, conversations with my dad over the years, alongside experiences with my sisters and brothers, provided a lens through which to engage the possibilities and fault lines of adoption's multicultural promise. Dad and Abby, thank you for your support and being there, especially over the recent years. To Bob, for continuing to be a support as I wrote my manuscript over the last few years and for your willingness to always care for the little dude. To Bev, thank you for your support of my work. To my sisters and brothers, our experiences together influenced this manuscript in ways you may not realize. To my omma, the more that I visit, the more I realize how much I am you. To my appa, thank you. To my Korean siblings, you give me a glimpse into what life could have been. Thank you to Tasha for providing care to the little dude as I wrote this book. The completion of the manuscript owes many thanks to York, who's been supportive of my work for more than a decade. Ashley, Max, and Jaire, the best is yet to come. Parker, you've been a much greater gift than one could ever imagine.

The Limits of Multiculturalism

The Asian girl's position at the intersection of numer-
ous aestheticized and sentimentalized identities—the child,
the feminine, and the Oriental—illuminates the stakes of
equating people with aesthetic objects in ongoing histories of exclusion from immigration and citizenship.

—Erica Kanesaka[1]

For white racial formation, racial liberalism renewed white
privilege by constituting the white liberal American as
the most felicitous member of the US nation-state on the
grounds of his or her liberal antiracist disposition.

—Jodi Melamed[2]

The story according to my father is that my mother was worried no one would want to date me when I became a teenager. She was worried about racism. Clearly, she had no idea about the Asian fetish. He tells me this story more than once without pause except to tell me I am pretty. Pretty or not, as that is neither here nor there when thinking about sexual fetishes, it is an exchange that sticks with me because it captures how unaware my white adoptive parents were about what it means to raise an Asian American daughter. But mostly, I think about the moments of racialized, sexualized harassment I experienced while out with my parents, as well as my friends, and wonder if it even registered with my parents. I never asked. Instead, I ignored those moments or laughed girlishly and nervously in the face of street harassment because I did not know what else to do beyond recognizing that sometimes silence meant safety.

For many Asian adopted women and girls, being Asian (American) and adopted into white families often means we navigate these uncomfortable realities alone—in my case, as a teen surfing the internet in the late 1990s.[3] Reading about Asian Americans and Asian American activism occurring on the coasts as a high schooler provided an avenue to a world that I would learn to inhabit in my twenties. I can count only a handful of Korean adoptees in my high school that I was aware of in addition to another handful of South and Southeast Asian American students. Beyond that there were some other

Asian American classmates, but more often than not, there were just a few of us here and there. This is why when a white girl classmate decided to call me Janet after the Asian American woman in the 1998 Seattle edition of *The Real World* (1992–2017), I did not bat an eye nor recognize the microaggression.

Adoption Fantasies: The Fetishization of Asian Adoptees from Girlhood to Womanhood is a love letter to Asian adopted women and girls. It's designed to call attention to the ways we find ourselves situated at a nexus of objectification—as adoptees and as Asian American women—and how we negotiate competing notions of what adopted women and girls should be like based on sensationalist and fictional portrayals of adoption found in US popular culture from 1992 to 2015. This period is significant because adoption from mainland China reached its zenith, following the opening of China to international adoption in 1992, and the largest wave of adoptees from Korea (late 1970s and early 1980s) and Vietnam entered adulthood at the turn of the twenty-first century. The 1990s also marked a shift in the formation of Asian adoptee communities due to internet technologies. Email discussion groups and Yahoo! Groups paved the way for connections made on Facebook and other social media platforms. These digital, deterritorialized communities should be seen as an outgrowth of the connections forged within local adult adoptee organizations that emerged in the late 1980s and early 1990s. One of the longest-running Korean adoptee organizations was established in New York City in 1996, and the First International Gathering of Adult Korean Adoptees occurred in Washington, DC, in 1999. Such efforts represent some of the earliest iterations of Asian adoptees building intentional adult adoptee communities within the US. Pan-Asian adoptee-led coalitions often feature Asian adoptees from South Korea, Hong Kong, and Vietnam who came of age during this period.[4] And since 1999, children adopted from South Korea, Vietnam, and China represent 80 percent of all adoptions from Asian countries. As someone who came of age during this period, I intersperse personal anecdotes alongside my scholarly prose to underscore the value and significance of recognizing how the personal is political. To pretend I have never borne witness to racialized sexual harassment, racism, or other forms of violence would be erroneous and disingenuous.

In tracing the life cycle of the adopted Asian woman, from the rendering of our infant bodies in the white American imaginary to Asian American fantasies of adoption to what it means when adopted Asian girls and women find themselves hypersexualized in popular culture, *Adoption Fantasies* reveals the intricacies of the mundane. Racialized and gendered Orientalism renders cisgender, Asian adopted women and girls vulnerable to a mythic "Asian patriarchy." This vein of Orientalism is intimately connected to white American sensibilities of adoption—whereby the Asian adoptee is both a voiceless, innocent child worthy of rescue and a potential sexual threat in adulthood. Asian adoptee womanhood and girlhood is anchored in racialized and gendered heteronormative stereotypes of women of Asian descent. This is not to ignore the experiences of Asian adopted men and boys nor of gender nonbinary or transgender adoptees. I am aware of the different ways that Asian American men and LGTBQ+ Asian Americans encounter racialized and gendered stereotypes and have interrogated Asian American masculinity as it relates to adopted Asian, cisgender men elsewhere.[5] While some of the experiences of queer Asian Americans may overlap with the pernicious ways feminized tropes are written onto their bodies, that analysis falls outside the scope of this monograph.[6] *Adoption Fantasies* makes visible the nuances that shape the nexus of objectification experienced by Asian women and girls as a lens through which to consider the ethics of representation and the ramifications of how racialized and heteronormative gendered tropes become operationalized on a specific subset of adoptee experiences.

I attend to the invisible strings informing Asian adoptee women's and girls' interactions with consumers of this media—adoptive parents and families and strangers alike—and how those exchanges and that media influence our negotiations with the world. Prior to the turn of the twenty-first century, limited depictions of Asian adoptees existed in mainstream US popular culture outside of the sensationalist coverage of Woody Allen, Soon-Yi Previn, and Mia Farrow, jingoistic Korean War movies, and human-interest stories documenting adoptees' arrival in the US. Allen's affair with Farrow's adopted Korean daughter, Previn, and the public outcry at Farrow's discovery of nude Polaroid photographs of her daughter in Allen's apartment remains a cultural touchstone (see the 2021 HBO television miniseries *Allen v. Farrow*). Previn's racialized sexualization reverberated in the lives of Asian adopted teenagers coming-of-age and those in adulthood, which is why it serves as a case study in chapter 3.

WHOSE FANTASIES OF ADOPTION?

Adoption operates as what Mimi Thi Nguyen conceptualizes as a "gift of freedom," whereby adoptees exist in a cycle of indebtedness to their adoptive parents. While Nguyen deploys the concept in her discussion of refugees, this intervention builds on Douglas S. Ishii's discussion of transnational adoption in *Modern Family*. Ishii notes that Mitchell Tucker and Cameron Pritchett's adoption of Lily from Vietnam "gesture[s] to, but never name[s], the US war in Vietnam as a point of sympathy, suggesting that her white American parents, as per dominant discourses about transnational adoption, 'rescued' her from violence."[7] While Operation Babylift may have been a generation prior, the legacy of war and the emotional affective response produced by adopting children in times of crisis never fully disappears from the US cultural imaginary about adoption. To this end, as I have argued elsewhere, adoptees are not only unable to repay the costs associated with their adoptions; they also "encounter the weight of the financial expenses in combination with the incalculable load of savior narratives."[8]

Adoption's "success" is contingent on the gratitude of the adoptee. Their affective behavior is the linchpin upholding the valuation of adoption as the best option. Those who do not are adoptee killjoys—who disrupt the notion of adoption as a happy object—the recipient of "good feelings."[9] As killjoy, the adoptee fails to adhere to the fantasy of adoption as an act of humanitarian rescue; instead, the adoptee killjoy elucidates the failures of the adoption project, drawing attention to the ways adoption is violence and imbricated in broader systems of anti-Blackness, settler colonialism, militarism, and imperialism. Carefully articulating the adoptees' object status—for they embody adoption's "good feelings"—Kathryn Mariner writes,

> For prospective adoptive parents, the imagined future child is a happy object—both in the sense that the child is imagined to be happy to be adopted, happy to have new parents, but also in the sense that through the child as an end, the prospective parents imagine they will be made happy. . . . Complicating this affective portrait is the fact that prospective adoptive parents so often derive happiness from a(n) object/subject—the child—that at the same time may be a source of despair for a(n) expectant/birth mother. One's utopia is another's dystopia.[10]

While Mariner discusses domestic adoption, her assessment can easily be applied to transnational adoption, especially when accounting for those adoptive parents whose motivation for looking abroad is to ensure a wider gulf between adoptee and birth family.[11] The idea of adoption as "happiness" arises out of a savior narrative that presumes adoptees are moving into economically stable families from poor and working-class families and, in cases of international adoptions, moving from the developing world to the developed world.

This book elucidates white American and Asian American fantasies of adoption and their attachments to those stories. It grapples with how Asian adopted women and girls negotiate these fantasies and considers what it means when adoptees traffic in those tropes. *Adoption Fantasies* recognizes how transnational, transracial adoption is not just a tool of white supremacy to effectively manage racial difference in a palatable manner through rescue under the auspices of racial liberalism and multiculturalism. Discussions of the transnational in feminist studies and Asian American studies historically elide international adoption. Transnational feminist calls for reproductive justice must include adoption when investigating how the reliance on the reproductive labor of Black, Indigenous, and other women of color mirrors the shifts in other forms of labor. This includes recognizing adoption as a reproductive justice issue.[12] Such a lens requires white, Western feminism to confront its complicity in upholding adoption as an institution for family-making. What would it look like if white feminists took stock of their role in fetishizing Asian adoptees and other adoptees of color? Or, how can we consider our complicity in family separation policies including the family policing system, which implicitly upholds white supremacy, when we participate in domestic and transnational adoption? To be certain, I am calling attention to systems and patterns, not individual choices. This is important to highlight given the ways adoption strikes a hyperpersonal nerve and can derail conversations if adoptive parents fail to see how adoption is not solely about their choices but also about the system and institution of adoption and its associated assemblages.

Simultaneously, I pay attention to Asian American investments in adoption. Often adoptees are held in contrast to non-adopted Asian Americans in discussions of a presupposed Asian American "authentic" identity. There is an emphasis on a "lost" sense of Asian American identity—one rooted in being raised by biological Asian (American) parents, whereby adoptees must always be in a state of melancholy. Such a hyperdetermined definition of Asian America omits adoptees, as well as multiracial Asian individuals and interracial families, from the vast heterogeneity of an already heterogeneous community. Not to mention, such an approach ignores the histories of Asian Americans' intermarriage and interracial kinship formations since the arrival of Asians to the US.[13] At the same time, adoption is situated as a recuperative strategy to make sense of US militarism in Asia. This includes the construction of militarized humanitarianism, whereby in the case of Korean adoption, the US military is viewed as aiding and supporting Korean orphans and children in the post–Korean War period.[14] I also am attentive to the ways that adoption as an analytic is not readily apparent in Asian American studies. The field must reckon with how adoptees are "more than an outcome of war" and not solely a vehicle to interrogate presupposed notions of an authentic identity whereby adoptees often are seen to exist in a state of lack.[15] Deploying adoption as analytic results in the interrogation of imperialism, militarism, settler colonialism, and access to immigration and citizenship in order to reveal the inconsistencies and incongruities shaping the Asian American experience.

Adoption Fantasies weaves together transnational feminisms and Asian American studies with critical adoption studies as I explore what it means when white and Asian American fantasies of adoption fail to see adoptees fully. I engage with the legacies of that erasure and disavowal to elucidate what's at stake, as those fantasies have real implications in the lives of Asian adopted women and girls. This monograph extends conversations ignited in scholarship that situates Asian adoption within broader histories of transnational adoption, explores Asian adult adoptee communities, examines white adoptive parents' attitudes toward transnational Asian adoptions, and discusses Asian adoptees' identity development.[16] This interdisciplinary scholarship informs my interventions from exclusively documenting the system and institution of adoption and its attendant effects on members of the adoption constellation to questions related to representations of adoption in cultural form. The latter gestures toward the origins of adoption studies, as an interdisciplinary humanities field, within English literature.[17] In doing so, this monograph joins the scholarship interrogating the manifestation and representation of adoption in contemporary popular culture.[18]

I build on scholarship that acknowledges adoptees as objects fulfilling hetero- and homonormative desires for family and underscores the marketing of children for consumption by US adoption agencies, orphanages in sending countries, and others whereby they are reduced to tangible objects in the public eye.[19] This work reflects on how the transnational adoption industrial complex—the neocolonial, multimillion-dollar industry that commodifies children's bodies—reckons with the racial capitalist project that is adoption.[20] Asian adoptees' bodies are fetishized through a particular racialized and gendered lens. Our stories and experiences are packaged for public consumption in media. I pay careful attention to how white American and Asian American conceptualizations of adoption are invested in the commodification of adoptee affective performance. Whether it is the adopted child securing the reproductive futures of white families or adoptees as an apparatus to explore racial self-loathing or romanticized notions of return to their countries of origin, these fantasies are applied to adoptee bodies without regard to the actual lived experiences of adoptees themselves.

Adoptees must negotiate these fantasies and confront how fantasies of rescue or internalized racism become mapped onto their own understandings of adoption. As infants, they are fetishized as adoptable commodities. They are the objects of prospective adoptive parents' desire, and the specific "country fees" associated with transnational adoption costs are also attached to their bodies. As adults, their bodies become attached to legacies of Oriental fantasies and anti-Asian racism. These bodies are sites of contestation—objects onto which anxieties of reproductive futurity and fear of the Oriental Other are projected in childhood and adulthood, respectively. Orientalist views ascribing innate hypersexuality to Asian women can be traced to the earliest examples of sexualized racialization encountered by Asian immigrant women in the US and Canada. Real and imagined links between Asian women and sex work cement this sexualized racialization. After all, as Leslie Bow reminds us, "Their portrayal as having 'nothing else' but sexuality defined their relationship to the American state: the conditions under which Asian women were granted permission to immigrate, first as prostitutes, then as picture brides, war brides, and now mail-order brides, reflects the centrality of sexuality as a determiner of inclusion."[21] At the same time, adoption discourse rooted in humanitarian rescue and legacies of US militarism and imperialism influences Asian American perspectives of adoption. Together, these fantasies inform the messages of adoption consumed by adoptees, even as adoptees and demands of their affect are the ones commodified.

Media representations that engage white and Asian American adoption fantasies elide the inequities undergirding the transnational adoption industrial complex, overlook the abuses within adoptive families, and superficially render adoptees that fail to demonstrate gratitude as melancholic. An ethics of representation that challenges the ways fantasies of adoption circulate engenders more nuanced engagement with adoption and opens opportunities for multiple truths of adopted women and girls to circulate in the popular imaginary. Recognizing the power of representation and arguably cinema as part of a wider windows-and-mirrors discourse—here, applying the children's and youth literature terms broadly—facilitates a greater awareness of the media's framing of one's sense of self.[22]

"I DON'T SEE YOU AS ASIAN, I SEE YOU AS MY CHILD"[23]

Transracial domestic and transnational adoptions demonstrate the ways that racial liberalism, according to Jodi Melamed, "introduce[s] flexibility into white supremacist ascriptions of privilege."[24] The racial difference produced by transracial adoption left a profound mark on the American psyche. More than 200,000 Asian children have entered American families since the end of World War I.[25] In the case of adoptions from Asia, the access that adoptees had to the US drastically differed from the reception of other Asian immigrants, given anti-Asian immigration laws from the 1870s onward. Naturalization rights were only granted to all Asian ethnic groups in 1952 under the auspices of the Immigration and Naturalization Act.[26] The postwar adoptions of children from Japan and Korea and the adoptions of children from Hong Kong in the 1950s and 1960s signaled the liberalization of immigration restrictions.

The majority of these Asian children entered white families, and the first legally recognized transracial domestic adoption occurred in 1948 in Minnesota. Nonwhite children were in the care of white adoptive parents prior to the legalization of interracial marriage at the federal level, as the US Supreme Court decision in *Loving v. Virginia* (1967) occurred nearly twenty years after. The juxtaposition of transracial adoptive families and mixed-race or interracial families reveals the hypocrisies and contradictions at the core of US conceptualizations of race. Adopted children of color and Indigenous children were seen as distinct from other racial and ethnic minorities. And unlike children in interracial families, transracially adopted children with white adoptive parents are more likely to live in monoracial white communities. According to Rose Krieder and Elizabeth Raleigh, "foreign-born [Asian Pacific Islander] children who were transracially adopted live in counties with less diversity than the counties of the average white child with white parents."[27] The lack of racial diversity in the communities where Asian adoptees are raised is significant because these adoptions are touted as exemplars of the nation as a melting pot.

Asian adoptees' reflections expose the fallacy of racial liberalism and the speciousness of multiculturalism. Whether adoptive families are unable to recognize that Asian adopted women and girls are exoticized and hypersexualized unlike their white peers or unable to fully grasp what it means to be considered the perpetual foreigner in a country that you consider home, adoptive parents' inaction in response to racism underscores the limits and failures of multiculturalism. The ideals espoused by Americans concerning the racial progress made by transracial adoptive families downplays how, in practice, these families failed to prepare adoptees to negotiate a racist world. Anti-Blackness informed white adoptive parents' engagement in the transracial adoption of Asian children as they simultaneously crossed the color line without confronting their anti-Black racism.[28] This is not to say that mixed-race Black Asian children were not adopted; rather, it's to call attention to the fact that anti-Blackness informed both the adoption of these mixed-raced adoptees and their experiences growing up in the mid-twentieth century.[29] Accounts from mixed Black Korean adoptees document the racism they encountered both in Korea and the US, offering insight into how their multiraciality shaped their negotiation of identity in Black adoptive families.[30]

Transracial Black adoptees have also shared experiences of anti-Blackness within their families and/or communities.[31] Adoptive parents who desire to display their commitments to diversity fail to understand how inclusion and equity go hand in hand. Yet, more concerning are those parents who adopted without considering the ways racial difference would affect their children's experiences and those whose white adoptive parent fragility becomes exposed when racism and other microaggressions are brought to their attention.[32]

Adoptees of color, broadly, routinely discuss how their families fail(ed) to protect them from racism and racial microaggressions in their extended families and local communities. Those families evoke Cathy Park Hong's discussion of Claudia Rankine's speaker in *Citizen*. Hong writes, "She saw what she saw, she heard what she heard, but after her reality has been belittled so many times, she begins to doubt her very own senses. Such disfiguring of sense engenders the minor feelings of paranoia, shame, irritation, and melancholy."[33] That dissonance is reminiscent of when adoptees recount in formal and informal spaces the ways their adoptive parents, siblings, extended family members, and, sometimes, white partners, minimize or elide the racism they experience. This is particularly acute for those whose white loved ones fail to see how their support of white supremacist policies, institutions, and politicians or disregard of social justice movements clearly signal that they do not see them—the adoptee—as a person of color. Adoptees often experience a broad disconnect from many white family members, even those who claim to love the adoptee and their children.

Adoption's incorporation of multicultural rhetoric reflects what Mary Thomas identifies as *banal multiculturalism,* which describes the everydayness of multiculturalism that bears little nuance, context, or explanation. The celebration of difference is limited to tokenized moments of inclusivity with little to no acknowledgment of the historicity of racial injustice.[34] Kate Driscoll Derickson further argues that banal multiculturalism operates through the denial and silencing of past and present forms of racial inequality, flattening difference under the guise of achieved equality in neoliberal society.[35] This form of multiculturalism fuels the fetishization of Asian adoptable children and can be seen in adoptive families that create racially diverse households but fail to comprehend how race affects their adopted children's interactions with the world. Adoptive families must be cognizant of how multicultural rhetoric is deployed and reconstituted to shape the institutions their children engage with to ensure a critical discourse on race. Although I only examine multicultural efforts in the US, given the increase of far-right political movements in the Global North, adoptive families regardless of location must be attuned to how racial discourse functions in these increasingly hostile climates.[36]

Transnational, transracial adoption, as a tool for managing racial differ-ence, exemplifies the failures of the multicultural project. Melamed writes, "A language of multiculturalism consistently portrays acts of force required for neoliberal restructuring to be humanitarian: a benevolent multicultural invader (the United States, multinational troops, a multinational corporation) intervenes to save life, 'give' basic goods or jobs, and promote limited political freedoms."[37] The gift of freedom, or in this case the gift of adoption, is only possible through the benevolence of (white) Americans, even as US militarism and empire generate the circumstances leading to those adoptions in the first place. James Kyung-Jin Lee's discussion of multiculturalism is useful for exam-ining the conditions that adoptees are subject to within their families: "The flexibility of whiteness to embrace the colored few forces open a split between a cultural whiteness that demands a fascism of homogeneity and a structural whiteness that accepts ethnic difference into racial similarity, as long as order is maintained, the Law protected, and the dynamic map of urban triage unfet-tered."[38] The adoption by predominately white parents facilitates Asian adop-tees' ability to become subsumed under this whiteness.

Acceptance of what Frank Chin and Jeffrey Paul Chan term "racist love" maintains adoptees' approximate whiteness.[39] Amy Tang writes, "Whereas African Americans, Latinos, and Native Americans have been targets of overt racial hostility, Asian Americans have been the objects of 'racist love'—atti-tudes of admiration and acceptance that nonetheless work to uphold white supremacy by valorizing nonthreatening attributes like industriousness and docility."[40] At the same time, Bow employs the term to describe how fan-tasy operates as "a screen for projecting cultural and political desires" as she explores fetishism of objects racialized as Asian American.[41] Bow observes the way racist love "vacillates between the philic and phobic."[42] The Asian adoptee is positioned within this discourse as a fetishized object of affection, whereby they exist as "familiar yet exoticized and differentiated" within their families.[43] The kinship forged by adoption is thus contingent. If adoptees are too willful, they find themselves rendered outside the adoptive family and labeled "angry." When adoptees cease their performances of gratitude, it becomes evident that adoption as a multicultural project is a sham. The racist love of adoption secures the legibility of adoptees as infants, yet its capricious nature renders them outside those supposed "forever families."[44] To ensure their belong-ing, Asian adoptees, like Black, Indigenous, and other people of color, must "put [their] minor feelings aside to protect white feelings."[45] Vocalizing their first-person experiences with racism and xenophobia, among other forms of oppression, risks destabilizing the contingencies on which their inclusion in their white families is based—one rooted in the colorblind, racial liberal philosophies underpinning transracial adoptions. Naming these oppressions upends the pro-adoption rhetoric espoused by adoption professionals and adoptive parents alike that focuses on "love is enough."

Affect theory lends itself to interrogating the demands placed on adoptees to behave *in the right ways* to secure their places within their (white) adoptive families. The language of love is weaponized as a tool to control adoptee affect, reinforcing beliefs of adoption as a happy object. Acknowledging their affective labor is critical; thus, Hong's concept of *minor feelings* offers a lens to sift through the residue of popular culture and middlebrow conceptualizations of adoption the lives of Asian adopted women and girls.[46] Building on Sianne Ngai's *ugly feelings,* Hong writes, "Minor feelings are not generated from major change but from lack of change, in particular, structural racial and economic change. Rather than using racial trauma as a dramatic stage for individual *growth,* the literature of minor feelings explores the trauma of a racist capitalist system that keeps the individual *in place.*"[47] Registering these minor affects offers an opportunity to interrogate demands on adoptee affect to fulfill the notion of adoption as the happy object, or in some cases, reunion as the happy object, while also exploring avenues for "emotion [to] be recuperated for critical praxis."[48] When the concept of minor feelings is applied to adoption, the illusion of fairy-tale adoptions is interrupted, uncovering how fantasies of saving children and reproductive futurity are limited by the very racism that white adoptive parents refuse to acknowledge.

Minor feelings capture adoptees' affective behavior in the face of what Kit Myers terms the *violence of love*—"the 'unmarked' symbolic violence that occurs in the process of making the transnational/racial adoptive family legible and how this violence can be produced by statements and acts of love."[49] Recognizing the cognitive dissonance experienced by adoptees when adoption fails to achieve the fantasies it promises, I consider Hong's recognition that "minor feelings arise, for instance, upon hearing a slight, knowing it's racial, and being told, *Oh, that's all in your head.*"[50] In articulating the realities of adoption, the adoptee as killjoy reflects this dissonance, as Hong notes:

> Minor feelings are also the emotions we are accused of having when we decide to *be* difficult—in other words, when we decide to be honest. When minor feelings are finally externalized, they are interpreted as hostile, ungrateful, jealous, depressing, and belligerent, affects ascribed to racialized behavior that whites consider *out of line.* Our feelings are overreactions because our lived experiences of structural inequity are not commensurate with their deluded reality.[51]

US middlebrow attitudes toward adoption surveil adoptees' affective behaviors to ensure that their acceptance into the multicultural family is contingent on "appropriate" levels of gratitude. *Adoption Fantasies* engages the sensationalist and fictional portrayals of adoption that shape the narratives adoptees encounter in their everyday lives in an analysis of literature, media, and the US public's reception to characterizations of Asian adoptee women as sexualized predatory objects. Normative adoption discourse found within mainstream US middlebrow culture ensures that those who deviate from positivist adoption accounts risk expulsion from their families.[52] Consequently, the cultural impact of the artifacts discussed herein should not be discounted.

ORIENTALISM'S CONTRADICTIONS: THE LIMITS OF "CUTE"

To understand how racialization and sexualization of Asian womanhood shape Asian adopted girlhoods, I situate my analysis within an examination of racialized girlhood. Thomas notes, "In the context of American girlhood, the feminine is idealized through the priorities of capitalism and whiteness and not least of all heteronormativity."[53] Girls of color and women of color are thus always seen as deviating from the norm. They can never be pure because they never *were* pure based on traditional constructions of American girlhood and femininity, which locate "white, cisgender, able bodied, middle/upper class, heterosexual [girlhood] . . . in opposition to and dependent on nonnormative girlhoods—non-white, working class, disabled, immigrant, queer, gender nonconforming."[54] I am attentive to Jennifer A. Ho's discussion of Asian American adolescence in coming-of-age novels, for she recognizes the additional emotional labor undertaken by racialized young adults to navigate white society.[55] Vanita Reddy also traces the central role of racialized girlhood and young womanhood in "the making of national and diasporic public cultures" in her discussion of South Asian American adolescence.[56] Similar to Ho and Reddy, I am invested in grappling with the intersectional identities of Asian American girlhood and accounting for the reverberation of adoption in Asian adopted women and girls' experiences negotiating the nexus of objectification.

This uneven positioning of femininity and understanding of sexuality is important when accounting for the adultification of Black girls and its application to other girls of color. Often used to describe the way Black girls are seen as less innocent and more adultlike than their white peers of the same age, the concept of adultification is useful for locating how white girlhood is protected while girls of color find themselves rendered outside that protection.[57] Whereas teens of color experience adultification, white adolescence is extended, as people ages eighteen to twenty-two are uniquely framed in US popular culture as on the cusp of adulthood.[58] The pervasive nature of anti-Blackness makes the liminal status bestowed on white youth inaccessible to Black, Indigenous, and other youth of color.[59]

Yet situating girls of color as "older" or more adult in contrast to white girls is not a new phenomenon.[60] In the context of Asian American teenage girl sexuality, Sarah Projansky juxtaposes the Hollywood film roles of Anna May Wong and Mary Pickford in the early twentieth century. Projansky notes, "Anna May Wong's non-child roles (performed when she was sixteen and seventeen) stand in sharp contrast to Mary Pickford's perpetual-child roles (performed well into her adulthood). As many scholars have argued, women of color are defined culturally as always already and perpetually sexual and as adultlike even as very young children. Thus teenage Wong's sexualized adult roles should come as no surprise."[61] *Adoption Fantasies* therefore engages with the racialized constructions of girlhood that frame the adoption of Asian girls.[62]

I am attentive to the racialized processes that disciplined the bodies of Korean children in the wake of the Korean War because specific narratives took hold in popular culture concerning their rescue and care in ways that did not occur alongside the adoptions of mixed-race Japanese children and Chinese children from Hong Kong from the 1940s onward. These bodies negotiated gendered scripts, and in the case of Korean girls, their bodies found themselves subject to what SooJin Pate describes as the militaristic gaze, which "is produced by the spatial intimacy between Korean children and US soldiers."[63] In connecting the experiences of Korean women and girls, Pate notes, "The code of militarized prostitution creates a gaze and culture that constructs female orphans in the image of the *gijichon* women, thereby turning the child into an object of pleasure and desire."[64] Korean orphan girls functioned to "lift the morale and spirits of American GIs by performing similar roles as entertainer and hostess," roles that circulated within popular culture via photographs, newsreels, and the *Pacific Stars and Stripes*.[65] Susie Woo elucidates the interconnected nature between the manufacturing of Korean adoptees and the GI baby and war orphan and traces the adoptees' ties to figures of the Korean birth mother, sex worker, and military bride.[66] The Orientalist belief that constructs the West as progressive encourages the notion that adoption provides ostensibly better opportunities to adoptees, but it fails to engage the conditions surrounding the traffic in Asian women.[67] The US military condoned American GIs' sexual liaisons with women in Asia and worked with nations to ensure an endless supply of women.[68] Attending to these overlapping genealogies elucidates modern transnational adoption's roots in the commodification of Asian women's and girls' labor and accounts for adoption's relationship with the US empire.

The fetishization of Asian adoptee girlhood is rooted in the mobilization of a "cute" affect to facilitate the incorporation of some objects/subjects while excluding others. In this case, it is the inclusion of Asian girls alongside the expulsion of Asian women's sexual and reproductive labor as sex workers and/or birth mothers. The incorporation of cuteness into a spectrum of fetishization and sexualization also accounts for the operation of power in relationships. This understanding of cuteness draws on Lori Merish, who notes,

> For its spectators, cuteness stages the assimilation of the Other ("uncivilized" child and/or "freak") into middle-class familial and emotional structures. As a performance aesthetic, cuteness can serve to mediate the subject's relationship to ritualized forms of social control: it can constitute a highly theatrical way of enacting familial allegiance and *choosing* the compelled, displayed, and erotically objectified body.[69]

Being defined as cute facilitates the adoptee's admittance into the adoptive family. Without access to *being* cute, the adoptee would be rendered outside US norms of acceptance.[70] Yet cute objects face a double bind in that cuteness elicits delight and suspicion.[71] A particular violence comes with being cute. Hong writes, "Cute objects are feminine, defenseless, and diminutive things, provoking our maternal desires to hold and nuzzle them. . . . But they can also unlock our sadistic desires to master and violate them."[72] This tension makes plain the current of aggression that frames the boundaries of inclusion. In the case of adopted Asian girls, their entry into the US is predicated on their ability to affectively belong as sanitized and moldable children, whereas in adulthood this belonging is precariously reliant on affective behaviors that require them to sublimate willfulness. Yet it's not just Asian adoptees who encounter racialized and gendered stereotypes that shape their experiences navigating the world.[73] Rather, *Adoption Fantasies* demands an ethics of representation to empower adoptee truth-telling and foreground adoptee voices in lieu of adhering to fantasies of adoption that create undue harm in minimizing the minor feelings of Asian adopted women and girls.

Chapter 1 considers how their cute, silent affect fulfills heteronormative desires for reproductive futurity in an analysis of depictions of Asian adoption in *Sex and the City* (1998–2004) and *Modern Family* (2009–20), which coincided with the height of infant adoptions from China. When examined together, the shows' transracial, transnational adoptions operate as a mechanism for interrogating the failures and limits of US multiculturalism in an era that would soon give rise to what many white American progressives hoped would be a postracial moment following the 2008 election of Barack Obama. Interrogating the television shows' adoption storylines reveals how the myths of humanitarian rescue and the ease of international adoption in comparison to domestic adoption circulate in US popular culture. My analysis addresses the fetishization of the Asian infant and toddler body as commodities to fulfill the fictional prospective adoptive parents' goals and aspirations.

At the same time, Asian adopted infant and toddler bodies become sexualized as a result of *what they will become* in adulthood. Popular culture exposes the sexual tensions produced by Asian adoptee women and girls. As an infant, the Asian adoptee is fetishized as if she were an inanimate China doll, a repository for adoptive parents' racist love. She's seen as pliable and assimilable to white culture, the latter often touted to prospective adoptive parents in the twentieth century. As an adult, she becomes a fetishized, hypersexed Asian woman rendered outside the construction of family whereby she is the repository for a different type of racist love. Both constructions of these two figures—adopted Asian infant and adopted Asian woman—rely on subsuming her as an object to be enacted on, a recipient of a fantasy. These young girls enter adulthood in families who fail to understand how the adoptee woman's body cannot be seen outside of racialized and sexualized depictions of women of Asian descent.[74] The assumptions concerning their bodies continue to exist given the longevity of Orientalism, a persistent factor in how women of Asian descent are fashioned in the American imaginary. This reveals the continuum of Asian adoptee women's and girls' legibility, for they exist as both legitimate and illegitimate subjects due to their object status.

Chapter 2 explores what it means to navigate society without the protection of the adoptive family. I trace how the lone Asian adopted woman and teenage girl protagonists in *Sideways* (2004) and *Better Luck Tomorrow* (2002), respectively, negotiate representation as adoptees and Asian Americans through the performative nature of mundane activities related to claiming family and encounters with racialized and sexualized stereotypes of Asian womanhood. Unlike the other chapters in this monograph, chapter 2 is less about adoptee affective behaviors; it instead points to the ways adoptees encounter racialized sexualization via the male gaze. I explore how the adopted characters in both films serve as "erotic object[s] of the gaze" and what this gaze signifies when deployed by white adult men and Asian American teenage boys.[75] Michele White notes, "Classical Hollywood cinema and contemporary media forms often depict women as objects and make them available for the pleasurable and controlling look, or gaze, of spectators, who are coded as white heterosexual men. Critical scholarship on the gaze is concerned with how gendered, raced, eroticized, and controlled bodies become visible within media and other texts, and how individuals look at, identify with, and are constructed by visual representations."[76] Probing how the gaze renders adoptees as Asian American women and girls is central to considering the reverberations of Orientalist projections of hypersexuality in their everyday lives. I ruminate about the possibilities for agency or whether these characters are bound to the gaze, while acknowledging how that gaze functions in the everyday lives of adoptees. I discuss adoptee disclosures of fetishization and violence in writings published prior to the release of the films as well as how Asian adopted women reflect on the history of being subject to that gaze in light of anti-Asian violence. The desire for a fantasy of an available Asian woman alongside fantasies that overlook the ways Asian adopted women and girls experience racialized sexual harassment like their non-adopted counterparts rely on ignoring the voices of actual adopted people.

Attentive to the tensions produced as fantasies of adoption held by white adoptive mothers come up against hypersexualized fantasies of Asian American girlhood and womanhood, chapter 3 turns to what happens when the adoptee finds herself cast out of the adoptive family in an analysis of the Woody Allen, Soon-Yi Previn, and Mia Farrow scandal. I interrogate Farrow's failure to protect her daughter, Soon-Yi, and the ways Farrow weaponized notions of adoption as rescue, pathologizing Soon-Yi as the daughter of a Korean sex worker. I trace the ways the trope of the birth mother as sex worker connected to Farrow's creation of a narrative that pathologized Previn as a defective, intellectually disabled adoptee. In re-examining this high-profile scandal, I pay attention to how the circulation of images of Asian adopted women and girls in popular culture informs contemporary middlebrow understanding of adoption.

The final two chapters in *Adoption Fantasies* examine Asian American fantasies of adoption. Chapter 4 turns our attention to *Seoul Searching* (2015). Arriving three years before the premiere of *Crazy Rich Asians* (2018), *Seoul Searching*'s Netflix release filled a void in films marketed to middlebrow consumers with its all–Asian American cast. Even as other Asian American independent films were produced, limited releases or screenings at film festivals inform who has access to those productions. While it did not receive the same success as *Always Be My Maybe* (2019), another Netflix-released Asian American film featuring comedians Ali Wong and Randall Park, *Seoul Searching*'s release offered a viewing opportunity to many who would not otherwise see a film featuring an Asian American cast.

Seoul Searching explores the multicultural Korean diaspora in 1980s South Korea from the perspective of high-school-age Koreans returning from Europe and North America for a summer of identity exploration. The film's plot offers an opportunity to situate Korea's participation in transnational adoption against notions of anti-Blackness and the relationship between the overseas Korean diaspora, Koreans in Japan, and Koreans living in Korea. I discuss the film's birth family search-and-reunion subplot, situating this analysis within broader scholarship on the South Korean government's reincorporation of adoptees as overseas Koreans and adoptee reunion narratives in Korean media. *Seoul Searching* mediates adoptee affect in the creation of a fictional narrative that accounts for demands to adhere to a script that seeks to absolve the sending country for its adoption participation while also engaging the belief of reunion as the happy object.

In chapter 5, I turn to the ways that adoptees' Asian American fantasies of adoption inform how they mediate their narratives in film and memoir through an analysis of *Twinsters* (2015), a documentary charting the reunion of two Korean adoptee twins, Samantha Futerman and Anaïs Bordier, who were separated upon adoption and reunited in adulthood, as well as the film's companion memoir, *Separated @ Birth: A True Love Story of Twin Sisters Reunited* (2015). Futerman is one of the documentary's directors. The adult adoptee must be seen as cute and innocent to the complexities of the transnational adoption industrial complex in order to retain her status as the good adoptee. A cute affect ensures Futerman's and Bordier's access to their adoptive families. That is, *Twinsters* frames adoption in a playful and relatable narrative that does not explicitly critique the fraudulent and deceptive nature of transnational adoption. Such an uncritical examination of adoption secures one's place in the adoptive family and stands in contrast to documentaries following Asian adopted women such as *Crossing Chasms* (1998), *Searching for Go-Hyang* (1998), *First Person Plural* (2000), and *In the Matter of Cha Jung Hee* (2010).[77]

In many ways, Futerman and Bordier represent the real-life articulations of the palatable infant and toddler adoptees discussed in chapter 1. The chapter foregrounds adult adopted women's strategies to maintain access to their adoptive families and offers an opportunity to consider how the fictional reunion narrative proffered in *Seoul Searching* mirrors some of the ways adoptee affect finds itself mediated to ensure that Futerman and Bordier comport themselves to the expectations of viewers and readers. My analysis explores how demands for adoptee gratitude shape their public reception and interactions with the world, and it raises questions about the ways Asian American cultural producers are complicit in the adoption fantasies perpetuated by white American middlebrow culture.

I focus on *Twinsters* because of the autonomy and agency Futerman and Bordier have over their stories. This is different from Jennifer Fero in *Adopted* (2009) or even Heidi Bub in *Daughter from Danang* (2002). Both *Adopted* and *Daughter from Danang* present narratives of adoptees that show their intimate vulnerabilities, some of which raises questions for me about dissemination and the choices made during the editing process. What does it mean to have your innermost thoughts shared with the world that risks pathologizing adoptees as perpetually wounded and broken, or as ungrateful and uncaring for being reunited, in the case of Bub?[78] My analysis of *Twinsters* aims to attend for the ways Futerman and Bordier exerted control over their narrative and the story that was shared in both the documentary and the memoir.

In a different vein, I have been cautious and reluctant about analyzing documentaries featuring teenage or young protagonists that premiered between 1992 and 2015. For instance, *Calcutta Calling* (2004), a documentary short that follows three adopted teenage girls raised in Minnesota who participate in the 2003 Ties program in India, is directed by non-adopted Indian American Sasha Khoka, while *Somewhere Between* (2011) is directed by Linda Goldstein Knowlton, a white adoptive mother of a Chinese daughter. That film tells the story of four Chinese adopted teenage girls raised across the US—Berkeley, California; Newburyport, Massachusetts; Lansdale, Pennsylvania; and Nashville, Tennessee. It is important to recognize these documentaries for helping to tell adoption stories; however, it is incumbent on viewers to be critical of what stories are told, how they are told, and who is doing the telling. What does it mean to document the experiences of teenagers on the cusp of adulthood? What would the story told of me, or others like me, be if only rooted in one snippet of our teenage girlhoods? I also wonder what is mediated by editing and production and who is behind the camera. I grapple with these questions elsewhere as I interrogate the voice of my younger self to ruminate over what it means when adopted teen voices are preserved in a moment of time.[79] *Adoption Fantasies* raises questions about the ethics of representation—who produces and distributes these stories is significant to considering how mediation of adoptee narratives occurs.

Foregrounding content that operates outside of niche adoption communities, I turn toward popular cultural artifacts to critically engage how adoption is packaged, commodified, and sold as a social good. Interrogating how US society employs representations of adoption at the turn of the twenty-first century, following more than five decades of adoptions from Asia, illuminates the contradictions in representation and the fetishization of the bodies of Asian adopted women and girls, first, as cute adoptable objects and then as potential sexual threats. Adoptees have been communicating and articulating the gulf between adoption's fantasies and adoption's realities for some time. I recognize these knowledges from below and make adoptee epistemologies legible, so adoptees no longer find themselves silenced because their experience was only their experience and seen as invalid or, in the least, an anomaly.

Tracing the contours of adoption through popular culture deepens our collective awareness of the demands placed on Asian adopted women and girls as subjects and objects onto which are projected fantastical desires. At a time when being an Asian woman means grappling with a combination of misogyny and anti-Asian hate, and for many adoptees, a time when they are first grappling with white supremacy, *Adoption Fantasies* should be seen as a mediation on our inclusion and acceptance in the white American family and its contingency on our behavior fitting within particular scripts, even as nonnormative families become more visible and see increased representation. Not only are adoptees expected to fulfill notions of gratitude and gratefulness; adopted women and girls must also negotiate centuries-old notions of hyper-sexual Asian womanhood.

CHAPTER 1

The Fortune Cookie and the Mandarin

Adoption in Modern Family *and* Sex and the City

> Despite the fact that American narratives of transnational adoption are premised on notions of unconditional colorblind love and inclusion, adoptees occupy a precarious space in which their adoptive families and nation both continue to Otherize and disavow themselves from their children's Asian origins while also claiming and possessing the adoptees as fully and seamlessly belonging to them. Or, conversely, these adoption narratives ignore the racial difference within the adoptive family while simultaneously flaunting it to demonstrate the United States' dedication to anti-racism.
>
> —Kira A. Donnell[1]

It is no surprise that as transnational adoption became a normalized method of family formation, US popular culture took notice. Television viewers at the turn of the twenty-first century witnessed an increase in programming featuring adoption as an integral part of the storyline or of characters' personal development. This is not to say that adoption was previously absent in television or film. Rather, a new trope in the portrayal of adoption on the small screen emerged—the Asian adoptee as a fetishized commodity for consumption.[2] This coincided with the popularity of infant adoptions from China, as the nation opened its doors to international adoption in 1992, and the changes in diversity rhetoric from assimilationist narratives to celebration of multicultural difference within adoptive families.

My interest in the adoptee as commodity in this chapter rests in the packaging and repackaging of the infant and toddler body for the viewing audience and, arguably, adoptive parents. Fantasies of adoption—both real and imagined—rely on a docile, feminized Asian body that is pliable enough to align itself with US interests. Sentimentality has guided adoption and in turn framed the way it is understood in the public imaginary, with adoption stories in popular media relying on a shared notion of rescuing children from unworthy families and bringing them to worthy families. The object status of adoptees can be traced to Orientalism's feminization and infantilization of Asian bodies, which have influenced public perception of Asian children.

Limited representation of Asian Americans and Asians in popular culture, in combination with Orientalist understandings of "Asian" culture, inform adoptive parents' notions of adoptions from Asia. Their fetishization of infant adopted girls results in adoptees' status as objects. Here, we see the descriptors for Oriental dolls in the early to mid-twentieth century—"femininity, exoticness, delicateness, silence, and docility"—become applied to their bodies.[3] This interchangeability between child and doll demonstrates the way in which the labor ascribed to both objects became aligned to serve a similar mission. In her discussion of the racialization of orphans in the wake of the Korean War, SooJin Pate asserts,

> The Korean social orphan as Oriental doll performs similar labor as the Japanese friendship doll [from the interwar period] in that she serves to ease political tension and build friendly relations between the two countries. In this way, she continues the work of the *gijichon* women but in a more palatable, G-rated way. Her labor becomes more palatable precisely because of her fetishized commodification. The Korean orphan as Oriental doll is more successful at disguising her relationship to her production (namely US military intervention and neocolonialism) than the *gijichon* women, who by definition and name denote American military occupation—not only because she is a doll (an object presumed to be ahistorical) but also because her consumption is framed within the context of humanitarian rescue, kinship building, and caretaking. Thus, the Korean social orphan as Oriental doll facilitates the expansion of US empire through the guise of benevolent consumption/adoption by the American consumer/adoptive parent.[4]

I quote Pate at length because her discussion of Korean orphans lays the groundwork for how Asian adopted infant girls across time have been rendered in the US imaginary. White progressive notions of liberating adopted Asian girls are refracted through Orientalism. Integral to these fantasies is the belief that these are innocent children in need of rescue and care. These prospective adopted girls are situated outside the material conditions that engendered their ability to be adopted throughout the twentieth century. In writing about the Japanese friendship dolls described by Pate, Erica Kanesaka captures the constraints placed on Asian girlhood: "In contrast [to images of Asian women], the [Asian girl] maintained an aura of innocence that depended upon her imagined asexuality. . . . The Asian girl became a figure for imagining racial difference without racial conflict, a 'friendly' ethnic other gently enfolding whiteness into dreams of interracial harmony and world peace."[5] While Kanesaka examines Asian girlhoods in the early to mid-twentieth century, the same logics of Asian girls as innocent, feminized, and exotic persist into the twenty-first century.

The Asian adoptee as "friendly"—or more assimilable—facilitates their entry into the US as model minority adoptable subjects. Andrea Louie comments, "As a group, Asian adoptees are viewed as innately intelligent and fairly trouble free to raise. The fact that most adoptees from China are female reinforces the latter image. . . . Stereotypes about Chinese girls portray them as both desirable and docile, malleable and intelligent."[6] Echoing Louie's statement about the fetishization of Chinese girls, Leslie K. Wang writes, "A white adoptive mother I interviewed in California in 2004 stated that she and her female partner chose Chinese because they considered it 'a privilege to give a girl a chance.'"[7] This gendered stereotype operates in conjunction with parents' references to their children as "China dolls," whereby child and Chinese doll are conflated and seen as almost interchangeable. That comparison offers a modern-day analogy to Pate's analysis of Korean girls. Sara Dorow highlights this conflation in her discussion of adoptive parents' considerations of Chinese Barbie within adoptive parent digital spaces.[8] Similarly, Heather Jacobson notes adoptive mothers' fixation on Asian girls' racial features and the way Asian adoptees are seen as "cute and special."[9] And sometimes adoptive parents make these claims explicitly. Discussing adoptive parent reactions to their adoptions, Christine Ward Gailey discloses that an adoptive father of a Chinese daughter exclaimed, "There she was in the airport—our little China doll," while an adoptive mother recalled, "We chose Karen because she was so sweet and delicate and fair—like a porcelain doll."[10] Tracing the connections between mid-twentieth-century adoptions and the rise of adoptions from China reveals the longevity of these myths and how Orientalism found itself repackaged to promote the adoption of subsequent generations of children from Asia.

Being cute and doll-like ensures that the adoptee as object is enshrined in a particular set of innocence and unencumbered by histories of Asian women's purported linkages to sex work. This results in a particularly insidious form of racist love wrapped up within white racial liberalism. It's not just that adoption animates the adoption of Asian dolls as adopted Asian girls fulfill that role. Rather, it's bound to a violence that demands a pliable adoptee to enact one's fantasies of child behavior—both grateful and malleable to adoptive parent desires. Adoption was never about the adoptee. It was always about the fantasies of adoption held by white adoptive parents.

Consequently, under the auspices of multiculturalism, adoptive parents can celebrate the racial difference of their families and claim a progressive stance on issues of race, even as they lack a deeper grasp of how racial difference and cultural diversity function in their children's lives. This construction of multiculturalism permits superficial acknowledgment of racial difference that often dismisses racism and tokenizes diversity.[11] Such banal multiculturalism often takes form in white adoptive families' celebration of racial difference and creation of ethnically mixed households, even as they are unprepared for or resistant to grappling with the effects of societal racism directed toward their transracially adopted children.

I examine characters' discussions of infant adoption in season 4 and the adoption process in season 6 of *Sex and the City* (1998–2004) and the arrival and inclusion of an Asian infant in season 1 of *Modern Family* (2009–20) to interrogate the manifestation of banal multiculturalism in popular culture. In both shows, the adoptees' racial difference is simultaneously normalized and othered. An adoptee character is not featured in *Sex and the City* until one scene in the series finale's final episode that features newly adoptive parents, Harry Goldenblatt (Evan Handler) and Charlotte York Goldenblatt (Kristin Davis), cradling the child. A more formal introduction of the Chinese adopted daughter, Lily York Goldenblatt, occurs in the first *Sex and the City* (2008) film, with subsequent appearances in *Sex and the City 2* (2010) and in *And Just Like That* (2021–present).[12] *Modern Family* introduces Lily Tucker-Pritchett (Jaden and Ella Hiller) as Mitchell Pritchett (Jesse Tyler Ferguson) and Cameron Tucker (Eric Stonestreet) bring her home to the US from Vietnam.[13] While *Modern Family* ran for eleven seasons, I center my attention on season 1, during which the adopted girl as infant is rendered an object lacking agency and discussions of adoption are enacted on her body. It is in those exchanges where we can interrogate the limits of the multicultural family through the lens of queer liberalism, whereas in *Sex and the City*, we can observe racism and xenophobia operating as undercurrents in transracial, transnational adoptions.

HBO's *Sex and the City*, with its postfeminist investments, created a shared language among (white) women around an aspirational lifestyle that resulted in the popularity of cosmopolitans, Magnolia Bakery, Manolo Blahniks, and other tangible material goods that laid claim to a particular upper-middle-class, feminine, white woman aesthetic as it followed the lives of Carrie Bradshaw (Sarah Jessica Parker), Miranda Hobbs (Cynthia Nixon), Samantha Jones (Kim Cattrall), and Charlotte York (Kristin Davis). Based on Candace Bushnell's columns in the *Observer,* the show's postfeminism is similar to that in *Bridget Jones's Diary* (2001) as analyzed by Angela McRobbie—it is rooted within a desire to "gently chid[e] the feminist past, while also retrieving and reinstating some palatable elements, in this case sexual freedom, the right to drink, smoke, have fun in the city, and be economically independent."[14]

An undercurrent of classed heteronormativity is what drives the show. Before Sheryl Sandberg popularized the concept of "leaning in," this aspirational lifestyle created a framework of possibilities for white women to have it all.

While *Sex and the City* ushered in a new phase of representation for cisgender, heterosexual, white women on screen, *Modern Family* offered an opportunity for (white) nonnormative family formations as it followed the Tucker-Pritchett family; Claire and Phil Dunphy (Julie Bowen and Ty Burrell) and their three children, Haley, Alex, and Luke (Sarah Hyland, Ariel Winter, and Nolan Gould); and an older white man, Jay Pritchett (Ed O'Neill), his Latina second wife, Gloria Delgado-Pritchett (Sophia Vergara), and her Latino son, Manny Delgado (Rico Rodriguez). Despite the seemingly nontraditional families it featured, *Modern Family* engaged traditional family structures to make them legible.[15] The series attempted to find footing in a rapidly changing US but proves to be an anchor point to middlebrow, conservative culture in its reification of both hetero- and homonormativity. As Douglas S. Ishii points out, "difference appear[s] manageable."[16] In the contained spaces of the three different households, the fiery Latina and the Asian adoptee, among other racialized, minor characters, operate within safe storylines in a fictionalized world of racial microaggressions. *Modern Family* thus portrays the racist love framing transracial, transnational adoptions from Asia.

These two series demonstrate that the act of adoption is both object- and outcome-oriented. The child is the commodity. Both shows depict the fetishization and commodification of infant Asian girls wrapped up in a discourse of benevolent rescue. The writers of the shows have the characters say the silent parts out loud—the microaggressions, anxieties about genetic-relatedness, and the commodified nature of adoptees—to the middlebrow viewer. Acknowledging adoptive parents' anxieties concerning adoption helps tell the stories of Asian adopted girlhood, specifically those narratives concerning the racial undercurrents driving expectations of adoptee affect. In the following sections, I first situate the emergence of these shows within a broader history of the connections forged among adoptees and adoptive families in the last decade of the twentieth century. Locating these shows in broader narratives of adoption communities reveals the conditions in which the shows entered popular culture. I then turn to an analysis of adoption's inclusion within *Sex and the City* and *Modern Family*, underscoring their postfeminist and queer liberal sensibilities, respectively. The chapter closes with a brief discussion on how rhetoric of "the priceless child" shapes middlebrow perceptions of adoptees.[17] Even as *Modern Family* and the *Sex and the City* films and reboot, *And Just Like That*, incorporate their respective Lily characters as they grow up, my interest in them as infants stems from a commitment to capture the operationalization of racist love in the discourse surrounding the adoption of infants.

BIRTH-CULTURE PEDAGOGY AND
FINDING ADOPTEE VOICES

Adoptive parents' participation in banal multiculturalism can most notably be attributed to their engagement in what Heather Jacobson terms *culture keeping*, a method employed by adoptive parents to ensure that the adopted child has access to their birth culture. Culture keeping risks adoptive parents "co-opting or at least selectively drawing from cultures that are not entirely their own."[18] This type of adoptive-parent-driven embrace of diversity manifested in early heritage camps for internationally adopted children. Kit Myers discusses this curriculum as *birth-culture pedagogy*, which "employs an Orientalist version of culture that enables adoptive parents to be a substitute for missing birth parents, thereby foreclosing discussions about the latter and reifying narrow conceptualizations of identity, culture, and kinship."[19] Despite this, Myers recognizes that "the camps help create an environment where Asian American adoptees realize that they are not alone."[20] Adoptive parents' investments in sanitized aspects of their adopted child's culture under the auspices of love reveal the complexities of adoption and its limits. Culture keeping and birth-culture pedagogy exemplify the mediation of access to racial or ethnic identity by the adoptive parents, whereby their desires and needs supersede those of the adopted child.

Additionally, adoptive families coalesced with the emergence of organizations such as the Korean American Adoptee Adoptive Family Network (KAAN) and chapters of Families with Children from China.[21] KAAN began as a national organization serving Korean adoptees, adoptive parents, and their families in 1998. The organization has since evolved to serve transracial and transnational adoptees and their adoptive families and is currently led by an adult adopted woman, the third executive director and first nonwhite adoptive mother. Families with Children from China emerged in the late 1990s as adoptions from China increased.[22] It is important to recognize that even though adult adoptees may have been included in such spaces, historically their voices have not been valued or centered in meaningful and intentional ways.[23]

The emergence of these organizations that served both adoptive parents and adoptees coincided with the deterritorialization of the global adoptee community. The international Korean adoptee community first came together for the Gathering of the First Generation of Adult Korean Adoptees in 1999, the same year KAAN held their first national conference for adoptees, adoptive parents, and families. An earlier gathering of adoptees occurred in 1997 as part of the Global Korean Network meeting in Los Angeles; however, the 1999 gathering is broadly cited as the coalescing point for Korean adoptees' efforts in deterritorialized community building.[24] The second worldwide gathering of adult Korean adoptees occurred in Oslo, Norway, in 2001, and the third occurred in 2004 in Seoul, South Korea. Following that global event, International Korean Adoptee Associations (IKAA) was established and has sponsored subsequent triennial gatherings in Seoul since 2007. For additional context, the Filipino Adoptees Network was launched in 2005, and the first meetup of Hong Kong adoptees only occurred in 2010, with a subsequent gathering taking place in 2015.[25]

Throughout the late 1980s and 1990s, Korean adoptees had come together in Europe and North America as part of local adult adoptee organizations. It was those connections that facilitated the larger gatherings among Korean adult adoptees.[26] For example, AK Connection in Minneapolis, Minnesota, and Adult Korean Adoptees of Portland were founded in 2000 and 2001, respectively. Prior to the establishment of AK Connection, Minnesota Adopted Koreans operated in the 1990s, after forming in 1991, and holds the distinction of being the first formal adult adoptee organization in the US.[27] Two of the longest-running adult adoptee organizations in the US are New York City–based Also-Known-As and Asian Adult Adoptees of Washington, both founded in 1996. The Association of Korean Adoptees San Francisco and Boston Korean Adoptees formed in 1997 and 1998, respectively. By the end of the first decade of the twenty-first century, more adult adoptee organizations had been established, including Adoption Links, DC (2002), Korean Adoptees of Hawai'i (2006), and the Chicago-based KAtCH (2008). While this is not a comprehensive list, it is important to recognize that during the period with which *Adoption Fantasies* engages, adult adoptees actively formed connections with one another to build community and engender change. These organizations demonstrate how those Oriental dolls fetishized by adoptive parents do in fact grow up and become adults, parents, and even grandparents. Yet only in the second decade of the twenty-first century have adoptees garnered sustained media attention for sharing stories that deviate from positivist adoption accounts.[28] Nonetheless, adoptees still encounter pushback and resistance for disrupting narratives of adoption as an act of altruistic love.[29]

Given when *Sex and the City* and *Modern Family* began their forays into adoption, it should not be a surprise that these shows failed to recognize adoptees as autonomous adults. Transracial, transnational adult adoptee experiences were rarely taken seriously and adoptive parents' and social workers' perspectives dominated narratives of adoption. These shows perpetuated long-standing notions of adoptees as perpetual children and, because they situated adoptees as objects on which to enact desires, are an opportunity to critique adoption's racist love. The adopted girl infant and child serve as a vehicle to consider adoptive parents' anxieties over kinship and the limitations of their understandings of multicultural families.

THE BACKUP PLAN:
ADOPTION AS SECOND BEST

Sex and the City illustrates the intersection of consumer choice—that is, the adoptive parent's choice—and ostensible investment in racial liberalism as Charlotte York contemplates adoption while married to her first husband, Trey MacDougal (Kyle MacLachlan), in season 4, and her second husband, Harry Goldenblatt, in season 6. Infertility and white reproductive futurity intersect with contemplations of transnational as well as domestic adoption. *Reproductive futurity* calls attention to the notion that all humans want to biologically beget a child, and, in the case of adoptive families, reproductive futurism provides fertile ground for considering the performative aspects of their desire to adhere to heteronormative constructions of family.[30] While José Esteban Muñoz contends that children of color, and families of color broadly, are not included in reproductive futurism, I argue that because adoptees of color fulfill the familial desires of white adoptive parents, transracial and transnational adoptions fit within this rubric of reproduction, even as these families elide procreative sex.[31] Charlotte's reproductive journey reveals the societal assumptions concerning motherhood, which informs the commodification of the adoptee infant including the infant's affective labor to shore up the heteronormative household.

At the end of season 6, Charlotte's fertility struggles serve as her main storyline. Fiercely desiring motherhood, she attempts acupuncture to facilitate reproductive success. Her investment in reproductive futurism is made particularly acute in the season's first episode during a conversation with Harry. When raising the question of how he would react if she could not bear children, his response, "We'll adopt or something," does not satisfy Charlotte, who states, "But they wouldn't be your own."[32] Her emphasis on a child being "one's own" is firmly positioned as the only possibility, with adoption as a second or even avoidable option. This may seem surprising to viewers who remember Charlotte's infertility struggles in season 4 with Trey, during which she undergoes fertility treatments and contemplates adoption. This attachment to fecundity is inescapable because of how *mothering* ideology functions in US society.

My attention to the biological underpinnings of Charlotte's character development is not a desire to diminish the emotional, physical, and mental health toll of infertility and miscarriage on people, including the fictional Charlotte. Rather, my analysis is concerned with the lack of parity between adoption and biological reproduction. To understand how adoption is rendered as a lesser option, consider the reception of Charlotte's interest in adopting a "Mandarin" child in season 4 by her then mother-in-law, Bunny MacDougal (Frances Sternhagen), who tells her, "Now, I know some things can't be helped, but I must tell you right now, I don't enjoy Mandarin food and I don't enjoy a Mandarin child."[33] That comment immediately follows Bunny's matter-of-fact statement that "MacDougal is one of the oldest highland clans in existence. We have a very proud lineage. One I hope you and Trey will be able to perpetuate." The use of the word *Mandarin* to describe adopting from China is jarring, not the least because it evokes the outdated term *Celestial* to describe nineteenth-century Chinese immigrants as well as images of the small citrus fruit or the actor Ben Kingsley playing Trevor Slattery as "the Mandarin" in *Iron Man 3* (2013) and *Shang Chi and the Legend of the Ten Rings* (2021).

Sex and the City's lack of updated language to discuss China is unsurprising if one considers the show's lack of diversity and its racism, homophobia, and transphobia. The term *Mandarin* is a stand-in for *Oriental,* making the exchange with Bunny evidence of *Sex and the City*'s Orientalism. The show was never a bastion of progressivism. Even if one situates Bunny as representing an outdated or racist family member, Charlotte's silence at the racism epitomizes adoptive parents' failures to protect their adopted children of color from racism. This type of representation and the lack of correction of the use of the term *Mandarin* reinforces stereotypes of Asian foreignness.

I contend that Bunny's judgment strikes a chord with Charlotte even as she feigns shock at her mother-in-law's staunch anti-transnational, anti-transracial adoption viewpoint. Bunny's stance, in combination with Charlotte's offhand remark to Trey that "the good news is, since we're both dark haired, people won't immediately know that she's not ours," seems to reveal an interest in "passing" as a biologically related family if they adopt.[34] It may be laughable to think about the mutability of race or that someone of Chinese descent could pass as white; however, this investment in "matching" has historically framed domestic adoptions.

To understand Charlotte's adoption hesitancy, it is important to acknowledge the way biological relatedness functions within the ideologies of mothering that frame the experiences of white, upper-middle-class women. Susan Douglas and Meredith Michaels describe the "new momism" as "the insistence that no woman is truly complete or fulfilled unless she has kids, that women remain the best primary caretakers of children, and that to be a remotely decent mother, a woman has to devote her entire physical, psychological, emotional, and intellectual being, 24/7, to her children," and as "it both draws from and repudiates feminism," they assert, it is merely a dressed-up version of the feminist mystique that provides the illusory notion that women have choices.[35] If *Sex and the City* is located within a postfeminist moment, then this attachment to biological reproduction by way of new momism squares with Charlotte's character development. To become a mother is the logical next step in her identity progression.

As Charlotte negotiates her feelings toward motherhood in season 6, viewers learn that Harry is considering adoption. In episode 16, "Out of the Frying Pan," he remarks that he is researching adoption as a "backup." Harry notes, "Maybe we put ourselves on some lists. By the time we know what's what, we'll have some choices. What do you think?" Charlotte responds, "That seems like the right thing to do." Patting Harry on the shoulder, she exits the room. While individuals who have used adoption as a method of family formation may initially take offense at Harry's comment that adoption is a backup, I suggest he uses the term in light of his wife's recent miscarriage. Pregnancy loss is not routinely depicted on screen, making this moment of tender care touching. Perhaps in off-screen moments, Charlotte revealed to Harry the emotional toll of her infertility experience with her first husband. In season 4, she refers to herself as "reproductively challenged" and "barren," raising questions about the emotional effects surrounding her ability to become pregnant. Thus, I am not attempting to minimize the toll of infertility, fertility treatments, or miscarriage; rather, I seek to discuss the depiction of adoption in *Sex and the City*. I read this scene as an attempt by Harry to normalize adoption as the best fit for his family.

Charlotte's inability to grapple with adoption is confirmed in the following scene. Sitting alone on a Central Park bench, she considers the recent exchange with her husband and bursts into tears over her infertility. This anxiety is reinforced in episode 18, "Splat!," when Charlotte learns that her new King Charles spaniel, Elizabeth Taylor, is pregnant and calls her future offspring a "trampy, pedigreed family." Transferring feelings about infertility onto a dog may seem comical; however, this type of resentment may also be found between women. We see a version of this in the dynamic between Charlotte and Miranda in season 4, when Miranda unexpectedly finds herself with child after a one-night stand with Steve Brady (David Eigenberg).[36] Charlotte's reaction to both human and canine pregnancies offers an opportunity to examine societal awareness of infertility and the (limited) support offered to women. How does society perceive infertility alongside its focus on biological reproduction and monetary support for assisted reproductive technologies? When it aired, *Sex and the City* provided one of the few nuanced portrayals that confronted women's reproductive lives, including discussions of abortion.

At the end of the episode, Charlotte is overjoyed at the birth of Elizabeth Taylor's three puppies, and it is hard to imagine her accepting adoption, even though in season 4 she had placed herself and Trey on a waiting list for a "Mandarin" baby. Charlotte's response, then, to Harry's suggestion to consider adoption, in combination with her drive to biologically reproduce, counters any notion that adoption is a viable alternative for forming a family. And yet, by episode 19, "An American Girl in Paris (Part Une)," viewers witness a shift in the Goldenblatt household. Reviewing paperwork at the dining room table, the couple discuss their adoption applications:

> CHARLOTTE: Oh, where is the recommendation from your friend, the judge?
> HARRY: Hmm . . . here.
> CHARLOTTE: And Carrie left hers at home, so I can pick it up when I go get her mail later in the week.
> HARRY: It's amazing that with all the unwanted children, we have to do all this.
> CHARLOTTE: Well, this private adoption is a very competitive market.
> HARRY: More competitive than China. We've got like a year's wait on that list.
> CHARLOTTE: Honey, God is gonna send us a baby. From somewhere. And it's just our job to file all the papers and be as aggressive as we can to the point of obnoxious.

In this exchange, it is clear that Harry and Charlotte, like many prospective adoptive parents, inherited the widespread belief that there were more than 140 million orphans in the world by the 2010s.[37] Yet, as Kathryn Joyce points out, "Only about 10 percent . . . are 'double orphans'—children who have lost both parents—but many of them likely live with their extended family."[38] This also does not take into account those families who use orphanages as a means of temporary care because of economic precarity and children who may be considered vulnerable for other reasons.[39] Nevertheless, the circulation of this figure in society upholds the underlying belief that adoption agencies create roadblocks of bureaucracy despite the need for "good" homes like the fictional Goldenblatts' Upper East Side family. This fictionalized storyline mimics reality in that prospective adoptive parents frequently bemoan long wait times or delays with little regard for how these changes are designed to protect the rights of birth families and adoptable children, including considerations for family preservation.

Adoptive parents' desires are central to the workings of adoption agencies since they are, as Elizabeth Raleigh notes, "the paying customer."[40] Overlooking adoption's function as a market discounts the ways children are seen as commodities and adoptive parents as buying a particular good. This may be an unpopular opinion; however, the dynamics surrounding the "gift of adoption" as discussed in the introduction reveal the sometimes competing and contradictory interests of waiting prospective adoptive parents and children in need of families.[41] Raleigh's work foregrounds an important consideration regarding those interested in private adoptions: "Considering that parents pursuing private adoption are willing to wait years for a baby, while 23,000 children 'age out' of the US foster care system every year without being adopted, it is clear that foster care is not seen by many as a desirable market alternative."[42] Raleigh reflects on the fine line that adoption agencies maintain between explicitly centering adoptive parent needs and framing adoption as being about child welfare. Cloaking the consumerism within adoption, the "adoption winnowing process [is rebranded] in terms of the euphemism of finding the right fit."[43] Raleigh's assessment echoes Christine Ward Gailey's: "The neoliberal emphasis on choice, for those who can afford it, is unvarnished in these promotional materials, although the language used is often that of altruism. Implicitly, the language of choice presumes that the goal is a child as much like the adopters as possible."[44] This emphasis on fit conceals adoptive parents' consumeristic desires as a method of selection that "implies an innocuous individualized preference."[45]

The adoptive parents' perspective of adoption permeates the final episode of the series, "An American Girl in Paris (Part Deux)." Charlotte and Harry are on the cusp of becoming parents. Viewers learn that an interview with potential birth parents has been scheduled as Charlotte shops for the "perfect outfit" in Chanel. At the time of the visit, the social class differences between the adoptive and birth parents are firmly cemented, with the white birth parents speaking in class- and region-inflected English that highlights their lower social standing and potential lack of education. The birth father's unfamiliarity with lox serves as a visible marker of difference and comedic fodder for the presumably well-educated, affluent viewer. The assumed parental deficiencies of the birth parents are exacerbated as Charlotte explains how the child will have access to "the best grammar schools in Manhattan." This coded comment signals that the child will gain entry to elite private schools and not enter the New York City public school system. Viewers are also left visual cues to determine that these birth parents should not be the child's parents. The deficiencies of the birth parents are reinforced when we learn that they had intended to keep the child and only met with the Goldenblatt family because "[they'd] never seen New York."

The interactions between the birth parents and prospective adoptive parents are meant to illustrate a clear comparison between the two women—birth mother and prospective adoptive mother. This postfeminist show and specifically that scene underscore what McRobbie wrote concerning "successful" decision-making: "The individual is compelled to be the kind of subject who can make the right choices. By these means new lines and demarcations are drawn between those subjects who are judged responsive to the regime of personal responsibility, and those who fail miserably."[46] Charlotte's pedigree falls within this postfeminist invitation as well as under the tenets of new momism and Sharon Hay's articulation of intensive mothering—"a gendered model that advises mothers to expend a tremendous amount of time, energy, and money in raising their children."[47] Throughout the series, Charlotte's tendency toward mothering, including giving advice to an expectant Miranda in season 4, demonstrates her keen interest in investing her time in child-rearing. Charlotte would be able to engage in intensive mothering, which, according to Hays, requires the following: "A mother must put her child's needs above her own. A mother must recognize and conscientiously respond to all the child's needs and desires, and to every stage of the child's emotional and intellectual development."[48] Intensive mothering is seen as "the *proper* approach to the raising of a child by the majority of mothers" and "the dominant ideology of socially appropriate child rearing in the contemporary United States."[49] The birth mother operates with an inherent inability to fulfill those particular needs by virtue of her lower-class status, regardless of the fact that both women are white.

After the devastating blow of not becoming parents to the white, newborn infant, Harry and Charlotte are offered the second-best, or at least most comparable, alternative—an infant from Asia. This is not to minimize one form of adoption over another. The scene highlights the clear hierarchy that exists within adoption circles. It is common knowledge within the adoption community that domestically adopted, Black infants and children cost markedly less than their white counterparts.[50] In the context of transnational adoption, the model minority myth shapes prospective adoptive parents' desires to adopt from East Asia. Intersecting with these gendered and raced constructions of Asian adoptee girlhood is the belief that Asian Americans, especially those of East Asian descent, are honorary whites.[51]

As a result of the nature of adoption economics, these adoptive parents find that demand outweighs supply in adoptions from China and Korea, giving rise to higher fees and longer wait times. Regarding girls from China,

Wang notes that their "overwhelming popularity goes far beyond issues of supply and demand, as Western applications have vastly outweighed the number of available children for years."[52] A Google search for "Chinese adoption wait times" or any variation populates multiple websites discussing the wait times between completion of the adoption dossier, referral of a child, and when the child can be adopted from China to the US. For the purposes of television, these wait times do not translate to the fictional world of Harry and Charlotte. At the end of the final episode, Harry announces to Charlotte that they will receive a baby from China in six months.[53] The couple, unlike adoptive parents in real life, do not have to travel to China to meet their newborn. With no mention of this part of the adoption process, the writers of *Sex and the City* neatly package international adoption as a mail-order process. One can easily see the conflation between adoption from China with adoption from Korea, whose program historically relied on chaperones to shuttle adoptees from South Korea to the West. The made-for-television adoption storyline only strengthens the Goldenblatts' ability to assert a particular postfeminist, multicultural ethos, whereby a Jewish family welcomes a Chinese daughter home under the celebrated umbrella of liberal multiculturalism.

THE FAMILY AS A SITE OF
RACIAL MICROAGGRESSIONS

Although postmodern families have existed throughout history, families who depart from the heterosexual nuclear household, built on the male breadwinner and female housewife model, only gained legibility in popular culture at the turn of the twenty-first century.[54] Homonormativity renders these families part of the postmodern ideal through the deployment of queer liberalism. David L. Eng notes, "Queer liberalism marks a particular confluence of political and economic conditions that form the basis of liberal inclusion, rights, and recognition for particular gay and lesbian US citizen-subjects willing and able to comply with its normative mandates."[55] Transracial adoptive queer families gain access to the polity by virtue of their willingness to comply with "normative dictates of bourgeois intimacy."[56] Here, I am interested in how single queer parents or partnered queer parents, such as Cameron and Mitchell from *Modern Family,* adopt and align with homonormative constructions of family. This is not to elide LGBTQ+ individuals who use reproductive technologies to biologically reproduce a child; rather, in the desire to parent, the Tucker-Pritchett household demonstrates homonormative conformity to ideals of family. Their reproductive futuristic desire to propagate relies on gendered tropes of labor, whereby Cameron is coded as more effeminate and nurturing than his spouse. Investments in whiteness and a certain kind of family manifest within this adoptive family much like they do within hetero-sexual couples adopting children across racial lines.

The adopted Vietnamese child, Lily, becomes a catch-all for Asian differ-ence. So too, does her country of origin. As Ishii notes, "The Pritchetts are founded on a legal impossibility, as Vietnam does not allow same-sex couples to adopt."[57] By overlooking the legal fictions necessary to render their adoptive family possible, *Modern Family* is complicit in reducing adoption to ahistori-cal narratives designed to bring joy to white consumers—those viewing the series as well as (prospective) white adoptive parents who see themselves rep-resented in the Tucker-Pritchett family. Queer liberalism facilitates the inclu-sion of the Asian adoptee in the homonormative family. On this point, Eng writes, "I would suggest that the possession of a child, whether biological or adopted, has today become the sign of guarantee both for family and for full and robust citizenship, for being a fully realized political, economic, and social subject in American life."[58] Eng's analysis of a 2000 John Hancock commercial featuring the adoption of a Chinese adoptee is useful in locating Lily's role in the Tucker-Pritchett household. In his discussion of the commercial, Eng notes, "Through her adoption and crossing over an invisible national bound-ary, a needy Chinese object is miraculously transformed into an individuated and treasured US subject, one worthy of investment—that is, economic pro-tection (capital accumulation), political rights (citizenship), and social rec-ognition (family)."[59] Even as Lily is from Vietnam, because of the conflation of all things Asian with her body and experience, we can see how the Asian adoptee writ large finds herself incorporated as a future American within her home. Unlike her Asian parents, and arguably other Asian Americans, the Asian adoptee is believed to be able to actualize US belonging, even though we know the perpetual foreigner myth and anti-Asian racism preclude this from being true.

The *Modern Family* series premiere propelled viewers into the initial first days of the life of Lily Tucker-Pritchett and her fathers.[60] Viewers first encounter the newly formed family on a plane bound from Vietnam to the US. Mitchell announces to his fellow passengers, "We just adopted her from Vietnam and we're bringing her home."[61] The scene captures what many adult adoptees realize: the plane is the site where the adoptee experiences (re)birth—becoming an American—or in Lily's case going "home."[62] Erasing her status as a Vietnamese subject, Mitchell acknowledges the *social death* Lily must endure to become a member of the Tucker-Pritchett family narra-tive. This social death involves the severing of ties with her birth family and country of origin to facilitate her (re)birth as a Western subject.[63] Yet even as he recognizes that she no longer and will never be a Vietnamese subject by virtue of her (re)birth as an American, Mitchell remains unaware of the long-term implications of this logic. He displays ignorance in his inability to discuss or even recognize the loss associated with adoption. Furthermore, Mitchell demonstrates his adherence to the tired trope of adoption as rescue, noting, "This baby would have grown up in a crowded orphanage if it wasn't for [adoption]."[64] By positioning adoption as better than orphanage care and rendering orphanages as unloving, decrepit entities, Mitchell inadvertently promotes the Christian notion of adoption that can be traced back to early international adoptions from the mid-twentieth century and the work of organizations such as World Vision and the Holt Adoption Program (now Holt International Children's Services).[65]

At the outset of season 1, it becomes clear that members of the Tucker-Pritchett extended family may not know how to grapple with the newest, non-white family member. Upon hearing his niece's first name, Phil Dunphy says, "Lily . . . isn't that going to be a little hard for her to say?"[66] His wife, Claire, interjects before Phil can comment further. Given that viewers have been conditioned to expect accented English by Asian and Asian American characters, it is no surprise that the writers included this classic racist microaggression in the first episode. Since Lily cannot mispronounce her name herself, as she is an infant and soon-to-be native English speaker, the writers rely on the audience's grasp of racial dynamics in the US and the perpetual foreigner myth. Rendering his niece an inscrutable Oriental, Phil precludes Lily's fully becoming American. This stands in juxtaposition to Eng's assessment of the Hancock commercial yet also reveals Asian adoptees' tenuous belonging within the US. They are simultaneously accepted and foreign.

The Orientalization of Lily is similar to the repeated use of *Mandarin* to describe the potential Asian adopted child of Charlotte and Trey in season 4 of *Sex and the City*. Here, I borrow Aki Uchida's concept of Orientalization to account for the objectification process experienced by Asian women in the US.[67] Uchida writes, "The discourse serves important functions to perpetuate not only the image itself but also the message around the image, which also functions to Orientalize Asian women, either directly or indirectly. The signifier Oriental Woman directly affects the signified Asian woman, in terms of her life experience in the United States."[68] Although Uchida discusses adult women, it's important to recognize the ways such Orientalism does not just occur when one is of age and to consider the spectrum of Orientalization that occurs from infancy to adulthood. More importantly, perhaps what ties the two shows together beyond their Orientalism is the screenwriters' use of the name "Lily" and the name's popularity among Chinese adoptive parents for their daughters. Evoking images of water lilies and Asiatic lilies, the name Lily gestures toward an elusive Asian femininity and long-standing Orientalism. It also is reminiscent of Asian American woman writer Edith Maude Eaton's pen name—Sui Sin Far, which means "water lily" in Cantonese.

Adult adoptees routinely recall multiple examples of their adoptive nuclear and extended families perpetuating Orientalist stereotypes and contributing to the racial microaggressions they encounter in their daily lives. Joining these voices is scholarship that documents adoptive parents' racialized assumptions concerning Asian countries and their adopted offspring. Whether it is through fetishizing Asian culture via an alleged celebration of multiculturalism or by deploying terms such as *China doll* to describe their newly adopted daughters, as discussed earlier in this chapter, adoptive parents are complicit in the commodification of adoptees as consumable Orientalist products to purchase and flaunt as examples of "their commitment to diversity." Adopted persons and researchers were aware of these microaggressions within the family, but it was not until season 1 of *Modern Family* that this racist love was aired unabashedly on prime-time television.

While *Sex and the City* captures the anxieties of adoptive parents during the pre-adoption phase, *Modern Family* season 1 demonstrated the "they're just joking" discourse operating within adoptive families. This statement illustrates the way adoptees' vocalizations of racism are disregarded, rendering them as people who "can't take a joke." *Modern Family* capitalizes on this discourse, using racial difference as a comedic prop, whether it is Jay Pritchett simultaneously claiming his newest granddaughter while calling her a food— "She's one of us now. Let me see that little potsticker"—or Lily practicing tai chi with Mitchell's mother, DeDe Pritchett (Shelley Long).[69] Jay returns to his food metaphors in episode 12, asking Lily, "How's my little fortune cookie?"[70] His use of "fortune cookie" as a descriptor construes Lily as a static object, one that is a Western signifier of Chineseness even though its origins are thought to lie in Japan. Here, Jay flattens the differences between Asian ethnic groups with the "all Asians look the same" outlook. Many Asian countries have versions of the potsticker (e.g., dumpling, *mandu*, *gyoza*), but to believe that the Pritchetts recognize the differences would be a leap given the various racist and racialized interactions the family has with their newest member. Food descriptors serve as a racialized containment strategy.[71] Jay's engagement with Orientalist stereotypes operates against the way he is contrived to be somewhat racially open-minded; after all, he is married to a Colombian woman and has a Colombian stepson. He becomes the stand-in for the "I'm not racist, I have a Black friend" family member within adoptive families. In other words, Jay is the ignorant and occasionally racist family member whom adult adoptees typically recount in reflections of their childhood.

Self-awareness of these racial microaggressions and the lack of Asian Americans in their social circle lead Mitchell and Cameron to two distinct and racially problematic encounters with their pediatrician, Dr. Miura (Suzy Nakamura). These encounters are less about Lily and ensuring she has an Asian American woman role model as a racial mirror or window and more about alleviating Mitchell and Cameron's adoptive parent needs. Lily is a commodity for their racial anxieties to be enacted on, and Dr. Miura serves as someone who can relieve them of their guilt. We first meet Dr. Miura in episode 6, "Run for Your Wife," when Mitchell and Cameron become concerned that Lily may have been severely injured after bumping her head on the ceiling. Clearly unsure of how to address the racial difference between himself and his daughter, Cameron states, "You should be happy to know that Mitchell and I intend on raising Lily with influences from her Asian heritage." He then follows this comment, noting, "We've hung up some Asian art in our rooms. And when she's ready for solid food, there is a fantastic pho place right around the corner from our house. Am I pronouncing that right? Is it *pho* [fə]? . . . It's a soup." Dr. Miura provides an almost canned, automatic response: "I don't know. I'm from Denver, we don't have a lot of pho there." With his racial ignorance clearly evident, at the end of their doctor's visit, Cameron bows to Dr. Miura, who is exiting the patient room. Her one-word response, "Denver," captures the frustration of many Asian Americans. The perpetual foreigner myth resurfaces in the lives of persons of Asian descent regardless of age. Cameron and Mitchell fail to understand that Cameron's racial Othering of Dr. Miura and his Orientalist assumptions concerning her upbringing could just as easily be experienced by Lily.

When viewers encounter Dr. Miura for a subsequent time in episode 16, "Fears," she joins the Pritchett-Tucker family for a meal. Immediately as the scene progresses, we see Lily calling Dr. Miura "mommy." Obviously uncomfortable, Cameron excitedly utters, "You know it's because you're Asian, right?" This racist comment results in the following exchange:

MITCHELL: Cam.
CAMERON: No. I'm sorry. What? Am I just supposed to ignore the giant panda in the room?
DR. MIURA: Pandas are from China. I'm . . . well . . . it doesn't matter.
MITCHELL: I think what my hysterical partner is just trying to say, if I may, is that for the first six months of her life, Lily was raised by very loving

Asian women in an orphanage with whom she clearly bonded. And then suddenly you come in with all of your . . . Asianness and breasts and womb and lady bits. And it all just comes rushing back to her.

DR. MIURA: You guys are overreacting. I'm sure Lily just strung a couple of random syllables together and they just happen to sound something like that word. That's all.

Whether it is Cameron's insecurity or ignorance concerning his ability to successfully parent his daughter, his conflation of pandas with anything and everything Asian, or Mitchell's linking of Dr. Miura with Asian women orphanage workers, their response cannot be left uninterrogated. They both use the logic of "all Asians look alike" to justify why Lily may consider Dr. Miura her mother, though Dr. Miura is Japanese American and Lily is coded as ethnically Vietnamese. Even if Lily were a child of a minority population in Vietnam, she would more likely be a descendant of someone who was Thai, Chinese, Lao, Khmer, or Hmong than be part Japanese.

The conflation of all things Asian is underscored by the fact that Lily is never her own person. She is continually attached to histories and legacies of US Orientalism. In locating adoption within frameworks that focus on adoptive parents, this analysis elucidates how meanings of Asian girlhood are mediated through the use of the child in the lives of adoptive parents.

THE NORMATIVITY OF ADOPTION

Whether it be the actual purchase of a child in question or the consideration of an adopted child as an object to fulfill reproductive futurity, the adoptees in *Sex and the City* and *Modern Family* signify adoptive parents' consumerism. The fetishization of girlhood reflects the treatment of adopted infants and children as dolls. Adoptees are not subjects with agency in these scenarios. Their inclusion and depiction rely on their object status to ensure that they can propel a particular adoptive parent narrative.

This valuation of the child is most apparent when considering the inclusion of adoption in *Smash* (2012–13), a two-season television series that traced the production of a Broadway musical. The figure of the adoptee is invoked in the adoption subplot involving Julia and Frank Houston (Debra Messing and Brian d'Arcy James) in the first season. The adoptive child is seen as making the family, fulfilling the dreams and promises of an intact family engaged in reproductive futurism.[72] Similar to Kathryn Mariner's use of the term *imagined / future child,* I, too, am interested in "emphasizing the child's ability or potential to be adopted in the future."[73] Mariner further notes, "Although technically the object of investment is a fetus, or the mere idea of one, the word 'fetus' was rarely, if ever, uttered in my field site, further underscoring the social import of the child as anticipatory subject. By referring only to the 'child,' 'baby,' or 'adoptee' (not 'child-to-be' or 'fetus') when discussing the contents of a pregnant women's uterus, social workers and prospective adoptive parents discursively create a speculative future. They are hailing a child—and a future—that does not yet exist."[74] While the child Mariner references in her examination of a single midwestern US-based adoption agency is Black, this discussion of the future child, regardless of race, is significant because reproductive futurity manifests this not-yet-born object that is sentimental and available to become attached to.

Viewers witness the figural conjuring of the daughter as the Houston family negotiates the adoption process. They are privy to the struggles and internal conflicts between the prospective adoptive parents. The examination of the pre-adoption finalization process allows viewers the opportunity to sympathize and perhaps even empathize with the stress that prospective adoptive parents encounter. In placing primacy on the adoptive parent, *Smash*, similar to *Sex and the City*, emphasizes adoption as an exchange of market goods—children—with the adoptive parent being the consumer. Viewers are positioned to sympathize with the arduous process of completing paperwork and screening, with the assumption that fertile couples can easily have children and reproduce regardless of parental fitness. Mariner provides insight into the home study process as she writes about domestic adoption in the US: "It pries open intimate aspects of (often) white middle-class subjectivity in ways to which many prospective adoptive parents are not accustomed, so that social workers can make informed decisions about the granting of future kinship."[75] Individuals deciding on transnational adoption also undergo this process and trainings associated with the adoption process. Nonetheless, as Raleigh reveals in her examination of US-based adoption agencies, those trainings may be online in addition to in-person offerings, thus raising questions about their efficacy, even as these home studies serve as a metric for determining a person's ability to raise a child.[76] Home studies are meant to prevent abuse or to reduce the chances that children will be placed into abusive homes. This is an imperfect system and fails to account for how implicit bias rooted at the intersections of race, gender, class, and sexuality may result in abusive individuals passing these checks and harming children.

Attending to these fictionalized representations makes visible the ways in which Asian adopted women and girls must confront these portrayals of infant orphan rescue and stock adoption stories. Situated at the nexus of objectification, the innocent, infant adopted girl is the repository of adoptive parent desires for an infant that conforms to specific understandings of racialized girlhood. These voiceless children's bodies also are sites of adoptive parents' anxieties about racial difference and culture keeping. While both Lilys in *Sex and the City* and *Modern Family* grow up and those narratives reflect an evolution of the writers' and producers' knowledge of adoption, I focus on the initial introductory moments of adoption to delineate what it means to say that adoption serves the needs of adoptive parents. A more recent example of this fetishization of Asian infant adoption is *Little Fires Everywhere*, the novel and the Hulu-released series, underscoring the staying power of fantasies of adoption.[77] The best interests of the child are mitigated and mediated through a lens that recognizes that the act of adoption can only be fulfilled by adoption consumerism. Thanks to the persistence of such fantasies of adoption as rescue, adoptees writ large find themselves negotiating these troubled tropes and reflect their internalization of demands for gratitude. The next chapter interrogates what happens when their white adoptive families are relatively absent and they must negotiate racialized and sexualized understandings of Asian American womanhood as Asian adopted women.

CHAPTER 2

Just Another Asian (American) Woman in *Better Luck Tomorrow* and *Sideways*

Images of Asian women . . . have remained consistently simplistic and inaccurate during the sixty years of largely forgettable screen appearances. There are two basic types: the Lotus Blossom Baby (a.k.a. China Doll, Geisha Girl, shy Polynesian beauty), and the Dragon Lady (Fu Manchu's various female relations, prostitutes, devious madams). There is little in between, although experts may differ as to whether Susie Wong belongs to the race-blind "hooker with a heart of gold" category, or deserves one all of her own.

—Renee E. Tajima[1]

To be an Asian woman in America means you can't just be what you are: a fully enfranchised human being. It means you are a blank screen on which others project their stories, especially, too often, their sexualized fantasies—because US culture has long presented Asian women as sexualized objects for White male enjoyment.

—Jennifer A. Ho[2]

On April 7, 2021, I participated in a roundtable discussion for adoptive parents with another adopted Korean woman and a white adoptive parent as part of Community Conversations offered by the Korean American Adoptee Adoptive Family Network (KAAN). That event, titled "Supporting Asian Adoptees: A Conversation for Parents in a Time of Violence," arose in the wake of the tragedy in Atlanta, Georgia, the murder of eight people, six of whom were Asian or Asian American women, on March 16, 2021. The deaths of Soon Chung Park, Hyun Jung Grant, Suncha Kim, Yong Ae Yue, Delaine Ashley Yaun, Paul Andre Michels, Xiaojie Tan, and Daoyou Feng galvanized broader support for efforts to combat anti-Asian violence, which increased markedly after the onset of the COVID-19 pandemic as a result of the xenophobic and racist rhetoric from the Trump administration and members of the Republican Party. In the aftermath of the deaths, there was increased recognition of the relevance of Asian American studies as a field as well as the need to acknowledge the histories and contributions of Asian Americans in the US, as their experiences have been overlooked as a result of the persistence of the forever foreigner myth.

As the Asian adoptee community processed that act of terror in relation to their own experiences with anti-Asian violence and racial aggression, many turned to social media to reflect on how their white adoptive families had failed to check in with them to see how they were doing. The tropes of the hypersexual Asian woman invoked in discussions of the women who worked at the Atlanta spas were familiar to Asian and Asian American women. Essays by women scholars in Asian American studies contextualized what happened within Asian American history and frequently highlighted their own experiences with racialized misogyny.[3] To this discourse, many Asian adoptees, including me, added our accounts of encounters with that same racialized misogyny.[4] From my own experience, I know that all too often unsolicited remarks are followed by sexual innuendo.[5] These comments are more than just racial microaggressions. For many it begins with an innocuous "hello" in an Asian language.

Throughout my teens and twenties, I found myself going about my daily life or walking around in a city and encountering "ni hao" or "konichiwa" more times than I care to admit. This racialized sexual harassment occurred so frequently on a 2007 trip to Porto, Portugal, with friends from my master's program in London that I titled my photo album documenting the trip on a popular social networking site "Ni Hao Kiss Kiss," as that phrase targeted me throughout our travels. While the album's name may seem flippant, it captures the everyday realities of being a woman of Asian descent in a world where unwanted racialized sexual harassment is commonplace. I draw on Sumi K. Cho's discussion of *racialized sexual harassment*—"a particular set of injuries resulting from the unique complex of power relations facing [Asian and Asian American women] and other women of color in the workplace"— to make sense of how this form of racialized misogyny manifests itself as a result of a confluence of "racialized ascriptions (exotic, hyper-erotic, masochistic, desirous of sexual domination) that set them up as ideal-typical gratifiers of Western neocolonial libidinal formations."[6] Those "hellos" operate as a violent white noise. Simultaneously as the hundredth hello in Chinese or Japanese barely registers, they also signal a need for hypervigilance about my surroundings.[7]

Although I cannot remember the first time I encountered "hello" in an Asian language (it was sometime in high school), one incident from my freshman year of college in Washington, DC, is fresh in my mind. Walking from my dorm to class, I had gotten into a conversation with a man doing work on the parking meters on Virginia Avenue across from the Watergate building. He mentioned his service in the Vietnam War and "those nice Vietnamese girls." At the age of eighteen, I was all too aware of what was implied by that simple phrase. Now almost forty, I recognize that, no matter my credentials, to some I am only defined by my race and gender—a stark reminder of how the model minority myth, in combination with the legacies of US militarism abroad and Orientalism, affects popular American beliefs about Asian and Asian American women.

My experiences are part of those of a larger generation of Asian adopted women who came of age in an era celebrating multiculturalism while simultaneously not discussing racial difference within their adoptive families. Prior to the late 1990s, parents had been told to raise their adopted children as their very own—as if begotten. Parents who discussed race were rare. Asian adopted girls and women adoptees find themselves sexualized and racialized in ways that may be unfamiliar, as their white adoptive parents may not have facilitated an environment conducive to addressing encounters with the racialized gaze.[8] Except even if no formal discussion occurred within the family, by a certain age as we crossed into adolescence, we somehow felt the shifting tides from being a cute infant to a sexualized being. Broadly, the marketing of childhood innocence in advertisements is tied to sexualizing precocious girlhood.[9] In the context of Asian adoption, the innocence of the Asian girl adoptee as a cute addition to the white family ceases as her adolescent body encounters adultification. While this is rooted in perception, these perceptions hold power and influence.

There is a reason why Asian adopted women will loudly and conspicuously proclaim their relationship to their white fathers, brothers, and other male relatives. We learned the pernicious ways racist stereotypes of Asian women and white men operate and disavow our familial ties.[10] The nexus of objectification means kinship is never a part of our potential futures. This is not to erase or further marginalize sex workers or to make light of trafficking; rather, I seek to make visible society's gendered racism that fails to imagine anything but racist, sexualized fantasies of Asian women and white men.

Notions of consensual interracial relationships, transracial adoptive families, or mixed-race families fall outside of this gaze, for this particular gaze relies on eliding Asian and Asian American women as subjects. Instead, we are merely objects to fulfill racialized, sexual desires. This becomes evident when considering white supremacists' desire for and relationships with Asian women.[11] The Atlanta spa shootings, among other examples of sexual violence against Asian and Asian American women in the US and abroad, also demonstrate this fact.

I ruminate on what it means for Asian adopted women and girls to grapple with questions of safety, anti-Asian racism, and misogyny, because this chapter wrestles with what happens when Asian adopted women are not viewed as part of an adoptive family. What happens when the presence of adoptees is naturalized in the popular culture landscape? The adoptee becomes just another Asian woman, devoid of nuance. The fantasy of the Asian woman writes itself onto our bodies. Through an analysis of the films *Sideways* (2004) and *Better Luck Tomorrow* (2002), I consider what it means when adopted women serve as signals of a broader racial liberalism while also operating as the only or one of the only women protagonists in a film. I situate this examination within a reflection on how Asian adopted women and girls make sense of racialized misogyny and how we claim autonomy and agency to push back against Orientalist notions of our racialized (hetero)sexuality.

Exploring the friendship of Miles Raymond (Paul Giamatti) and Jack Cole (Thomas Haden Church), *Sideways* centers on their adventures in California's Santa Ynez wine country on the weekend prior to Jack's wedding and is based on Rex Pickett's novel of the same name. The appearances of the women protagonists Stephanie (Sandra Oh) and Maya Randall (Virginia Madsen) are secondary to the white middle-aged men's negotiation of the precarity of life and relationships. While the focus is on the crisis of white masculinity affecting Jack and Miles, the women enter the film and function as props to shore up their manhood, which has suffered losses from the castration by marriage for Jack and the inability to become a successful male breadwinner for Miles. One of the more incisive critiques of the film comes from Sally Quinn, who writes,

> "Sideways," the low-budget Oscar contender, is a guys' movie that celebrates a certain cultural fantasy: Set off on a drinking-carousing-debauching adventure for a week with your buddy, seduce two great-looking girls and then dump them and go home. What fun! . . . The two leads, played by Thomas Haden Church and Paul Giamatti, are losers. They are unattractive—at times repulsive—stupid, and gross. They are also untalented, cowardly liars with no sense of humor. They are self-absorbed, undisciplined, navel-gazing failures. They have no redeeming qualities.[12]

Quinn's excoriating review hints at what makes the film successful. The male characters' navel-gazing makes *Sideways* appear as if it is about "real life." The film exposes the fragility of white men as they cling to their previous successes—in the case of Jack, as he confronts the slowing of his acting career, and Miles, as he aspires to become a renowned author. The film's insight into failed white manhood appealed to viewers.[13]

Focused on the friendship between four high school Asian Americans living in Orange County, California, *Better Luck Tomorrow* is loosely based on the December 31, 1992, murder of Stuart Tay.[14] The Justin Lin–directed film captures suburban youth culture as viewers watch Ben Manibag (Parry Shen), Virgil Hu (Jason Tobin), Han Lue (Sung Kang), and Daric Loo (Roger Fan) negotiate model minority stereotypes and seek to define a masculinity in opposition to hegemonic masculinity, which Asian American men are routinely denied access to and which the group's nemesis, Steve Choe (John Cho), seems to embody effortlessly. In the middle of this dynamic is Stephanie Vandergosh (Karin Cheung), Steve's girlfriend and Ben's high school crush. Lab partners in chemistry class, Stephanie and Ben develop a friendship, and, at the end of the film, viewers see Stephanie pull up in her Audi convertible alongside Ben, who is walking on the sidewalk, and drive off with him. This is immediately after viewers see Ben and Virgil sitting together in the backyard on a sunny day near Steve's buried body.

The film garnered excitement among Asian Americans because, as Noy Thrupkaew writes, "no mainstream film has shown us the way we see ourselves: people, not *a* people, with individual quirks and dilemmas not accorded to characters forced to 'represent' (positively or not) 'their community.'"[15] The film also appealed to a broad audience. Brian Hu and Vincent N. Pham note, "*Better Luck Tomorrow* (Justin Lin, 2002) rocked the 2002 Sundance Film Festival, legendary for its conflict-ridden question-and-answer session that spurred Ebert to come to defend the movie against hostile audience members, and became the first movie acquired by MTV Films."[16] For many, the film's distribution by MTV Films represented a shift in Asian American representation in that the protagonists operated outside the confines of "traditional" Asian culture (e.g., *The Joy Luck Club* [1993], *Crouching Tiger Hidden Dragon* [2000]), something that independent Asian American cinema had been critiquing for years.

Sideways and *Better Luck Tomorrow* are neither adoption-focused nor even tangentially related to adoption. This chapter is thus attentive to what is at stake when viewers do not recognize the characters as adoptees and what this erasure tells us about middlebrow culture's racialization of Asian American women and girls—adopted and non-adopted alike. Adoption goes unmentioned in *Sideways* and barely receives verbal mention in *Better Luck Tomorrow*. A person's status as an adoptee operates invisibly. When adoptees are considered on their own, outside of the white privilege afforded by their parents, they are seen only as persons of Asian descent. There is no neon sign above us indicating that we were adopted and, in the majority of transracial adoption cases, that our parents are white. This is particularly important to understanding how Asian adopted women encounter racialization as Asian American women.

FICTIONAL ADOPTEES AND THE REALITIES
OF GENDERED RACIALIZATION

I began this chapter with quotations from Renee E. Tajima and Jennifer A. Ho. While Tajima's reflection on the representation of Asian American women in cinema was published in 1989, her assessment of how they are categorized in the US imaginary still holds true, as expressed in Ho's words in the wake of the 2021 Atlanta spa shootings. More than thirty years separate their conclusions about the racialization of Asian American women. The longevity of these stereotypes cannot be disregarded. This is not to erase Asian American feminisms and the work of Asian American activists; rather, I underscore the inscription and reinscription of these tropes onto our bodies without our consent.

Using *Sideways* and *Better Luck Tomorrow* as case studies offers an opportunity to interrogate the operationalization of the heterosexual male gaze at the turn of the twenty-first century. The male gaze's rendering of women as objects must be seen from a racialized lens to account for how women of color and women of Asian descent in particular encounter and negotiate raced sexualized fantasies. Useful in situating this understanding of the gaze is Janet McCabe's analysis: "Chief among the pleasures offered is that of voyeuristic-scopophilic gazing, where the spectator gains gratification from indulging in unlicensed looking at an image, typically of a woman. The active and curious (male) gaze translates the (female) image into an object of sexual fantasy, so granting the voyeur a position defined by control and mastery with its implied separation from the source of erotic stimulation."[17] This gaze cannot be seen as something only deployed by white men. Men of color are complicit in the creation and consumption of white women and women of color in media. bell hooks attends to the role of the Black male gaze in the reception of Black women in Black independent films.[18] I pay attention to hooks's caution about Black men's phallocentric gaze toward Black women in my own understanding of Asian American men and their engagement in a similar gaze in their interactions with and reception of Asian American women on screen. The comparison of the white male gaze in *Sideways* with the teenage Asian American male gaze in *Better Luck Tomorrow* illustrates Asian American hegemonic masculinity's complicity with white supremacist ideologies that harm Asian American women.

Asian American women's representation in cinema is bound to racialized and gendered stereotypes associated with their bodies. Orientalism manifests perniciously in that as consumers of this media, Asian and Asian American women must confront how their seemingly perverse sexuality informs "an imaginary construction of *her desire*," which assumes they consent to participate in these erotic desires.[19] The fetishistic male gaze that operates and results in the stereotypes that render women of Asian descent as hypersexual, submissive, and devious is applied to Asian and Asian American women writ large, including those who are adopted.[20]

Given that the male gaze circumscribes engagement with media texts, I draw on hooks's concept of the *oppositional gaze*.[21] Operating as a recuperative strategy, the oppositional gaze allows Black women spectators to engage in the production of counternarratives that locate their subjectivity. The oppositional gaze is useful in considering Celine Parreñas Shimizu's discussion of the *bind of representation* facing Asian American women, whereby "the hypersexual Asian woman in representation haunts the experiences and perceptions of Asian women across different contexts."[22] Shimizu and hooks engender space for women of color to reclaim agency through a transgressive understanding of their subjectivity. My interest in how the oppositional gaze functions and its possibilities for resistance frames my engagement with the two films. What does resisting dominant narratives as spectators require from us? I consider the moments of potentiality in the films to imagine a different future or at least to more fully tease out the ways adoption operates latently within them.

Sideways and *Better Luck Tomorrow* capture the realities Asian adopted women encounter as they negotiate the world as racialized subjects. We cannot disconnect the adopted body from the Asian American body, as that overlooks how race and sexuality intersect and affect a person's lived experiences. Understanding how popular culture and middlebrow cultural representations of Asian American women penetrate and circulate within society vis-à-vis the nexus of objectification is critical in the examination of adopted women in film as well as in other forms of media. No longer is the adoptee a cute infant or toddler signaling their adoptive family's racial tolerance and investments in multicultural rhetoric (never mind that racial microaggressions are commonplace within the family). I pay attention to how adopted teenage girls and women undergo such transformation along the spectrum of fetishization of Asian bodies from infancy to adulthood. The invisibility of adoptee status shapes the reading of Asian adopted women characters and has real-life implications for Asian adopted women and girls.

The period in which *Sideways* and *Better Luck Tomorrow* debuted coincides with when Korean adoptees who were sent abroad as part of the nation's peak transnational adoptions in the early to mid-1980s reached their late teens and twenties alongside Operation Babylift adoptees and other Korean adoptees nearing their early thirties. While this may seem irrelevant, the turn of the twenty-first century saw international and transracial adoptee voices claiming space in mainstream narratives of adoption. Yet it was still rare to encounter an Asian adopted woman or girl publicly disclosing their experiences to a wide audience. Documentaries featuring Asian adopted women and girls were few and lacked broader dissemination beyond PBS, and they predominately focused on the adoption journey writ large, including adoptees' return to South Korea or Vietnam, with less emphasis on encounters with stereotypes of Asian (American) womanhood.[23]

Similarly, even as first-person writings from Asian adoptees found an audience, it was rare to see adoptees calling attention to explicit forms of racialized sexual harassment or violence.[24] A notable exception is Jane Jeong Trenka's memoir *The Language of Blood* (2003), which not only weaves these stereotypes and their attendant effects into a memoir but also recounts the author's experience of being stalked and the stalker's racialized motivations. Upon arrest, the stalker was found to be in possession of what "authorities would dub the 'Rape and Murder Kit': cotton gloves, a shower cap, a bull whip, Vaseline, four tent stakes, rope, duct tape, a video camera and tripod, a hunting knife, one Rossi .38 Special with five live rounds in the cylinder, seventeen rounds of extra ammunition, and a shovel" as well as a copy of a paperback about Pearl Harbor.[25] While the book on Pearl Harbor may seem irrelevant, the stalker had previously accosted Trenka and said, "You're nothing but a Korean in a white man's society. You're a gook, you're a chink."[26]

Interspersed throughout the memoir are instances where Trenka calls attention to racism and misogyny with examples such as "ASIAN WOMEN: exotic, petite, lotus blossoms, pale, fragile, docile, geishas."[27] Trenka also includes the following "advertisements" for submissive Asian women:

Advertisement 1[28]
SWM, 29, SEEKS ASIAN
You: Submissive, petite, long hair.
Your master is 6'1", brown/brown,
185 lbs. Looking for fun. Will
Respond to all that send pictures.
Mailbox #14520

Advertisement 2[29]
www.seeasiangirls.com
Thousands of streaming hardcore
Videos and movie clips with sound.
Watch our young Asian girls scream
As they get fucked for the first time.

Trenka's recollection of being propositioned as a sex worker while at the grocery store follows the website description for www.seeasiangirls.com. She notes how it took her time—merely seconds or minutes—before "a lightbulb in [her] head finally went on" during the interaction for her to realize he was propositioning her.[30] These examples call attention to racialized misogyny and its implications on her life as a Korean adopted young woman. And for adoptee readers at the time, this was one of the only examples that validated their lived experiences negotiating such sexual harassment and violence. For me personally, I remember an adult son of a family friend wondering whether I was the mother of my younger sister, who was then a toddler. I was in middle school. Yet that type of assumption is directly linked to stereotypes of Asian girls and women and girls of color writ large as a result of adultification. To pretend otherwise discounts how girls of color are denied access to girlhood.

In my examination of adoptee writings in anthologies published prior to 2004, there's a paucity of adoptees explicitly reflecting on hypersexual stereotypes. Peter Kearly gestured to these tropes when reflecting on who he did not want to date in high school, writing, "I didn't want to ask an Asian girl on a date just because she was 'Asian,' at least the kind of Asian female that American movies have men fantasize about. I didn't want to believe that I wanted a geisha or a dragon lady or a cute lotus blossom."[31] This stereotype also surfaced in Kari Smalkoski's recollection of an exchange she had with another adopted Korean woman. Smalkoski recounted her friend saying,

> You ever notice how it's always the geeky, weird white guys that are with Asian women? The worst part is, you get the feeling a lot of these women are just with the guy because he's white. Either way you look at it, it's gross. And yet, look at me, who am I to point fingers? I've never personally known any Asian American guys. My whole family is white. Every guy I've dated is white. What am I supposed to do about it?[32]

The exchange may initially appear benign and the stereotyping less obvious compared with Trenka's explicit reference to non-Asian men's Asian sexual fetishes, but it nonetheless acknowledged adoptees' recognition of how Asian (American) women are sexualized.

Such interventions have been few and far between. Most notably, the 2019 publication of Jenny Heijun Wills's *Older Sister. Not Necessarily Related.* calls attention to the sexual violence that occurs within adoptee communities. Her accounts of adopted Korean men's enactment of sexual violation toward her remain one of the only disclosures by adopted Korean women. The dearth of writings aligns with the broader absence of Asian American feminist scholarship concerning sexual violence as noted by erin Khuê Ninh.[33] The "#WeToo: A Reader" special issue of the *Journal of Asian American Studies* attends to those absences. The special issue editors erin Khuê Ninh and Shireen Roshanravan note, "[The reader] insists that Asian Americans be heard, believed, and backed up in their experiences with sexual violence—not in an additive sense, but with syntactical difference. The 'we' of the title casts for Asian Americans as subjects, not merely objects, inside rape culture."[34] Assumptions of Asian American women's submissive nature also result in the erroneous notions that these women are unrapeable subjects who, as such, are unable to experience sexual violence more broadly. In claiming subjecthood, Asian American women, adopted and non-adopted, assert autonomy and control over the narratives written onto their bodies.

This is not to say that adopted Asian girls and women weren't aware of how they are rendered into parts as objects nor conscious of rape culture and sexual violence. Rather, recognition of these stereotypes necessitates confronting the realities of Asian adopted women and girls as they exist outside the protection of their white adoptive families. Personally, I remember being thrilled while reading Kristina Wong's essay in *YELL-Oh! Girls: Emerging Voices Explore Culture, Identity, and Growing Up Asian American* satirizing the Asian fetish, as it offered me a lens to articulate what I experienced in isolation.[35] To return to my discussion of Trenka, even as her family sought to protect her from her stalker, campus security and law enforcement failed to take the stalking against her seriously and instead labeled the terror she was subjected to within the framing of an overzealous boyfriend.[36] Advice from a local women's group specializing in domestic and sexual abuse guided Trenka through the restraining order process.[37] The ways Asian and Asian American women alongside other women of color fall outside of protection and are seen as disposable should not be ignored.

This chapter elucidates the tensions produced by the (hyper)visibility of adopted characters as they are rendered hypersexualized Asian women and teenage girls. Underscoring the need to situate adopted women as adults, Ho writes, "The figure of the adult adoptee is rarely found in public discourse or popular culture. The standard images that we have within orphan narratives are of babies and children—subjects in need of protection and victims of tragic circumstances (death of parents, causalities of war, loss of fortune or social standing)."[38] *Sideways* and *Better Luck Tomorrow* draw attention to the women and teenage girls who must negotiate representation as both adoptees and Asian Americans through the performative nature of such mundane activities as claiming family and through encounters with stereotypes of Asian womanhood. These seemingly disparate films are useful for thinking through representations of Asian adopted women and girls precisely because their Asian adopted characters function as minor love interests to the protagonists. Reduced to their affective roles as love interests, these women are not seen as autonomous subjects.

POSSIBILITIES FOR RESISTANCE AND SEX-POSITIVE ENACTMENTS OF SEXUALITY

A sanitized version of wine country is proffered in *Sideways*. Co-written by Alexander Payne and Jim Taylor, the film focuses on the existential midlife crises of Miles and Jack and captures a particular nadir of white masculinity. Women are seen as both critical and disposable in their lives. The California of the two protagonists is noticeably white, with diversity inhabited only by Jack's Armenian fiancée, Christine Erganian (Alysia Reiner), and Stephanie. In many respects, the setting recalls *Friends*—an all-white Manhattan; in this case, it is an all-white Santa Ynez, though demographics tell a different story. The 2000 Census reports that white people composed 59.5 percent of the total population of California and 72.7 percent of Santa Barbara County, where much of the film is set.[39] The unbearable whiteness of the film stands in stark contrast to reality.

The erasure of the Latino migrant laborers, primarily from Mexico, who work the vineyards illustrates how the film and arguably white Hollywood would like to see wine country—devoid of people of color and immigrants, though they are who make the cosmopolitan scenes of wine tasting and eating at Michelin-starred restaurants possible. This romanticized and celebrated wine country arose with the 1976 Paris Wine Tasting, which, according to Garrett Peck, "put Napa Valley on the wine map as one of the premier winemaking regions in the world."[40] He further notes, "Here was proof that California could produce not just good, but great wines. The event—and the victory—brought worldwide attention to Napa."[41] The popularity of wine and its entry into mass consumption eventually resulted in "Two-Buck Chuck," sold at Trader Joe's locations across the US in 2000. "Wine, Inc." has made few inroads in Santa Ynez Valley, a region with a range of microclimates similar to Napa and Sonoma and home to more family-owned and -operated vineyards.[42]

When situating Stephanie's fictional existence within the Santa Ynez Valley, we should note that the 2000 Census reports 238 and 343 people who identify as Asian and mixed-race, respectively, among the 21,859 inhabitants in the area.[43] More important, however, is that the lack of discussion of Stephanie as an Asian American occurs within a broader history of Asian adoptees as one of the only or few in their communities. Because even if a large Asian American population existed, it does not necessarily equate to Asian adoptees self-identifying with those communities. Adoptees raised in Minnesota and elsewhere across the US attest to this fact when they connect to the adoptee community in adulthood.[44] Thus the lack of discussion of Stephanie's racial identity tells the story of Asian adopted womanhood—one that is invested in seeing her as just like anyone else (in this case, approximately white), even if she's subjected to racialized misogyny. Sandra Oh's body personifies the stereotypes of Asian women's sexuality, even as Oh in an interview on NPR's *Fresh Air* indicates a keen sense of autonomy over the scenes with her character. She reveals, "I want[ed] to pack as much story about Stephanie the character in the film as possible. My character is not on screen very much and doesn't have a lot of dialogue. She's there visually a lot. So I was very, very conscious to try and pack as much character into every moment as possible."[45] Her body language, in conjunction with Jack's description of her sexual prowess, further highlights her presence as the only woman of color in much of the film. The lack of explicit sexual chemistry between Maya and Miles only amplifies the heterosexual fire between Stephanie and Jack.

We first meet Stephanie when Miles and Jack visit the winery where she is employed. The initial conversation is flirtatious, with Stephanie and Jack engaging in a highly sexually charged exchange as she pours the pair wine. Jack lasciviously comments, "You've been a bad, bad girl." Stephanie replies, "I know, I need to be spanked." She positions herself in a service role when she flirtatiously comments that she needs to be spanked. Even as Stephanie engages willingly in this exchange, her demeanor plays into Orientalist constructions of Asian femininity, as someone who is sexually aggressive and simultaneously docile, compliant, and ready to please. Stephanie's employment in the service industry underscores the latter description.

Jack's subsequent revelations to his traveling companion reveal Stephanie's hypersexual prowess. Following his initial sexual encounter with her, Jack tells Miles, "She fucks like an animal." Through this comparison, Jack erases her status as an equal and represents Stephanie as the exotic Other and an object to fuck. The erotic possibilities that Stephanie opens up in their initial flirtation reach their peak in this first sexual liaison. Her sexually depraved nature is further intimated following a subsequent sexual encounter. Speaking to Miles in his hotel room, Jack declares, "She is nasty, Miles. Nasty, nasty, nasty." His repeated use of the adjective "nasty" evokes the excessive nature of Stephanie's sexuality. This characterization is linked to the erotic possibilities associated with hypersexual Asian womanhood and the nonexistence of boundaries concerning sexual foreplay and sex acts. Sexual piety is not an issue.

Operating simultaneously in the racialization process of Stephanie as the Asian Other is the insertion of her intergenerational mixed-race family into the film. Jack, Miles, and viewers are introduced to her biracial daughter and white mother, two peripheral characters who further complicate the racial coding of Stephanie. Viewers encounter the first misrecognition of Stephanie when Miles sees photos of her daughter, who at first glance looks half Black, half Asian, on the refrigerator. Miles turns to Maya and asks, "Is that Stephanie's kid?" His disorientation over the nontypical "Asian" family member becomes irrelevant when Maya affirms that the girl is Stephanie's daughter. This less-than-thirty-second glimpse of Stephanie as a mother humanizes her, the woman who seemed to only exist vis-à-vis her status as sexual object. The rendering of Stephanie as a three-dimensional character is furthered upon the formal meeting between her mother, Jack, and Miles in a local bowling alley. Yet the racial difference is not discussed or acknowledged.[46] Rather, the class difference of Stephanie and her mother, Carol, in contrast to Miles and Jack is what separates them. The fictional household of Stephanie aligns with Census findings that 55.7 percent of Santa Ynez Valley households were women-led and included children under age eighteen.[47] Within one character, the film showcases diversity while simultaneously reinscribing stereotypes concerning Asian women's sexuality onto her body. By placing the labels "single mother," "adoptee," and "Asian" on the character of Stephanie, the film consumes difference in a manageable bite. Difference becomes embodied by a single character. Appearing diverse, the film perpetuates the pathologization of women of color in its desire to appeal to a mainstream audience while "pushing" boundaries at the same time. This is not a transgressive articulation of Asian American womanhood, because she seemingly doesn't adhere to a model minority stereotype of financial success. Any hint of nuance is erased given the fact that the combination of her working-class profession, sexual appetite, and single motherhood reifies reductive stereotypes of women of color broadly.

While some may argue that these two brief exchanges underscore how mixed-race and transracial families have become the norm in twenty-first-century society, these scenes render Stephanie hypervisible. Even as we see Stephanie as a mother and daughter, those identities do not erase how she is positioned as an insatiable lover. The way in which Oh's body is simultaneously raced and erased is important, for it illustrates how latent stereotypes concerning Asian American women's bodies circulate within popular culture. These fictional representations have real-life implications, as the writings of adoptees discussed earlier in this chapter indicate, in shaping public perceptions. The lack of racial diversity in white Americans' friendship networks results in many of their perceptions being shaped by media framing of racial and ethnic groups, among other minoritized communities.[48] The circulation of degrading pornography in contrast to sex-positive, feminist pornography also contributes to racialized misogyny.

Since Stephanie as a character is a prop to Jack's desire to reclaim his white masculinity, viewers are not privy to her innermost thoughts, including whether she reclaims her sexuality, even if as an actress Sandra Oh made intentional choices in how she played the character. Instead, we see how Stephanie's lasciviousness is perceived and how her body is acted upon by Jack. Still, I am reminded of Shimizu's desire to read Sandra Oh's character against the grain, arguing: "She will not die for the white man who relegates her love as worthless. Instead, she will beat him up till he bleeds. She establishes a viable subjectivity that brings together the gaps between fantasies of Asian women and the lived realities of Asian American women."[49] What Shimizu gestures toward is what Peter X. Feng argues: "When we speak of resistance within texts, we speak about moments. But when we speak of resistance within spectators, we speak of the mobilization of those moments into a new narrative space, one that transcends the narrative logic of the movies."[50] Reading the film against the grain reveals how women of color resist the gaze and claim subjecthood outside of dominant constructions of their identities.

Nonetheless, while I concede that Stephanie "rejects this classification" as she physically assaults Jack at the end of the film, I remain wary of what this violence signifies to the audience. Perhaps Stephanie regains the agency she lost through her supporting role in shoring up Jack's virility; the fact remains that she is bound to her hypersexualized and racialized body. Scripts girding her sexuality, or at least what popular culture considers her sexuality, remain intertwined with her assertion of agency. And even if an oppositional gaze is deployed by Asian American viewers, this does not guarantee that white or non-Asian viewers of color will also see Oh's performance as transgressive. The physical assault could be read as only playing into ball-busting dragon lady stereotyping or resulting in a male gaze that renders Stephanie a "frigid bitch" for desiring recognition as a consenting equal. To claim agency means to go against tropes of being nasty, submissive, and looking for fun.

My analysis of Stephanie does not intend to elide her autonomy, nor Oh's commentary about this particular role. Rather, I am invested in how the gaze renders Stephanie as someone whom one can engage as a disposable sexual conquest. How do Jack's assumptions about Asian and Asian American women's sexuality permeate his interactions with Stephanie? And how does the gaze of the spectator function in this regard? Capturing the gaze's intersection with potentialities for resistance, Cathy Park Hong writes,

From invisible girlhood, the Asian American woman will blossom into a fetish object. When she is at last visible—at last desired—she realizes much to her chagrin that this desire for her is treated like a perversion. This is most obvious in porn, where our murky desires are coldly isolated into categories in which white is the default and every other race is a sexual aberration. But the Asian woman is reminded every day that her attractiveness is a perversion, in instances ranging from skin-crawling Tinder messages ("I'd like to try my first Asian woman") to microaggressions from white friends. I recall a white friend pointing out to me that Jewish men only dated Asian women because they wanted to find women who were the opposite of their pushy mothers. Implied in this tone-deaf complaint was her assumption that Asian women are docile and compliant. Well-meaning friends never failed to warn me, if a white guy was attracted to me, that he probably had an Asian fetish. The result: I distrusted my desirousness. My sexuality was a pathology. If anyone non-Asian liked me, there was something wrong with him.[51]

Hong's comments drive my questions as I wrestle with recognizing potential moments for resistance within *Sideways*. How does disavowal of those stereotypes circulate outside of Asian American or other marginalized communities in the face of fetishization? If the infant and toddler adoptee is fetishized as an object, the adult version of this objecthood is the rendering of her body in the imaginary by that same gaze. For Stephanie to have a fling with Jack that acknowledges her excitement to have non-vanilla sex tinged with aggression, biting, and rough foreplay means that she also needs a partner who is capable of separating her sexual proclivities from racialized misogyny. To resist means to recognize how an Asian or Asian American woman's sexual kinks and fantasies exist outside of Orientalism. We must be more than a fetish. And yet, Jack's reactions to sex with Stephanie appear to be rooted in just that—she is a sexual conquest, nothing more. A story to tell his buddy Miles.

As I rewatch *Sideways,* I recognize that seeing Oh on screen allows me to see an Asian American womanhood that I intimately know, but I also grapple with how that same womanhood is weaponized against us to tell the story of hypersexual Asian women. My reaction to and analysis of the film remains linked to the fact that we need more productions heralding what Shimizu describes as *race-positive sexuality*. She asserts, "The representations of Asian women fucking, touching, kissing, and engaging in other bodily acts by themselves or with others—can be deployed toward new freedoms, forms, and structures of recognition and legibility in culture, fantasy, and imagination."[52] Perhaps that is why my engagement with *Sideways* still vexes me as I struggle to make sense of the notions of resistance put forth by Shimizu, hooks, and Feng while acknowledging how Hong's words hit close to home. If casting had been reversed and Oh had played the role of Maya, what would we be saying about her caretaking and the emotional labor Giamatti's character required? In creating possibilities to see Asian American women's sexuality go beyond stereotype and in offering the chance to read it for new possibilities of sensuality and sexuality, *Sideways* demonstrates Asian American women's recognition of how the gaze shapes their interactions with the world.

While this may not be a similar analogy, my issue with the Jack and Stephanie's sexual coupling makes me return to a conversation from more than fifteen years ago that I had with someone I dated in graduate school in London—a white British man in his twenties. I mentioned craving Americanized Chinese food, which, thanks to colonization and immigration, I believe, is different from British Chinese food, but I digress. It was a brief exchange where I mentioned this to him, and I recall him asking me whether I only liked to eat Chinese food. My Korean American body was subsumed under "Chinese," which in a British context is unsurprising given how Asian British communities encounter racial categorization. Nevertheless, the point of this brief personal narrative is to underscore the way that my interest in Chinese food must be tied to some racial or ethnic identity that I possess. It could not just be that my nostalgia and desire for Chinese food always happened to coincide when I saw him. I disclose this here because if a person cannot separate one's seemingly benign food cravings from a person's racial/ethnic identity, why should we believe people can separate race/ethnicity from their partners' sexual proclivities if it's a fling?

"THE PARENTS I HAVE NOW
ARE MY REAL PARENTS"

In my examination of the entanglement of the bodies of Asian adopted women and girls in a web of racialized sexual harassment, I now turn to the stereotypes inscribed on the adoptee's body before she even speaks in a film and regardless of racial coupling. My analysis of *Better Luck Tomorrow* focuses on how same-race, heterosexual romantic couplings are complicit in the inscription of racialized notions onto girlhood. The sexualization of Stephanie Vandergosh establishes that this racialization process is not limited to white-Asian couplings. Her age also provides the occasion to interrogate the sexualization experiences of high school girls, especially girls of color, whose experiences are shaded by racialization and racism. Personally, I recall being sexually harassed and catcalled from eighth grade onward by teenage boys. This type of sexualization is not unique, which is why exploring how Asian adopted

teenage girls encounter these stereotypes is significant. Capturing the mutability of girlhood, Anita Harris writes, "The category of 'girl' itself has proved
to be slippery and problematic. It has been shaped by norms about race, class
and ability that have prioritized the white, middle class and non-disabled, and
pathologized and/or criminalized the majority outside this category of privilege."[53] This discussion offers insight into the liminal space of girlhood and
womanhood in the teenage years, which, for girls of color, renders them older
as part of adultification.

In *Better Luck Tomorrow*, which features an all–Asian American cast, the
character of Stephanie Vandergosh offers an opportunity to interrogate Asian
American masculinity. As the love interest of both Ben Manibag and Steve
Choe, Stephanie serves as the site of male sexual fantasy for the protagonists
and the viewers. No attention is given to Stephanie's character development
beyond a brief appearance of her white brother. In my analysis of the stereotypes of Asian womanhood inscribed on Stephanie's body, my interest is particularly rooted in her interactions with Asian American teenage boys, as she,
in her role as the high school ingénue, is the sole Asian teenage girl supporting character. Her introduction to viewers highlights her status as the "dream
girl": we see her from Ben's perspective as he opens his locker while staring at
Stephanie, who is wearing a cheerleading uniform and talking to Daric Loo
against the lockers. Ben comments, "Stephanie Vandergosh. It's girls like her
who make you realize that life's not fair," as the camera zooms in on her face
and a photo montage of her appears on screen. This introduction of Stephanie,
in combination with the high school setting, sets the stage for a coming-of-age
tale similar to *Can't Hardly Wait* (1998) or even *Varsity Blues* (1999), but with
a darker twist given that the film ends with Steve's murder at the hands of the
other main protagonists.

Better Luck Tomorrow captures the tensions that Asian-ethnic adolescents
encounter in coming-of-age novels, as Ho describes: "For adolescents of color,
this process [of moving into adulthood] is obviously complicated by the additional cultural strain of trying to locate themselves as minority subjects in a
predominately white society. . . . The cultural specificities of adolescence make
the recognition of its racial and ethnic particularities especially critical."[54] It
is important to situate *Better Luck Tomorrow* within the genre of high school
films at the turn of the century, as well as within the Asian American cinematic canon, because addressing the intersections makes space to consider
what it means to capture Asian American adolescence on film.[55]

Viewers do not see Asian American teenage girls rendered autonomous
fictional subjects not prone to slippage into racist or sexist caricature on
screen until a decade and a half later with Lara Jean Covey (Lana Condor) in

To All Boys I've Loved Before (2018) and the subsequent sequels, Devi Vish-wakumar (Maitreyi Ramakrishnan) in *Never Have I Ever* (2020–present), or Claudia Kishi (Momona Tamada) in *The Baby-Sitters Club* (2020–21). The films and two television shows were released on Netflix and bypassed traditional commercial outlets. While it falls outside the scope of this chapter, considering what it means for Lana Condor, a Vietnamese adoptee, to play a mixed Korean-white character is a worthwhile endeavor that someone whose work bridges young adult literature and cultural studies should take up for analysis. Other examples of teenage representations of Asian girlhood that coincided with the release of *Better Luck Tomorrow* include Parminder Nagra as Jesminder "Jess" Bhamra in *Bend It Like Beckham* (2002) and the characters of Cho Chang and sisters Parvati and Padma Patil in the *Harry Potter* series, whose first four books were published prior to 2002 and first two films released in 2001 and 2002.[56] This is not to overlook mixed-race Neela (Nathalie Kelley) in *The Fast and the Furious: Tokyo Drift* (2006) or to dismiss the work of Keiko Agena in *Gilmore Girls* (2000–2007) and Brenda Song on the Disney Channel in *The Suite Life of Zack and Cody* (2005–2007) or *Wendy Wu: Homecoming Warrior* (2006). I highlight the dearth of representations of teenage Asian girlhood to consider what it means to see a character who is not some reductive depiction of Asian girlhood. It's worth acknowledging Lin's directing of *Tokyo Drift*, as it was his first *Fast and Furious* franchise film. Perhaps bound by genre, the character of Neela vacillates between ingénue and tragic mulatta stereotype. At the same time, the work of Song on the Disney Channel lacked broader appeal to an adult audience.

Locating *Better Luck Tomorrow*'s presentation of Asian American masculinity is central to interrogating the racialization of the only girl protagonist. The film is a mediation on Asian American complicit masculinity.[57] Only through crime can the teenage boy protagonists access hegemonic masculinity.[58] The film excavates Asian American boys from renderings in American popular media, such as Long Duk Dong (Gedde Watanabe) from *Sixteen Candles* (1984), Short Round (Ke Huy Quan) from *Indiana Jones and the Temple of Doom* (1984), and Data (Ke Huy Quan) from *The Goonies* (1985).

While other representations of Asian American masculinity have entered the mainstream (e.g., Dante Basco as Rufio in *Hook* [1991]) and Asian American cinema, to pretend that Long Duk Dong, Short Round, and Data did not have a cultural impact ignores the reductive narratives of Asian American masculinity the three characters supported.[59] Recognizing how *Better Luck Tomorrow* grapples with Asian American cisgender, heterosexual manhood, erin Khuê Ninh notes, "And that is the last indispensable point about *BLT* as fantasy: it operates as tonic for wounded masculinity."[60] She further points out, "Aggrieved (straight) masculinity has been the way we talk about Asian men in the West since the launch of Asian American identity politics in the 1960s, into the present day. In Lin's film, its injuries take two forms: disrespect by white men and rejection by (Asian) women."[61] By the same token, Shimizu notes, "Films by Asian American men intervene in what can be described as the torturous experience of enduring images of asexuality and abnormality, suffering as the butt of jokes, and being relegated to peripheral status in a world of white women and women as central and heroic figures."[62] Addressing the ways Lin seeks to assert a complex Asian American masculinity provides a lens to situate *Better Luck Tomorrow*'s sexualization of Stephanie.

A teenage boy's sexual fantasy, Stephanie is broadly linked to hypersexualized representations of Asian girls. She is a stand-in for Asian American girls and women negotiating Shimizu's bind of representation. Immediately following Ben's voice-over introduction of Stephanie, his friend Virgil mumbles, "I swear I saw her in a porn." This reference to Stephanie in a porn is brought up twice more, once when the viewer sees "Stephanie" in a low-budget pornographic film and again when Ben mentions the porn rumor to her. Shimizu writes, "The chance that she may be a porn star points to the projection of hypersexual fantasy upon Asian American women."[63] Stephanie wears the burden of US Orientalist constructions of women of Asian descent even as a teenage girl. Here, I am reminded of Laura Mulvey, who notes,

> The presence of woman is an indispensable element of spectacle in normal narrative film, yet her visual presence tends to work against the development of a story line, to freeze the flow of action in moments of erotic contemplation. This alien presence then has to be integrated into cohesion with the narrative. . . . Traditionally, the woman displayed has functioned on two levels: as erotic object for the characters within the screen story, and as erotic object for the spectator within the auditorium, with a shifting tension between the looks on either side of the screen.[64]

In this case, Stephanie functions as both a love interest and, for the spectator, a repository for our collective desires for racialized girlhood. For Asian adopted girls, she was one of the only fictional portrayals of teenage adoptee girlhood on screen. Prior to this period, to find Asian adoptee teenage girls in popular culture, one had to look at the work of non-adopted Korean American writer Marie Myung-Ok Lee, whose young adult novels *Finding My Voice* (1992), *Saying Goodbye* (1993), and *Somebody's Daughter* (2005), alongside short stories such as "Summer of My Korean Soldier," featured young adopted women protagonists.[65] More generally, Stephanie provided a new opportunity besides Claudia Kishi in *The Baby-Sitters Club* book series (1986–2000) and movie (1995) for Asian American girls to see ourselves on screen, and even as *Better Luck Tomorrow* called attention to the hypersexualized stereotype of Asian American women and girls, Stephanie was never relegated to this reductive trope.

Viewers do not have to read resistance onto her body like they do watching Oh in *Sideways*. An oppositional gaze is not necessarily needed even when Stephanie is recognized as the subject of teenage male fantasy. The repeated invocation of "I swear I saw her in a porn" becomes farcical by the third iteration and depicts the unwanted sexualized objectification of Asian American girls and women. This functions as a "wink and nod" moment to Asian American women by *Better Luck Tomorrow* writers Ernesto Foronda, Justin Lin, and Fabian Marquez. Unlike the way Sandra Oh's Stephanie is rendered as hypersexual and insatiable such that she plays into racist stereotypes, *Better Luck Tomorrow* makes explicit Stephanie's Asian American and an Asian (American) girlhood through the satirical notion that she starred in a pornographic film. Even if this is a more extreme example of how Asian adopted girls encounter racialization, it depicts the undercurrent of hypersexuality that frames their interactions, as well as non-adopted Asian girls, with society, recalling performance artist Kristina Wong's spoof website Big Bad Chinese Mama.

Stephanie's sexuality is juxtaposed against her image of innocence as seen in her interactions with both Steve and Ben. Positioned as Steve's girlfriend, Stephanie is a naïve young girl, ignorant of his other, white girlfriend at a different high school. At the same time, with Ben, Stephanie is the girl next door, happy to be friends with her complement, the boy next door. She has no knowledge of the illegal activities of Ben and his friends; nor is she aware of the arrangement Steve makes with Ben concerning her "emotional needs" in high school, such as attending the winter formal. The latter example involves Steve asking Ben to take Stephanie to the formal without her knowing about the arrangement and evokes the scene in *Sixteen Candles* (1984) in which Jake Ryan (Michael Schoeffling) asks The Geek (Anthony Michael Hall) to drive Caroline Mulford (Haviland Morris) home. While there may not be a clear alignment of the two films, I mention *Sixteen Candles* because the male protagonist and heartthrob relies on his envious, hegemonically masculine but inferior classmate to do the emotional labor and caretaking that he is uninterested in doing. Aware of the sexual assault and violence toward women in John Hughes's films, including *Sixteen Candles,* I recognize that this comparison relies on the way hegemonic masculinity is grounded in the belief that a subordinate masculine man would engage in the emotional labor in an effort to claim access to hegemonic masculinity. A deeper discussion of Hughes's work and the representation of women in his films occurs in chapter 5, where I reflect on director Benson Lee's inspiration from Hughes in the creation of *Seoul Searching* (2015). Consequently, although Ben's genuine interest in Stephanie positions her as a subject, Steve and Ben's interactions reveal that she, like the Stephanie in *Sideways,* is also an object of male desire.

Yet Ben knows little about the personal life of the object of his desire. This is evident in Ben's surprise when a young white boy, Stephanie's brother, answers the door to her house one evening. As Ben surveys her room and asks questions about the Chinese décor, Stephanie asserts her status as an adoptee. Moreover, unlike the lack of formal conversation concerning adoption in *Sideways,* in *Better Luck Tomorrow,* Stephanie's adoptee status enters in more direct language. In a brief exchange following their high school formal, Ben asks Stephanie whether "she knows her real parents," and Stephanie responds that even though she has a tattoo of her Chinese name, she "still wants to find out who she is."

The carefulness in her responses indicates a cautiousness in how one discloses information. She both clearly articulates her relationship to her white family in claiming her brother as her brother and gestures toward a willingness or at least an openness to discuss the Chinese signifiers in her bedroom when she and Ben study together. There is a palpable ambivalence about what it means to be adopted from China and how Stephanie asserts those aspects of her identity. And given the fictions that go into creating the Asian names of Asian adoptees at orphanages, there's a particular finality in how she asserts her Chinese identity with a tattoo. That name regardless of its provenance is her name and cannot be taken from her.

The fact that Stephanie's adoption is more visible in the film's subplot comprising her and Ben's relationship is directly attributed to director Lin's interest in adoption. Lin commented in an interview, "That became the fun part, to complicate the role of Stephanie [Karin Anna Cheung], who could have just been the Pretty Girl. I had just done a documentary on Korean adoptees from Minnesota, and I thought, 'That's an interesting identity that I want to explore.'"[66] The deliberate positioning of adoption as a subplot device to strengthen the supporting character's backstory highlights Lin's recognition of not only how adoptees are included within the Asian American experience but also how this inclusion renders Asian adopted girls susceptible to racialized sexual harassment.

While Karen Fang contends that Stephanie's status as an adoptee complicates possible cultural stereotypes concerning academic drive, this read of adoption is faulty, as it relies on the notion that because her parents are white, the model minority myth somehow does not shape her engagement with the educational system.[67] Just because one does not have a Tiger Mom does not mean assumptions of an innate Asian intellect are not made by teachers or peers. This reading of Stephanie assumes that her adoptee status takes precedence, as if the adoptee never undergoes involuntary racialization.

Better Luck Tomorrow offers an opportunity to trouble fantasies of adoption in that the film creates a lens to imagine a different fantasy of adoption, one that tells the story of an adoptee who has access to an Asian American community, unlike many adoptees of this period. The film crafts a narrative that recognizes how mundane, day-to-day interactions shape one's experiences, whereby Stephanie can be seen as just like everyone else and not fetishized because of adoption, even if she experiences the fetishistic male gaze. This is not to minimize the male gaze nor elide sexual violence; rather, it's to highlight what it means to operate independently of adoption, as though adoption is not the sole defining characteristic of one's identity. That engenders the conditions to hold the intersectional identity of the adopted Asian woman and girl and see what it means when she is seen as parts of who she is—adopted, Asian, woman/girl—and as a subject with multiple identities. It is the latter that calls attention to the ramifications of racialized misogyny and associated violence in the actual lives of Asian women and girls, adopted and non-adopted.

ADOPTION AS (IN)VISIBLE

Perhaps adoptees were never supposed to grow up. The myth of adoptees as perpetual children persists and exposes the failure of white adoptive parents to recognize that their children of color will navigate the world as adults of color. This forgetting that Asian adopted infants and children become Asian American teenage girls and adults lays bare the complexities of attending to the racialized sexual harassment they encounter in their everyday lives at the nexus of objectification. To overlook this process of racialization is grossly problematic, for it also means that Asian adopted girls, as well as their adult counterparts, may be under- or unprepared to respond to various sexist remarks. Adoptive parents must engage with their discomfort concerning how Asian fetishes operate even as they may be complicit in their Asian adopted daughter's fetishization considering the tropes discussed in chapter 1.

As someone who engaged in such conversations during the decade I volunteered with a national organization serving Korean adoptees and their families, I have seen the uneasiness produced when Asian adopted women call attention to how they experience racialized sexual harassment like their non-adopted Asian American peers. One incident comes to mind. In my capacity as a social media operator for the organization, I posted the YouTube spoof video "How to Hit On an Asian Girl" in September 2011.[68] Fifteen seconds into the video, the following subtitle appears: "How Not to Harass an Asian Girl." The video offers six "recommendations" and ends with the note "All the scenes in this video are based on real experiences of real live Asian American females." The video calls attention to the lasting imprint of Stanley Kubrick's *Full Metal Jacket* (1987), which resulted in phrases such as "Me so horny" and "Me love you long time" becoming racist cultural mainstays and Asian food being randomly invoked in reference to Asian and Asian American women— both as a descriptor for women and as a demonstration of interest in Asian culture. Various commenters on the social media post stated that they felt the video was inappropriate. It is unclear why they thought sharing the video was inappropriate since it reflects the reality of Asian and Asian American women and girls. At the time and even now, I consider whether this reaction of outrage could have come from people who did not participate in the organization's annual conference regularly and who were less familiar with the content of the workshops, many of which addressed various iterations of this type of racialized sexual harassment, or simply people who preferred to think racist misogyny does not affect Asian adoptees. Regardless, the incident remains with me because the uneasiness toward contending with Asian American women's experiences of anti-Asian racism and misogyny cannot be overlooked.

I return to where this chapter began and explore how Asian adopted women mourned the Atlanta spa shootings and reflected on the ways adoption intersected with their grief. Reflecting on increasing anti-Asian violence, Korean adoptee Stephanie Drenka writes, "Thinking about the White mommy bloggers who have touted their adorable adopted Asian babies, but continue to ignore the racist violence happening to people who look like them. Who are more worried about losing followers than honoring and supporting their children."[69] A similar sentiment is raised by Chinese adoptee Grace Newton: "I saw a statement by a white adoptive parent, who stated that her dream was to adopt a child from China, not to have a white child. These fetishizing remarks contextualize the rise in hate crimes against Asians as a part of delegitimizing her dream rather than focusing on the needs of the AAPI [Asian American Pacific Islander] community right now."[70] Fetishization facilitates adoption's promotion and adoptees' inclusion within the white family; yet this does not mean that there is an awareness of how the logics of fetishizing Asian bodies operate as adoptees move toward adulthood. Korean adoptee writer Nicole Chung reflects, "Even after I grew up, I cannot recall having a single conversation with [my parents] about anti-Asian racism specifically. Not the 'model minority' myth. Not perpetual-foreigner syndrome. Not the exotification and fetishization of Asian women. Not the history of American imperialism that is partially responsible for my birth family's and my presence in this country."[71] If parents lack awareness of the stereotypes concerning Asian women that circulate in the US, how will it impact the racialized sexual harassment of adoptees?

More explicit about adoptees' negotiation with the Asian fetish is Midnite Townsend, a Korean adoptee and the 2014 Burlesque Hall of Fame's Queen of Burlesque. Writing in April 2021, she shared her experiences of negotiating consent and fetishism, disclosing, "I often wondered if my partners' interests were in me or in my stereotype. I accepted harmful behaviors in an attempt to fulfill the 'Asian woman experience.' This stifled my own sexual development and disabled my ability to give real consent. When I internalized fetishizing myself, I internalized dehumanizing myself." She further noted, "Asian fetishism was the perfect storm to exploit my dream. Without it I was bullied, with it I was eroticized. The transition from social pariah to romantic fantasy was overwhelming. My white family and friends had no idea what I was going through. I had no idea what I was going through."[72] Townsend's comments surrounding how Asian fetishism operates stand in contrast to, or at least run parallel to, Hong's discussion of fetishism as a perversion. Townsend's reflections reveal that after playing into the fetish as a result of internalized racism, she found herself feeling desired and desirable. Escort services and strip clubs advertising "Blondes and Asians" allowed her approximate access to the white ideal in ways she was unaccustomed to. These adopted women readily evince why addressing racialized misogyny is needed within adoptive families. Their comments offer reminders for why an ethics of representation is vital to combat the fantasies of adoption found in popular culture.

Both an awareness of racialized sexual harassment and an exploration of Asian American women and girls—adopted and non-adopted alike—cleave open space to claim agency over their sexuality is necessary. Even so, as the next chapter makes evident, the weaponization of the Asian American woman as hypersexual trope exposes adoptees' tenuous kinship ties to their families. Not only is the positioning of adoptees as part of their (white) adoptive families precarious in young adulthood and adulthood because of misrecognition by society at large; if they fail to perform gratitude or recognize the "gift of freedom" bestowed by adoption, they risk expulsion from the family.

CHAPTER 3

The Contingencies of Belonging

Soon-Yi Previn

The 2021 release of the HBO television miniseries *Allen v. Farrow*, along with the 2020 release of Woody Allen's memoir, sparked renewed interest in Mia Farrow's allegation that Allen molested their adopted daughter Dylan in the early 1990s. Both texts also drew attention back to his wife, Soon-Yi Previn, and the 1992 scandal that ended his relationship with Farrow, Previn's adoptive mother. This scandal demonstrates the uneasiness that accompanies Asian American young women's sexuality and adoptive family kinship. More importantly, Farrow's characterization of Previn in the press as intellectually disabled and in anti-Asian terms illustrates adoption's racist love. An analysis of what transpired elucidates broader anxieties concerning families who transgress the boundaries of heteronormative kinship.

Asian adopted women become trespassers in their own families, however, in adulthood as they come to represent the potential Oriental fantasy. It is this possibility that circumscribes their adult existence because adoptive families are unprepared and ill equipped to recognize how the hypersexualization and racialization of women of Asian descent affect adopted Asian women and girls. This vexing position illuminates how the nexus of objectification informs their interactions with the world and families. The narrow conceptualizations of what it means to be "Asian" molded Previn into two tropes: the rescued orphan and the seductive daughter. Asian adoptee girls are only welcome when they fulfill the fantasy of reproducing the future.

At the time of the scandal, Allen and Previn's relationship was framed in the media as a notorious affair. However, in the wake of the #MeToo movement, which gained social media attention in early 2018, it's unmistakable that the intersection of gender and race informs society's understanding of incest as evidenced by the public's uneven reaction to Allen's marriage to Previn and the alleged assault of his then seven-year-old, white adopted daughter, Dylan O'Sullivan Farrow. The failure to see Previn as anything but complicit in her affair and subsequent marriage reveals the frailties of transracial adoption and the limits of the celebrated multicultural adoptive family. This chapter deploys the lens of incest to analyze the public discourse surrounding Allen, Previn, and Farrow. I situate Farrow's and Allen's writings (e.g., memoirs, op-eds, social media posts) alongside biographies, interviews, and the miniseries, tracing Farrow's and Allen's attempts to construct two contrasting and competing narratives, in which one is either upstanding or abusive, and, in Allen's case, a child predator. My analysis attends to the operationalization of fantasies of white adoptive motherhood that circulate alongside and in contrast to presumptions of adoptee affective behavior and performances of gratitude. This line of inquiry reveals the ways adoption as rescue becomes weaponized to be punitive in the lives of Asian adopted young women.

Prior to 1992, the world knew little about Soon-Yi Previn outside of her role as the rescued orphan daughter of Mia Farrow. Adopted in 1977 from South Korea during the waning years of Farrow's marriage to the composer André Previn, the young girl received little attention from the press or public following her adoption.[1] Yet at the end of 1992, Soon-Yi 's face was splashed across television and print news. The media and Farrow characterized her as the seductress of her mother's long-term boyfriend, Allen, who is also the long-presumed biological father of Farrow's youngest child, Ronan (née Satchel) O'Sullivan Farrow.[2]

Society lacks the language to grapple with Allen's sexual exploitation of Soon-Yi because hierarchies of kinship privilege legal marriage and historically marginalize nonnormative kin relations. The public overlooks abuse in nonnormative families when it limits its definition of family to legal marriage and legal adoption, which masks familial violence. On this point, Nancy Fischer writes, "Blood relations play a strong role in this argument, providing a rationalization for why the relationship between Woody Allen and Soon-Yi Previn was legitimate: Real relatives are related by blood; therefore, they were not committing incest. Such an argument employs a traditional definition of incest—limited only to sexual relations between blood relatives—that cannot encompass alternative family arrangements where family ties are not defined by law or blood."[3] By asserting that what transpired between Soon-Yi and

Allen was *not* incest or a form of manipulation and violence, society reinforces heteronormative and biological determinist notions of family. Placing primacy on legal marriage and legal adoption obscures the violence against Soon-Yi and focuses on Allen's adoption of Farrow's younger two children—Moses and Dylan—and fathering of Ronan. The youngest three Farrow children are often discussed together because of the custody hearings that occurred in the immediate wake of the scandal.

Simultaneously as Soon-Yi and Allen's "affair" scandalized the nation, Farrow accused Allen of molesting Dylan at her Connecticut home. Both Farrow and Dylan maintain that this abuse occurred, even though formal charges were never filed against Allen.[4] These accusations resurfaced when Allen received the 2014 Golden Globes' Cecil B. DeMille Award and again in 2018, following a December 7, 2017, op-ed by Dylan in the *Los Angeles Times*.[5] It is this juxtaposition—Farrow's reaction to the alleged molestation of Dylan versus Soon-Yi's rendering in her eyes—that underscores the uneven legibility of the Asian adoptee within the adoptive family. Public fascination with familial sexual violence extended only to Dylan because of the logics of family and white girlhood that protected her sexuality. The lack of legal charges was not considered an impediment to extending the framework of incest to Dylan's story as it was when considering Soon-Yi's. Dylan was seen as a child victim in need of protection and saving, whereas Soon-Yi was foreclosed from this possibility. As an adult Asian adoptee, she was seen as both the forever foreigner and the hypersexual Oriental woman. The latter characterization is particularly insidious, as she was automatically cast as a consenting equal with little to no recourse to be considered anything else. Contrasting the sexual violence enacted on Soon-Yi and on Dylan magnifies the failures of society and the media to acknowledge the violence in Soon-Yi's case. Not only did Soon-Yi's transracial adoption and her mother's nonnormative relationship with Allen, their not being legally married, fail to protect her, but the fact that she was on the cusp of young adulthood also meant that her Asian body was read as a threat.

The analytic of incest as a category of sexual violence serves as a lens to see how adoptive and other nonnormative family formations exist at the tenuous crossroads of legitimacy. I focus on how power functions within these kinship units, specifically between fathers / paternal figures and daughters, to make incest within adoptive and other nonnormative families legible.[6] Intimate father-daughter relationships in these families cannot be understood as only "cross-generational" because this fails to recognize the sexual violence and predation committed by men who possess paternal authority (e.g., parent's partner) in nonnormative kinship formations. If these articulations of family had been truly seen as *families*, then the discourse created by Farrow and the media surrounding the affair would not have positioned Soon-Yi in competition with her mother for Allen's affection. Rather, she would have been seen as an adolescent vulnerable to the incestuous sexual attentions of a parent. The adoptive family and the promises of adoption failed to protect Soon-Yi. She was envisioned as neither the legible daughter of Farrow nor a plausible victim of a sexual predator. The hypocritical response to the sexual transgression between Allen and Soon-Yi exposes the limitations of colorblindness and multiculturalism in understanding transracial adoptive families.

THE LIMITS OF ADOPTIVE MOTHERHOOD

In her memoir, *What Falls Away* (1997), Mia Farrow depicts herself as a parent guided by humanitarianism when discussing her multiple transnational and domestic transracial adoptions. Prior to the adoption of Soon-Yi, Farrow adopted two Vietnamese girls, Lark and Daisy, in 1973 and 1976. The children joined her and André Previn's biological sons, Matthew, Sascha, and Fletcher. It seems almost natural that Farrow, spurred to adopt because of the horrors of the war in Vietnam, turned to South Korea following the closure of Vietnamese adoptions as Americans exited the war. In the mid-1970s, South Korea was recovering from the Korean War and was witnessing rapid industrialization under a military dictator. Reflecting on her earliest international adoptions, Farrow comments, "For those children who had been abandoned, I felt I could give them that home and I would love them with all my heart. It was my way of trying to give back because my childhood was interrupted when I was nine, um, by polio. . . . When possible, if you can alleviate suffering, you should try. And then I thought it would be wonderful to adopt an older child because they don't get the chance. And so we adopted Soon-Yi."[7] Due to assumptions concerning the similarities between the plights of Vietnam and South Korea, as well as the Korean adoption program's reliable reputation, Farrow's decision to adopt from South Korea is unsurprising.

In many respects, the adoption of Soon-Yi mirrors other stories of 1970s Korean adoptions. Abandoned and found living on the streets of Seoul, Soon-Yi was given an age and name by the orphanage. Her age was estimated to be five, and its reported that a document bearing the signatures of both adoptive parent lists her date of birth as October 8, 1970.[8] While it does not seem like a pertinent detail, her age became a point of contention when her affair with Allen was revealed decades later and controversy arose over whether she had been of legal age to consent to sex with Allen.[9]

André Previn and Mia Farrow, like other adoptive parents across the US, turned to their congressional representatives, who passed individual pieces of legislation facilitating the entry and adoption of the child in question. Their adoption of Soon-Yi had been hindered by existing legislation regulating transnational adoptions, which limited the number of nonquota immigrant visas for eligible orphans to two per family. On May 15, 1978, Private Law 95-37 was passed by the US Congress to allow for Soon-Yi's legal adoption.[10] Adoptive families regardless of socioeconomic class used this practice if they exceeded the two orphan visas allotted per adoptive couple until the law changed with the passage of Public Law 95-417 on October 5, 1978.[11]

Yet, in other ways, Farrow's adoption was very much an exception. Unlike other adoptive parents at the time who would meet their children at an international airport in the US, Farrow traveled to Seoul. In the case of US adoptions of Korean children, adoptive parents were not required to finalize the process in the child's country of origin. It was not until the Korean government enacted the Special Adoption Law in 2013 that adoptive parents had the option to finalize their child's adoption in South Korea. Historically, adoptions were finalized in the country of adoption.[12] Implicit in Farrow's reflection on her travel to Korea is her belief that she is an exceptional parent. She writes, "But Soon-Yi was not a baby, and I felt it was important to go there and bring her home myself . . . I wanted to see the orphanage where she had spent more than a year, to meet her friends, and to take plenty of pictures for her scrapbook."[13] Farrow constructs a narrative of commitment to learning more about her child's ethnic heritage and life in South Korea. In doing so, she positions herself as a paragon of love in comparison to the absent birth family.

Soon-Yi has subsequently challenged this characterization of their earliest interactions from May 1977. In a rare interview, Soon-Yi recalls, "I remember the second I laid eyes on her. There was a big excitement and hoopla around her. And she came to me and she threw her arms around me to give me a big hug. I'm standing there rigidly, thinking, *Who is this woman, and can she get her hands off of me?* She didn't ring true or sincere."[14] Despite how Soon-Yi experienced the interaction, Farrow's depiction evoked images of a caring mother, and that image is what circulated in the media for decades, feeding into notions that demand the adoptee's gratefulness for their rescue.

Coinciding with the arrival of Soon-Yi was the demise of Farrow's relationship with André Previn. Her crumbling marriage did not deter her from further adoptions. With input from Previn as well as other close friends and family, Farrow adopted a young Korean boy with cerebral palsy in 1979. Arriving in January 1980, Moses Amadeus Farrow became the newest addition to the Farrow household. Coupled with Soon-Yi's purported intellectual disability, Moses served as a harbinger of future Farrow adoptions of disabled children.

During this period, the newly divorced mother of seven became the new muse for Woody Allen. The fifty-seven-year-old Allen seemed an unlikely match for Farrow given his "zero interest in kids" by Farrow's account.[15] Nevertheless, Allen contradicts this notion in his memoir, writing, "I liked kids and always got along with them. I never had any pronounced feelings about having any of my own."[16] He characterizes himself as seemingly ambivalent to fatherhood when he met Farrow and even comments, "Mia having seven kids caused me no anxiety."[17] This ambivalence may be more representative of Allen's feelings as he became enmeshed in the lives of the Farrow children, visiting with them in Manhattan and then in Connecticut, where Farrow maintained a summer home.

Even if Farrow believes Allen initially had no interest in children, her recollections alongside her children's memories indicate that Allen accepted her large family. Farrow discloses, "He started spending more time with the kids, and he gradually warmed up to them, and he was sweet to them. You know, nice to them. He was the person I loved, and as such, they loved him too."[18] Fletcher Previn also comments, "[Allen] very much was a father figure. I mean, I had my actual father, but, um, he was not around day-to-day, and Woody very much functioned in that capacity. He would have meals with us. We'd fish in the pond together up in Connecticut."[19] Moses recalls that Allen would come over each morning, often with muffins and two newspapers, the *New York Times* for himself and the *New York Post* for Moses to read the comics and do the word puzzles, and sit with the children as they ate breakfast.[20] Daisy Previn affirms her brothers' recollections, noting, "I would get up in the morning and he would be there, you know, waiting for us kids to wake up. We would go to his house on the weekends and spend the night when my mom would spend the weekend with him. In the back of his apartment, he made bunk beds for us . . . and a living space for us . . . so we'd feel comfortable."[21] Farrow's own reflections in her memoir support these sentiments: "At first we carried our stuff back and forth across [Central Park] with us. . . . In time, shelves appeared in the back bedroom, then a bunk bed, and we began to leave things there. The kids brought their friends along for sleepovers."[22] She further notes that, as a family unit, they began new traditions, including dining at the Russian Tea Room to celebrate birthdays.[23]

As their relationship progressed, so did Allen's ability to accept more children. He relented to the concept of adoption in the mid-1980s once Farrow assured him that the child would fall under her purview. In summer 1985

Dylan joined the family. Two years later, as her eldest son, Matthew, entered college, Farrow discovered that she was pregnant with her ninth child, Ronan.

Even though these memories have been publicly disclosed, Allen and Farrow dispute the nature of his involvement with the children. He counters her statements that he was involved and presents himself as merely her boyfriend with little to no involvement with the family. In his memoir, Allen writes, "We never even lived together, I never once in the thirteen years we dated ever slept at her apartment in New York. Apart from a small number of times that first year or two where she might stay at night at my place, we lived separately. The moment school ended, she lit out for Connecticut with her brood, and apart from a July Fourth weekend or a Labor Day weekend, I spent the summers alone in Manhattan."[24] Unsurprisingly, Soon-Yi stands by Allen's assertions of his limited involvement with her and her siblings.[25] The Allen and Farrow households' divergent memories of his involvement are significant given Allen's adoption of the younger Farrow children in December 1991.

Regardless, as primary custody of her youngest five children remained with Farrow (twins Sascha and Matthew remained in England with their father), they were exposed to the unmarried couple's forging of family ties and traditions. Farrow even built a separate bathroom for Allen at her Connecticut home, Frog Hollow, to accommodate Allen's neurosis and obsessive-compulsive disorder.[26] Allen engaged with the various Farrow offspring in a manner that suggests minimum participation as she actively tried to facilitate a relationship between him and her children. For example, Farrow encouraged Allen to take Moses to basketball games and Central Park prior to Allen's formal adoption of him. Allen also taught him how to fish.[27] Additionally, Farrow strove to nurture a relationship between Soon-Yi and Allen, recounting, "I worried that [Soon-Yi] had lacked a positive male role model in her life. So when she was little, I asked Woody several times if he would take her for a walk, buy her an ice cream or something, but he had declined."[28] Her persistence in fostering a relationship between the pair eventually succeeded. As Soon-Yi entered high school in the late 1980s and displayed an interest in basketball, she began to accompany Allen to New York Knicks basketball games. Moreover, Allen initiated a relationship with Farrow's son, Fletcher, casting him in *Radio Days* (1987). The other children also received bit parts in Allen's films. Ultimately, perhaps the truth lies somewhere in between.

The Farrow-Allen relationship deteriorated by the start of the 1990s. It came to a shocking end when Farrow discovered nude Polaroid photos of Soon-Yi at Allen's Central Park East apartment in December 1991. Allen admitted to Farrow that his relationship with Soon-Yi was sexual. This revelation was almost immediately followed by charges that Allen had molested

Dylan at Frog Hollow. While Connecticut State Attorney Frank Maco and the state police investigated Allen, Farrow sought dissolution of Allen's adoptions of Moses, Dylan, and Ronan and custody of these children in New York. The New York City Child Welfare Administration also investigated the molestation allegations. As information concerning the affair emerged, the media dissected the Farrow-Allen relationship and commented on whether incest had occurred. Much interest centered on whether Allen was a surrogate father to Soon-Yi and her siblings.

During the court proceedings, Judge Elliott Wilk found that Allen "demonstrated no parenting skills that would qualify him as an adequate custodian."[29] Judge Wilk's assessment relies on gendered stereotypes about reproductive labor and raises the question of whether fathers, biological, adoptive, or step, who are the primary breadwinners in two-parent households would also be considered inadequate custodians if they "lacked familiarity with the most basic details of the children's daily existence."[30] His conclusions echoed sentiments expressed by Farrow during the court proceedings as she portrayed Allen as uninvolved in the children's lives. This image of Allen as a deficient father figure relied on specific "good" fatherhood tropes. Lacking detailed knowledge about the children's academic performance or health meant that he was somehow a less "real" parent in contrast to Farrow. Allen's level of involvement remained at the crux of whether he acted as a surrogate father or not, and these matters received a level of critical attention that is rarely applied to fathers outside of nonnormative families.

Marilyn Strathern's work on postmodern kinship formations is helpful in contextualizing Farrow and Allen's nontraditional relationship. While maternity is often conferred via gestational birth, paternity is inferred and "fatherhood is constituted in [the father's] relationship to the mother."[31] According to Strathern, "Fatherhood has to be declared, whether through the public relationship of marriage or the private acknowledgement of the mother."[32] Although Farrow was the adoptive, not biological, mother of Soon-Yi and some of her children, her legal positioning as mother cemented her connection to them, especially her transnationally adopted children, whose presence in the US was predicated on their adoption. Biological relatedness was replaced by legal connectedness to her adopted children.

Farrow privately sanctioned Allen's social parenthood. By virtue of their decade-long romance, Allen easily slipped into the role of surrogate father, even if he argues that he was never comfortable with nor embraced the role. Allen's location as father was solidified not only through his adoption of Moses and Dylan but also through Farrow's integration of him into her family, including giving birth to Ronan, since Allen's paternity was established at the time and at the subsequent 1992 custody hearing. Allen's emotional and financial care for the children provides claims to fatherhood and normalcy in ways that should not be minimized or considered less than the same behaviors exhibited by emotionally distant and/or financially absent biological fathers.

LOCATING INCEST WITHIN ADOPTIVE FAMILIES

Adoptive families are often situated outside of normative constructions of incest because of the primacy placed on biological relatedness and the historical framing of incest in terms of consanguinity. The lack of genetic ties leads people to assume that incest cannot occur between adoptive family members. This notion exposes the outdated nature of conceptualizations of incest that overlook how adoptive families are equal to biological families. Diminishing the possibility of incest within adoptive families upholds the notion that adoption is somehow a lesser version of biological kinship while overlooking the psychological trauma of incest. This erroneous assumption does great damage to how we recognize sexual violence in adoptive families. These are also families wherein the adoptee may be reluctant to disclose abuse for fear of rejection. Often the abuse that adoptees undergo may not result in the perpetrator being punished or in adoptees being protected from future abuse.[33]

To better understand how this chapter deploys the lens of incest, I foreground its psychological dimensions to recognize exploitation and the role of power differentials.[34] Incest thus is not predicated on the biological. When considering the sexual exploitation of children, broadly, it is vital to underscore the position of authority the adult holds in that configuration. The parental figure in this relationship relies on manipulating the parent-child relationship. Judith Lewis Herman and Lisa Hirschman contend,

> Because a child is powerless in relation to an adult, she is not free to refuse a sexual advance. Therefore, any sexual relationship between the two must necessarily take on some of the coercive characteristics of a rape, even if, as is usually the case, the adult uses positive enticements rather than force to establish the relationship. This is particularly true of incest between parent and child: it is a rape in the sense that it is a coerced sexual relationship. The question of whether force is involved is largely irrelevant, since force is rarely necessary to obtain compliance. The parent's authority over the child is usually sufficient to compel obedience. Similarly, the question of the child's "consent" is irrelevant. Because the child does not have the power to withhold consent, she does not have the power to grant it.[35]

In this discussion of children and their lack of power, it is important to recognize that incest is fundamentally sexually exploitative as well as violent. A feminist definition of incest accounts for biopolitics and technologies of power, as articulated by Michel Foucault, whereby incest is a tool deployed to control populations.[36] Expanding the definition of incest validates the experiences of adoptees without minimizing the sexual violence as unfamilial because genetic ties are absent.[37] Such an expansive definition accounts for the power wielded by nonnormative fathers in these families, whereby a mother's boyfriend may wield as much control, if not more, over the lives of her children as the biological father.

Power dynamics are exacerbated when one considers how adoptees internalize messages of adoption as an act of saving for which they should be grateful to their adoptive parents. Adoptive families are imagined as normal and biological families as dangerous. Any type of sexual abuse, including incest, is considered an anomaly and out of public purview because it is believed that these families—screened and vetted by adoption agencies—could not be potential perpetrators of illicit abuse. Instead, victim-blaming rhetoric may occur or, even worse, a web of deep pathology whereby society overlooks this form of sexual violence because it only conceives of incest when thinking about the heterosexual, biological family. Emphasis on biological relatedness positions stepfamily, adoptive family, or foster family incest as either not quite as incestuous as biological family incest or not incest.[38] Interrogating incest exposes the limits of the legitimacy of nonnormative families, as unmarried, nongenetically related families operate in a world that often views these families as deviant in the absence of biological and sexual reproduction. As a result of this cultural assessment, abuse within households that exist at the fragile boundaries of illegibility and legibility falls through the cracks of society.

The postmodern family, including that formed through Farrow and Allen's long-term relationship, challenges widely held beliefs concerning incest in biological, legal, and social relationships. Farrow and Allen's long-term relationship, cohabitation, his adoption of her youngest three children, and the birth of his biological son solidified their familial ties. By providing financial stability and support to Farrow and ostensibly her children, Allen further positioned himself in the paternal role, irrespective of intention.

Regarding Allen's recognition of adoptive familial relationships, Judge Wilk commented, "[Allen lacked] understanding that the bonds developed between adoptive brothers and sisters are no less worthy of respect and protection than those between biological siblings," affirming that families are not merely biologically constructed.[39] In fact, his words recognize and make visible the familial ties that exist within adoptive families. Farrow's perception of their family was similar, as she is quoted as saying "You're not supposed to fuck the kids."[40] In her eyes, Allen had dutifully assumed the paternal role within their nonnormative family. Directly countering these claims, Allen contended,

> People can argue, "Well, symbolically you're her father," and that usually would be a very good point, but in this situation it doesn't happen to be true. Soon-Yi will tell you that she and Lark and Daisy and Fletcher and all those people never for a second thought of me in any paternal way. They thought I was a joke, they thought I was a silly person. Their father was André Previn. They knew it. They had no interest in me.[41]

However, it is precisely because of the nature of his relationship with Farrow that his actions with Soon-Yi come into question. If incest is predicated on power dynamics and exploitation of the existing power structure, then it becomes clear that an incestuous relationship occurred. Farrow carved out a space for Allen within her family, and he adapted his lifestyle to accommodate the ever-growing brood.

Allen's significant role in the Farrow family can be seen in how Farrow addressed the question of whether she engaged in other romantic relationships after her partnership with Allen ended. Indicating that she had dated since their breakup, Farrow comments, "I never brought them home 'cause I didn't want to risk anybody falling for one of my children or grandchildren. If I couldn't trust Woody after twelve years, I would never take another risk with anyone else."[42] Her disclosure implies that she believed any person she had a relationship with had the potential to be a predator, even though the majority of men are not child molesters. Perhaps Farrow's own formative experiences as a teenager and young adult with significantly older men, including ex-husband Frank Sinatra, impressed on her that all men are potential predators.[43]

FAILURE TO PROTECT THE CHILD OF COLOR

The media's depictions of Soon-Yi invoked the seductive-daughter stereotype when her relationship with Allen became public knowledge. Her age—nineteen—fed into the constructions of a barely legal nymphet. Discussing this trope, Herman and Hirschman note, "[She] lives on, an active inhabitant of the fantasy life of the millions of ordinary citizens who constitute the readership of *Chic, Hustler, Playboy, Penthouse,* and the like."[44] Herman and Hirschman were even more concerned with the fact that the seductive daughter had infiltrated professional clinical literature: "A few authors were apparently troubled by a need to account for those cases in which sexual relations between children and adults had undeniably occurred. In general, these investigators tended to focus on qualities in the child victims, which might have fostered the development of an incestuous relationship. They, too, conjured up the image of the magical child, the nymphet, who has the power to entrap men."[45] Placing blame on the child absolves the adult of wrongdoing. Steven Angelides finds that "as late as the mid-1970s psychiatric studies cited evidence that young children were capable of seduction and commonly engaged in it."[46] Emphasis on children's sexuality condones the predation of adolescent bodies by adults. This trope underpins the genre of barely legal pornography and sets the stage for applauding older men's relationships with younger women.[47] Fischer notes, "These rationales arguing that the Allen-Previn affair was not incestuous rest on the libertarian assumption that Allen and Previn were consenting adults who were free to become sexually involved as they so choose."[48] To dismiss the sexual violence Allen enacted on Soon-Yi means to be complicit in the pathologization of Asian women's sexuality. As a result of the eroticized stereotypes of hypersexualized Asian women, society condones the predation of their bodies. The seductive-daughter trope, in conjunction with the lotus blossom stereotype, cements Soon-Yi's status as perpetrator and sexually ambitious temptress. She is represented as someone who was never coerced or encouraged to take nude Polaroids of herself; instead, she is framed as a willing and consensual participant in the affair.[49]

Farrow's castigation of Soon-Yi illustrates the limits of colorblind love. As soon as the relationship between Soon-Yi and Allen became public, Farrow distanced herself from her daughter and pathologized Soon-Yi as a defective, intellectually disabled adoptee.[50] Disability feeds into tropes of adoption as rescue and links Soon-Yi to excessive sexuality vis-à-vis the birth-mother-as-sex-worker trope, discussed further in this chapter. The love Farrow professed for her daughter was contingent, or perhaps never really present, though she asserted nearly thirty years after the initial scandal, "I love Soon-Yi, you know."[51] Farrow's actions in the immediate aftermath of the scandal and in the ensuing decades make evident the precarious positioning of adoptees within their families—a presence contingent on fulfilling specific behaviors and norms typifying what it means to be a "good" child. There was no regard for whether Soon-Yi was exploited; rather, the photographs of her body made real the Orientalist fantasies of dangerous Asian sexuality, whereby the adopted Asian daughter seduces the father. Transnational, transracial adoption is thus perverted, and, more importantly, so is the multiculturalist idealism on which it rests.

Constructed as an adult, Soon-Yi fell victim to racialized stereotypes of Asian women. She was no longer a girl. She was a sexual being. Discussing the change in her relationship with Soon-Yi in the weeks after learning of the affair, Farrow writes,

> She was my child, but I could not help her. I could scarcely look at her. We had become something else to each other. We had to go through this separately. In anger she threatened to kill herself. In anger I told her I hated her. It was a relief when she went back to college. I loved her, I missed her, and I worried for her, but it was hard for me to be near her.[52]

Her statement that she loved her daughter does not discount the fact that in subsequent months Farrow and her supporters continuously and publicly doubted Soon-Yi's intellectual capacity. An antagonistic relationship was created and solidified. Reflecting on the months prior to learning about the affair, Farrow notes, "Now I understood the reason for the dramatic change in her attitude the previous year, the new little laugh of superiority, the smugness, and the coldness to the other kids."[53] This revelation situates Soon-Yi as someone with a secret who reveled in knowing that she had won the affection of her mother's partner. An adversarial relationship formed between mother and daughter instead of a relationship whereby the mother believed her daughter to be the victim of a sexual predator.

Soon-Yi was always a sexual subject in the public imaginary in ways that Dylan was not. The juxtaposition of Farrow's reactions to Soon-Yi and Dylan highlights the degree to which the multicultural experiment that is transracial adoption failed to protect Soon-Yi. The divergence between Farrow's reactions reveals the insidious effects of Orientalism on Asian and Asian American girls' and women's sexuality and their access to innocence and purity. Race cannot be ignored in our analysis of the public's reaction and even Farrow's response to the affair between Allen and Soon-Yi. Her status as "always sexual" underscores how the adopted Asian child is never really allowed to be a child. This is not to say that I elide children's sexuality, a critique that Angelides offers regarding feminist analyses of incest and molestation. Instead, I am interested in how the perceived sexual prowess of a teenager and child has been used and misused to justify treatment of Soon-Yi Previn and Dylan Farrow in the media.

Adult standards of sexual promiscuity attached themselves to Previn, as Farrow, in contrast, sought to protect her white adoptive daughter Dylan from Allen. This protection was seen before and after the initial accusation of molestation occurred. Rhetoric concerning the innocence of white girlhood shielded Dylan from the accusations Soon-Yi encountered, even though Allen is more than three decades her senior. In her memoir, Farrow provides the groundwork for positioning Allen as someone with indecent intentions toward Dylan, locating him as "obsessed" and overly affectionate, exhibiting actions that verged on inappropriate.[54] Farrow's children Fletcher, Dylan, and Ronan, as well as friends of the family Priscilla Gilman and Casey Pascal, echo these assertions in the HBO miniseries.[55] Consequently, when Allen is accused of sexually molesting Dylan in Farrow's Connecticut home, these allegations seem unsurprising. Not only did Farrow request an investigation be launched and record Dylan in the days after the molestation was said to have occurred; she also sought adoption dissolutions for Dylan, Moses, and Ronan, which were finalized less than a year prior to the allegations and the end of their relationship.

This critique is not offered as a tool to minimize or cast doubt on what happened between Dylan Farrow and Woody Allen. Rather, I am invested in how whiteness, racial difference, and sexuality are constructed. Mia Farrow overlooked the alleged bonds shared between adopted daughter and adoptive mother for one child while protecting another. Farrow did what many adoptees fear: she abandoned her child. Although legally the adoption still stands, as there are no accounts of a dissolution of her adoption of Soon-Yi, and while we may never know the inner workings of Farrow and Soon-Yi's relationship, the erasure of this maternal bond cannot go unnoticed. Farrow abandoned one of her children following the 1992 scandal but continued to adopt transracially and transnationally, raising the question of what it means to parent. The limitations of assimilation rhetoric, which encourages adoptive parents to treat their adopted offspring "just like their very own," are exposed.

What is even more disconcerting is when Allen's supporters claim that Soon-Yi and Allen never had a familial connection. Following renewed interest in Allen's alleged molestation of Dylan, Robert B. Weide, a longtime friend of Allen, penned a 2018 article publicly declaring that no father-daughter relationship had existed between Allen and Soon-Yi since he had never married Farrow or adopted Soon-Yi.[56] This was not a new claim. This same logic was invoked in 1992 when the scandal first emerged in the public eye. In defense of Allen, Michael Lewis wrote, "[His sexual relationship with Soon-Yi] was not child abuse. And it was not incest, for Allen was never a father to Soon-Yi Previn. Allen's crime was to fall in love in a way for which society was not really prepared."[57] These sentiments reflect Allen's initial assertion, "It wasn't like she was my daughter."[58] Yet this overemphasis on their lack of a prior legal relationship ignores the power dynamics between Allen and Soon-Yi. By delegitimizing the abuse that transpired between Allen and Soon-Yi, we become complicit in delegitimizing other familial bonds.

PATHOLOGIZING THE ADOPTEE AS DEFECTIVE

Farrow, as well as her friends and acquaintances, portrayed Soon-Yi as intellectually and potentially developmentally disabled while also invoking the seductive-daughter trope. Her cognitive abilities were routinely focused on, with an emphasis on how elementary school testing revealed "minor learning disabilities, including trouble in processing information as well as an IQ slightly below average."[59] Farrow's nanny, Kristi Groteke, recounted that Soon-Yi was slow, with an IQ of 94, and that she "*acts* like a kid."[60] Groteke further opined that "in person she looks no older than sixteen."[61] This subjective comment undermines her credibility because of her assumption that if one is over eighteen, one looks their age and is not immature or seemingly incapable. Given the continued infantilization of adult adoptees in mainstream society, it is unsurprising that Farrow and her supporters portrayed Soon-Yi as ill equipped to make decisions for herself.

Pathologized as defective, the adult adoptee is rendered powerless, incompetent, and in continuous need of parental support. Adoptees are presumed to be unable to cope with their adoption histories or to delve into nuanced adoption conversations without becoming emotionally involved given their adoption status. Their status as perpetual children removes any possibility for agency in mainstream adoption discourse. The media and Farrow's supporters created a new narrative of infantilization by portraying Soon-Yi as a child even as they questioned her age. The specter of the adult adoptee body cannot be properly read as an individual capable of making judicious decisions.

American perceptions of disability clouded Soon-Yi's framing within the media.[62] In the nineteenth century, beginning with the medicalization of disability and under the influence of French physician Edward Seguin, individuals associated with "feeblemindedness" were infantilized and presented as requiring consistent aid and support to encourage mental development.[63] While Seguin's rhetoric was produced during a wider medicalization of society, the institutionalization of disabilities and pathologization of non-able-bodied individuals generated conditions that lauded infantilization. Learning disabilities, real and imagined, became liabilities. I do not seek to assess Soon-Yi's intellectual abilities. My interest rests in how the discourses of ability and disability shaped popular culture's treatment of Soon-Yi and influenced whether she was viewed as engaged in a predatory relationship.[64] I am invested in how the accounts of Soon-Yi's cognitive abilities and their perceived origins informed discussions of her sexuality. In what follows, I explore how the intersections of adoption, ability, race, and sexuality create conditions that result in victim-blaming and further pathologizing of Asian American women's sexuality.

As Soon-Yi's age and intellect were questioned, Farrow reframed her narrative of adoption as humanitarianism. Farrow cast herself as Soon-Yi's protector, saving the intellectually disabled orphan while simultaneously positioning her daughter as the licentious Oriental seductress. To bolster this notion of adoptive mother as savior, Farrow shares recordings of a just-adopted Soon-Yi in the *Allen v. Farrow* miniseries. In one audio clip, Soon-Yi can be heard disclosing that her Korean mother did not hug her and recalling, "When I did bad. Soon-Yi did not eat."[65] This is followed by a subsequent recording of her saying, "Good mama say you want to come stay in my house? And I said yes. Then I said, good mama give me cuddle, give me kiss."[66] This recording is coupled with Farrow's statement: "Soon-Yi, I think had a complicated relationship with her biological mother. She left her out on the street. She said something like, 'We're going shopping. Be back in five minutes.' She put her somewhere to wait, and she never came back. So, she had been running wild in the street, with a group of other kids, boys. . . . And she referred to her mother on those tapes as 'naughty mama.'"[67] Yet this recollection proffered by Farrow counters Soon-Yi's own memories, such as one quoted in a 2018 interview:

> When Soon-Yi was a girl, she says, Farrow asked her to make a tape about her origins, detailing how she'd been the daughter of a prostitute who beat her. The request puzzled her, Soon-Yi says, since she had no memory of anything like that, so she refused. (Soon-Yi says she'd love to find her biological mother, but she assumes she's dead; a 23andMe kit she tried didn't turn up any promising matches.) "I had nowhere to go," she says of that period in Seoul, "so I was running around the streets, going through the garbage looking for food. And I ate a bar of soap. The soap was the worst-tasting—I could think of it now, it was just disgusting. And then I was looking outside a bakery, you know, because I was starving, and this woman asked if I wanted something to eat. She bought me something, and she was trying to get information from me about where I lived. I wouldn't answer, so she brought me to the police station and then the police sent me to an orphanage. I liked it there, and then some people came—and I remember hiding under a table— to take me away to a different orphanage."[68]

It is disconcerting on multiple levels to think about how the recordings Farrow had Soon-Yi complete as a child ostensibly for personal and family use have been broadcast worldwide in an effort to construct Farrow as a "good mother." Soon-Yi rarely speaks to the public, so her 2018 interview was a notable exception given her relative silence over the last two decades. Thus, publicly available information about her is primarily driven by Farrow's disclosures and what Allen reveals to the press. Although she is an adult woman with children of her own, the adoptee continuously finds herself spoken for by her white adoptive mother and her white husband, the latter evoking stereotypical images of Asian wives silenced by their white husbands. Over the last two decades, Farrow has crafted an insidious narrative suggesting that the apple doesn't fall far from the tree: if Soon-Yi had remained in South Korea, would she have become a sex worker like her birth mother?[69]

The stereotype of the mythological biological mother as sex worker is not new. Adoptive parents have routinely used this trope to demonstrate how they saved their children, especially for transnationally, transracially adopted Asian children. In the case of Soon-Yi, Farrow alleged that her birth mother had also physically abused her, "forcing her to kneel in a doorway and slamming the door against her head."[70] The birth-mother-as-sex-worker trope is intertwined with the nineteenth-century generalization that "giving birth to an illegitimate child was considered a sign of feeblemindedness."[71] The implication, then, is that Soon-Yi's mother, by virtue of her status as a sex worker and unwed mother, was at fault for her daughter's intellectual disability. The construction of the sex worker mother as bad mother informs the stereotype that these women were "directly responsible for producing degenerate children."[72] Compared with the mythic prostitute birth mother, Farrow is presented as the good and moral mother.[73] This rhetoric linking disability with sex work and illegitimate births fueled public assumptions regarding Soon-Yi's intellectual abilities.

Soon-Yi bore the shame of her biological mother's status and the stigma attached to Asian women's sexuality. The Polaroids in Allen's apartment seemingly proved her promiscuity. Her sexuality was unable to be contained, which is why she proved sexually available to Allen. The rendering of Soon-Yi as a hypersexed Asian American woman, in combination with discourses of promiscuity as a result of the circumstances surrounding her birth and early childhood, results in a lack of compassion or empathy for her vulnerability to abuse. She is never considered the subject of predatory behavior; rather, she is viewed as an instigator or, at the least, a complicit party. Yet the characterizations of Soon-Yi are contradictory, even as her body could be read as exemplifying the ways the nexus of objectification operates in shaping the perceptions of adopted women. The intelligence associated with being an Oriental seductress is negated by the vicious maligning of Soon-Yi's intellectual abilities by Farrow and her supporters. This rendering of her did not appear to be incongruent for many; instead, it preyed on broader Oriental beliefs that the savage body must be tamed. Because of her sexual excess, the Oriental beauty cannot be trusted on its own.

THE LIMITATIONS OF LOVE

Deviant. Foreign. Hypersexual. These three adjectives implicitly shaped how the media and even her mother understood Soon-Yi after the photos of her naked body surfaced. The case study of the dissolution of Farrow and Soon-Yi's relationship as mother and daughter and the eventual marital union of Soon-Yi and Allen highlight the complexities of adoption, kinship, and sexuality. Discourse concerning the erotics of Asian womanhood is intertwined with the trope of the seductive daughter. These pathological constructions allowed for Soon-Yi to be positioned as her mother's adversary for Allen's affections.

The rhetoric on Soon-Yi's ability status should have drawn more scrutiny over parental fitness and Farrow's status as a "good" parent. During the custody court proceedings of Ronan and Dylan, "Farrow admitted hitting Soon-Yi with a chair and locking her in her room."[74] Court testimony on behalf of Allen included allegations that she also mistreated her other children, with a movie producer noting, "Lark was viewed as a 'scullery maid.'"[75] Echoing this notion are Soon-Yi's own memories of being used as a "domestic" along with Lark and Daisy.[76] While status as a scullery maid may not explicitly conjure images of abuse, this maltreatment exposes systemic problems of violence within the family. Soon-Yi remembers, "Mia used to write words on my arm, which was humiliating, so I'd always wear long-sleeved shirts. She would also tip me upside down, holding me by my feet, to get the blood to drain to my head. Because she thought—or she read it, God knows where she came up with the notion—that blood going to my head would make me smarter or something."[77] She also shares instances of being slapped across the face, spanked with a hairbrush, and called stupid and moronic by Farrow.[78] In her press release following the media storm surrounding the news of her affair with Allen, Soon-Yi disclosed the physical and emotional abuse within the household: "It's true Mia was violent with me and I have conclusive proof. . . . I don't think you can raise 11 (and soon she will have 13) children with sufficient love and care. Take it from one who's lived through it—it can't be done. Some of us got neglected, some of us got smothered."[79] More recently, Moses Farrow shared about physical abuse within the family: "From an early age, my mother demanded obedience and I was often hit as a child. She went into unbridled rages if we angered her, which was intimidating at the very least and often horrifying, leaving us not knowing what she would do."[80] He also wrote, "It pains me to recall instances in which I witnessed siblings, some blind or physically disabled, dragged down a flight of stairs to be thrown into a bedroom or a closet, then having the door locked from the outside. She even shut my brother Thaddeus, paraplegic from polio, in an outdoor shed over-night as punishment for a minor transgression."[81] Farrow refutes these accu-sations, and her other children have praised her mothering publicly on social media and in the HBO miniseries. These accusations elicit uncertainty over whether Farrow treated her biological children differently from her adopted children, or whether she treated her children of color differently from her white children.

Though we may never know the extent of the physical or emotional abuse that took place in the Farrow home, we do know that far too often adoptees' allegations of abuse are dismissed and overlooked. The rhetoric of adoption as a humanitarian act supersedes the possibility that negligence or other mis-deeds could occur within the family. One only needs to read adult adoptees' reflections to witness the damaging psychological, physical, and sexual abuse that took place in otherwise "good" adoptive families.[82] This masking of injus-tice is exacerbated when one considers the deaths of adoptees at the hands of their adoptive parents.[83]

The assertions of abuse also call attention to Allen's ability to manipu-late Soon-Yi to leave one form of abuse for another. How might the emo-tional and physical abuse within the Farrow household have made Soon-Yi ripe for a subsequent unhealthy and manipulative relationship? Reflecting on Farrow's cruelty, she notes that Allen demonstrated affection in comparison: "So of course I was thrilled and ran to it. . . . I wasn't the one who went after Woody—where would I get the nerve? He pursued me. That's why the rela-tionship has worked: I felt valued."[84] Discounting how a person starved for positive attention and love may be drawn to another's kindness minimizes the manner in which predatory relationships arise and grooming practices. This also neglects to account for the influence of Farrow's own relationships with men on her daughter's understanding of what relationships look like.

Failure to read the decade-long Allen and Farrow relationship and their children as a family is why the incestuous nature of Allen's union with Soon-Yi is never legible. The media and society cannot comprehend the possibility of incest if the family environment they are a product of is never seen as *real*. Instead, their sexual liaison and eventual marriage was viewed as scandalous for her alleged seduction and not for his predatory nature. Even in the wake of the #MeToo movement and the excoriation of Jeffrey Epstein and Har-vey Weinstein, critics of Allen, including Ronan Farrow, whose investigative reporting exposed Weinstein, have failed to interrogate how uneven power dynamics affected his pursuit of Soon-Yi.[85] To include adoptive families and other nonnormative kinship relationships in discussions of incest accounts validates these formations as legitimate forms of family. In the next chapter, I shift from the interrogation of adoption's unmet promises and white fantasies of adoption to explore Asian American investments in particular narratives of adoption that emphasize adoptees in search of an intrinsic part of their identity. That fantasy of adoption relies on static notions of Asia whereby the adoptee seeks an elusive home. I return to fictional portrayals of adoption to attend to the invocation of sentimentality in adoption, exploring the adoptee's return to the motherland—their country of origin.

CHAPTER 4

Reimagining Korean Adoption in *Seoul Searching*

How the Asian American imaginary renders adoptees is important when interrogating representations of adoptees in popular culture. To limit society's encounters with adoption to mainstream American (read: white) portrayals or to adoptee first-person storytelling obscures the ways adoptees' interactions—both real and imagined—with Asian Americans, and Korean Americans in particular, shape both communities' understandings of one another. This chapter engages the question of representation by Asian American cultural producers, building on my prior examination of what happens when writers of color tell adoption stories.[1] While much has been written on white authors appropriating the experiences of people of color and Indigenous persons, little has been said about authors of color who write across race and the type of accountability needed to ensure that their work does not replicate the violence of appropriation and pathologization that exist in the words of white authors.[2] There is a need for an ethics of representation. I am cautious about how cultural producers may be inspired by adoptee stories but create cultural artifacts rooted in co-optation and exploitation. For example, *Losing Isaiah* (1995) and *The Blind Side* (2009), two films featuring the transracial adoption of Black children by white women, fuel notions of rescue with little account for the fictionalized films' role in perpetuating the pathologization of Black motherhood and Black families while upholding the notion of white families as saviors.[3]

This chapter contends with the use of adoptees as points of comparison by some Asian Americans to claim a more authentic Korean or Asian experience. I am reminded of season 1, episode 5, "BBQ" of David Chang's *Ugly Delicious* (2018–20) in which Chang sits down for Korean barbeque with performance artist David Choe, actor Steven Yeun, and Jenee Kim, the owner of Park's BBQ in LA's Koreatown, where the meal was filmed.[4] The four joke about Chang's wanting to open a Korean restaurant, and Choe remarks that it would have no authenticity. In response, Chang jokes, "Like I'm a Korean Vanilla Ice?" The banter ends with the following dialogue:

CHANG: I take Korean self-loathing to another level.
YEUN: Korean Vanilla Ice, though?
CHOE: Just do the rest of the show in Korean. Let's hear how good your Korean is.
CHANG: No. I'm like a Korean that was adopted by white parents that has an Asian woman fetish.

The scene closes with them laughing, and then viewers are transported to Chang's next location in Copenhagen, Denmark, also home to a sizable Korean adoptee population.[5] In the LA Koreatown exchange, adoptees are rendered approximate Asian Americans. Their belonging is contingent and inauthentic. Not only does Chang presuppose a singular authentic experience; he links Korean identity to being raised by Korean parents. Chang's comments may appear innocuous, but in giving them a platform on his widely acclaimed show, he feeds into stereotypes of adoptee Otherness, even though for all intents and purposes, as I have discussed throughout this monograph, Asian adoptees are Asian American.

When scholars such as David L. Eng and Shinee Han attempt to provocatively raise the question of whether the Korean transnational adoptee is an immigrant, Korean, or Korean American, Eng and Han engage in the same marginalization Chang does in *Ugly Delicious*.[6] This separating of adoptees from Asian Americans implies adoptees are not Asian American.[7] Korean adoptees, and by extension Korean adoptive families as well as other Asian adoptees and their families, represent a new strand of the Asian American experience. To elide these interventions—in who belongs within Asian America—participates in the erasure of adoptee experiences. There's a presupposed authentic "Asian" experience that adoptees are held up against. This structuring—Asian adoptee versus Asian American—contributes to adoptees' pathologization and reinscribes notions of adoptees' inherent lack. I reject this approach, as it overlooks the heterogeneity within the community including the fact that adoptees are Asian American. Whether Asian adoptees claim that identity is a whole other matter.

The question of authenticity is critical considering adoptees' self-identification. For Asian adoptees who never thought of themselves as Asian American or even Asian, the anti-Asian racism associated with the COVID-19 pandemic has placed an Asian (American) identity at the forefront of their minds. Media interviews demonstrate their complicated relationship with their ethnic/racial identities.[8] These media stories position adoptees as experiencing an "awakening" concerning racial identity and elide the experiences of adoptees—including me—who see themselves as Asian American.[9] After taking into account adoptees who may not see themselves as racialized subjects, adoptee-authored writings that demonstrate the desire for whiteness, and adoptees' cultural whiteness, the question remains whether there is something about adoptees claiming Asian America that assumes they operate with an inherent lack due to their adoption.

Perhaps the interpretation of Asian adoptees as approximate Asians is what feeds the perception of melancholia in adoptees. In framing adoptees as existing in a state of melancholia, we entertain reductive notions of what it means to confront the multiple, compounding losses, contradictions, and complications wrought by adoption. Melancholia reduces adoptee vocalizations of the inherent complexity of adoption to pathology. And while adoptees may experience bouts of melancholia like any other individual or experience depression or dejection, a hyperfocus on melancholic adoptees elides adoption's complexities in favor of pathologization. Ayla McCullough's use of Jasbir Puar's concept of maiming to understand adoptee subjectivity is helpful for thinking about how adoption curtails the growth of aspects of adoptees' selves.[10] Similarly, Jieun Lee offers transgressive melancholia as a concept to acknowledge melancholia as "a state of resistance, capacity, and possibility." She notes, "The performativity of melancholia [is] a transgressive force that (re)shapes Korean adoptee and orphan characters' experiences of loss, loneliness, dislocation, and alienation."[11] Lee's invocation of melancholia as a form of resistance accounts for the capaciousness of adoptee affect to account for the range of the minor registers of affect. Adoptees' interiority is thus influenced not only by their ability to negotiate minor feelings but also in their access to name those feelings without encountering labels of melancholia.

Adoptees seem to be a vehicle for non-adopted Asian Americans to grapple with being an approximate of something and not the ideal, evoking parallels to the fetishization of mixed-race characters as the tragic mulatta stereotype. In the case of mixed-race adoptees, this becomes a combination of the two. Scholars who apply the lens of melancholia to adoptees deny adoptee autonomy and agency by fetishizing adoption as something that is enacted on the bodies of adoptees and not experienced by adoptees in their daily lives. Adoption is not a singular act; and yet, if one engages in Asian American studies application of melancholia onto adoptee bodies, it appears as if the complexities of adoption do not exist. This reductive lens fails to account for the systemic nature of adoption and the ways in which adoption as an analytic reveals adoption's interconnectedness with broader structures (e.g., militarism, imperialism, settler colonialism, immigration).

The Asian American fantasy of adoption tells a story that plays with notions of a presumed "authentic" Asian American experience while trafficking in the same romanticization of adoption similar to white American / mainstream notions of adoption. I turn my focus to the Netflix-released *Seoul Searching* (2015), a John Hughes–inspired dramedy by Benson Lee. *Seoul Searching* explores the Korean diaspora's return to 1980s South Korea from the perspective of college-age Koreans who have grown up in Europe and North America. This summer of identity exploration draws on Lee's own experiences participating in a South Korean government–sponsored program. The film is one of the few representations of Korean adopted women produced by an Asian American in mainstream popular culture. Another example is Stephanie Vandergosh (Karin Anna Cheung) from *Better Luck Tomorrow* (2002); nonetheless, as discussed in chapter 2, Vandergosh was an ancillary character whose adoption did not serve as a focal point. Rather, her character advanced the plot involving the homosocial relationship between Ben Manibag (Parry Shen) and Steve Choe (John Cho). In my analysis of *Seoul Searching*, I am attentive to what it means when Asian American cultural producers "discover" adoption and elect to tell adoptee stories.

If adoptees exist on the periphery of Korean America, then it is important to consider what happens when their voices and perspectives are included in Asian American cultural productions. A close reading of *Seoul Searching*'s adoption subplot reveals how Koreans and Korean Americans, with their limited understandings of adoption, rely on adoptees' affective labor to confront the use of adoption as a social welfare support and a safety net for economically precarious Koreans and unmarried Korean women. The character of Kris Schultz (Rosalina Lee) provides a glimpse into the vexed positioning of a Korean adoptee who lacks cultural ties to Korea in a program for teenage members of the Korean diaspora. This is particularly important given the film's setting of 1986, which was only one year after Korean adoption's peak, when 8,837 children were placed out to countries in the West. In 1986 South Korea sent 8,680 children for adoption.[12] These numbers only began to decrease in 1988, when the nation hosted the Summer Olympic Games and encountered resounding criticism for its largest export being its children.

While *Seoul Searching* provides space to interrogate the question of what it means to be Korean—a question posed to the characters by one of their teachers—the film's anti-Blackness and explicit male gaze mean that some nuance is lost. The film cannot be simply lauded for providing a more expansive Asian American masculinity as a counterpoint to Hughes's Long Duk Dong, for it does so at the expense of Blackness, with an unbridled use of racial slurs and modern-day Blackface with three characters who speak with Blaccents. Even as it proffers nuanced women characters, the film's sexualization of them and engagement in some of Hughes's troubled tropes involving women (including sexual assault) cannot be overlooked. Lee's trafficking in anti-Blackness and gendered stereotypes creates a film reliant on toxic Asian American hegemonic masculinity to counter the stereotypes of Asian American men in 1980s mainstream American cinema. This is unsurprising given Lee's inspiration from Hughes's films. To overlook the pervasiveness of these discourses in my discussion of the film would undermine the intersectional, feminist media lens employed throughout this book to interrogate representations of Asian adopted women and girls. A critical examination of the film makes evident *Seoul Searching*'s complicit role in promoting reductive notions of birth family search and reunion and situates this analysis within broader scholarship on the South Korean government's incorporation of adoptees as overseas Koreans and Korean media's interest in adoptee reunion narratives.

Each of the characters in the film serves as an archetype, similar to how the five characters in *The Breakfast Club* (1985) are observations on the minutiae of suburban US high school life. In *Seoul Searching*, the main characters featured in the opening scene at Gimpo Airport include the rebellious punk, Sid Park (Justin Chon); the pastel-wearing feminine Brit from Wimbledon, Sara Han (Sue Son); the unnamed hip-hop Blaccent trio from the US; the taekwondo tomboy, Sue-Jin (Byeol Kang); the twin girls Jackie Im and Judy Im (Nekhebet Kum Juch and Uatchet Jin Juch); the racist cadet from the Virginia Military Academy, Mike Song (Albert Kong); Madonna's *Like a Virgin*–inspired pastor's kid, Grace Park (Jessika Van); and the adoptee, Kris Schultz. This does not include the German Korean Klaus Kim (Teo Yoo) or the Mexican Korean Sergio Kim (Esteban Ahn), whom we meet when Sid encounters his roommates at the university; nor does it include the only Black Korean character, Jamie (Crystal Kay). Describing the film in her review for the *New York Times,* Jeannette Catsoulis writes, "Set in 1986 and inspired by a now-defunct summer camp in Seoul designed to introduce these globally scattered youngsters to their heritage (a program the Korean-American writer and director, Benson Lee, once attended), the movie pokes at cultural identity with a very broad stick. Simultaneously whacking and embracing as many stereotypes as possible—the German-raised student is organized and polite;

the Mexican is a skirt-chasing hedonist—Mr. Lee paves a boisterous road to amity and understanding."[13] Yet what Catsoulis sees as a potential critique of stereotypes, I read as virulent anti-Blackness and as a foray into Hughesian misogyny, both of which I discuss further in this chapter.

The range of characters and their associated clichés give rise to broader questions about what it means to tell a story and to represent a distinct Korean diasporic experience to audiences whose understanding of Korea, and of Koreans, is mediated through popular culture. In a January 2015 interview published in the *Hollywood Reporter,* Benson Lee is quoted as saying, "One of our goals for the movie was to provide characters who are normal characters, not caricatures or stereotypes, which we quite often see in the movies when it comes to Asian characters."[14] Yet, as aware as he is of anti-Asian stereotypes, and here I contend with stereotypes specifically around Asian (American) masculinity, he is unable to critically reflect on his role in perpetuating other forms of damaging racist and sexist stereotypes.

NARRATIVE SCARCITY, ANTI-BLACKNESS, AND ASIAN AMERICA

Coming out two years prior to *Crazy Rich Asians* (2018), three years before *Always Be My Maybe* (2019), six years earlier than *Everything Everywhere All at Once* (2022), and more than a decade after *Better Luck Tomorrow, Seoul Searching* appeared to fill a void in the telling of Asian American stories.[15] Claire Jia notes in her review for *The Rumpus,* "These Korean teens create their own world so naturally in spaces traditionally claimed by white people that one wonders why it took so long for a movie like *Seoul Searching* to make it to the silver screen."[16] Similarly, Catsoulis remarks, "'Seoul Searching' is rude, funny, silly and poignant. Above all, it's kind; Mr. Lee understands that belonging is a feeling that many of us may never experience."[17] Even as she makes mention of "student interactions zinging with racial slurs," Catsoulis follows up with "but the movie's filthy mouth is balanced by its warm heart, an organ that gradually takes charge as the story progresses. Tonal shifts from ribald to sweet and from raucous to sensitive aren't always smooth, and the sentiment can get gooey."[18] Justin Chang's review in *Variety* continues this celebratory theme: "If you can get past the wobbly execution and the gentle groaner of a title, 'Seoul Searching' delivers a sweetly engaging tribute to classic John Hughes movies and a refreshing glimpse into the secret life of the Asian teenager."[19] I suggest that these reviews do not intentionally overlook the anti-Blackness within the film. Instead, they demonstrate anti-Blackness's function as an undercurrent within society, and the lack of discussion underscores its fixed nature in popular culture. Nonetheless, we must hold Asian American cultural producers accountable for trafficking in anti-Blackness.

The lack of engagement with the film's anti-Blackness is to be expected given the way *narrative scarcity* operates in determining what Asian American stories are available for public viewing consumption. Writing about ethnic literature, Viet Thanh Nguyen notes, "But while dominant Americans exist in an economy of narrative plenitude with a surfeit of stories, their ethnic and racial others live in an economy of narrative scarcity. Fewer stories exist about them, at least ones that leave their enclaves. Not surprisingly, both the larger American public and the ethnic community then place great pressure on those few stories and those few writers who emerge to stand on the American stage."[20] The lack of narrative plenitude often overshadows the need for meaningful critique because ethnic and racial minorities may accept what is presented versus asking for better representation when stories produced by one of their own garner mainstream media attention. The desire to be seen on screen, in combination with the pervasiveness of anti-Blackness in US popular culture, is why so few of the film's reviews address the problematic nature of Lee's representation of racial Others—in this case the mixed-race Jamie, the Mexican Korean Sergio Kim, and the hip-hop Blaccent trio.

Narrative plenitude thus must be extended beyond literature to other forms of media. If Asian American cultural producers replicate problematic tropes or traffic in stereotypes, they should be held accountable. And yet, as Nguyen notes in a *New York Times* opinion essay, "[Asian Americans] live in an economy of narrative scarcity, in which we feel deprived and must fight to tell our own stories and fight against the stories that distort or erase us. Many Americans will take these Asian images—which are usually awful—and transfer them to any Asian-American they encounter."[21] For this reason, it is imperative that cultural producers heed Helen Jun's comments on ethical representation:

> The representational *burden of ethicality* refers to a specific variation of the more general concept of the *burden of representation* facing nonwhite film-makers and artists. Because racialized communities have been historically denied institutional access to the means of representation and have been subject to representation by dominant (white) imaginings of racial others, minoritized artists confront an "imperative" to produce counterimages and narratives that effectively contest racist ideologies. The most common and readily available representational strategy in response to this obligation is

to directly invert dominant depictions, exchanging positive for negative images, good for bad, "real" for stereotypical, and so on.[22]

While this is part of Jun's analysis of Spike Lee's *Do the Right Thing* (1989), her incisive critique on representation illuminates the constraints that may control the production of counterimages. Although these images arise from an effort to contest racialized ideologies of a particular racial or ethnic group, there is no guarantee that they will not replicate other forms of racism.

Acknowledging *Seoul Searching*'s anti-Blackness should not be seen as a move to vilify Asian Americans nor as an elision of past or present Asian-Black solidarity. Rather, this exploration of anti-Blackness is linked to broader concerns about the operationalization of white supremacy within Asian American communities and the intersections between racial triangulation and narratives of multiculturalism.[23] Myra Washington notes, "Structural anti-Blackness and anti-Asianness work in both concert and contention with each other to highlight the ordering power of White supremacy as it forces groups against each other."[24] This observation captures Jun's exploration "of how Asian Americans and African Americans have been racially defined in relation to each other since the nineteenth century."[25] To understand Asian American model minority discourse means recognizing the adversarial positioning of the model minority against the purported failures of the Black community within a white supremacist society. One cannot exist without the other. This logic also fails to take into account the heterogeneity of Asian America, and while that discussion falls outside this monograph's scope, it is important to acknowledge how discourses of success contribute to the elision of who is included in Asian America. More importantly, exploring the function and circulation of both anti-Black and anti-Asian racism in popular culture facilitates a deeper interrogation of Asian Americans complicity in Black abjection.

To watch anti-Blackness unfold on screen is unnerving. Underscoring the role of Asian Americans in perpetuating anti-Blackness, Claire Jean Kim, in her analysis of the lone Asian character in Jordan Peele's *Get Out* (2017), contends, "Sometimes Asians are not unwilling conscripts. Sometimes they weaponize themselves."[26] In other words, Asian Americans engage anti-Blackness to ensure their positioning within existing racial hierarchies. Lauren Bullock recounts her experience of viewing *Seoul Searching* on the website Black Nerd Problems: "Not 15 minutes into the film and I felt as though I'd been slapped in the face repeatedly by a barrage of the n-word flying between the lips of a Hip-Hop caricatures influenced group of camp members and a staunchly racist soldier from Virginia. And for what, shock value?"[27] The dialogue, peppered liberally with the n-word and anti-Black racial epithets, does not move the plot forward. The film relies on outmoded and reductive stereotypes for what appears to be shock value. The militant nature of Mike Song, whose demeanor is linked to US militarism and his experience at a military school, and the culturally appropriative hip-hop trio could have been presented without trafficking explicitly in anti-Blackness. This was a missed opportunity to reflect on the differences between appreciation and appropriation, something that Bullock contends Lee should have been aware of. She comments, "Lee's first film *Planet B-Boy,* one of the highest grossing US documentaries in 2008, literally depends on carefully navigating the line between Asian appropriation and appreciation of Black culture. There are no excuses that can be made here."[28] Yet the same explicit attention Bullock gives to the function of anti-Blackness in the film does not appear in the mainstream outlets that lauded the film's success at dismantling Asian American stereotypes.

The anti-Blackness within the film affirms assumptions of an anti-Asian-Black coalitional politic that counters efforts at interracial solidarity and social justice in the past and present. Lee's incorporation of anti-Blackness overlooks the experiences of mixed-race Black Asian Americans, including Black Asian adoptees. There are other means available to demonstrate the racism its lone mixed-race Black Korean student encounters in South Korea or interrogate modes of cultural appropriation. The film could have engaged Hughesian tropes but committed to *do better.* This would include not making the Mexican Korean character a Latino caricature. Reflecting on the notion of narrative scarcity, Bullock notes,

> I in no way condone the deeply problematic aspects of this film (all this without even touching on the some of the [*sic*] emotionally triggering trauma tropes and homophobia brought up further into the story) and wholeheartedly believe that the treatment of Blackness was incredibly harmful at worst and stupidly sloppy at best. But I also can't deny the void that this movie fills in a country that continues to insist that people of color can only be sidekicks or tokens even when its [*sic*] our stories being told. It's a movie I'm still eager to share with my mother if only because for all its flaws it truly does reveal necessary truths. Like many loves, my feelings in the end remain complex. Perhaps the best step in the meantime is to hope that the next Asian American classic will come soon and swiftly, and that this time it will be one that all of us in the diaspora can cheer for together, with our whole hearts for once.[29]

Even as Bullock is only a single person reflecting on their experience, it is significant because the film forces viewers to make conscious decisions about why they remain engaged with the material. Narrative scarcity versus narrative plenitude marginalizes some of the most marginalized because they must settle for racism and misogyny in order to see themselves on screen. At the outset of the film during the opening credits, Lee brings a level of nuance in situating the Korean diaspora within Korean War history; yet this same care is absent when accounting for racial difference. Perhaps this is because he witnessed virulent anti-Blackness while participating in the program in the 1980s; nonetheless, it does not justify its replication on screen nearly thirty years later.

ASIAN AMERICAN MASCULINITY AND THE ROLE OF THE MALE GAZE

The struggle for narrative plentitude informs the toxic masculinity in the film through the sexualizing Asian American male gaze. While I discuss this particular gaze—of Asian American teenage boys—in chapter 2, it is worth repeating that the heterosexual male gaze facilitates access to the hegemonic masculinity routinely denied to Asian American, cisgender, heterosexual men. On Lee's taking inspiration from Hughes, Jia notes, "Lee demonstrates a familiar myopia when it comes to his female characters, and along with the 80s music and dress comes a sexism better left in movies of years past. *Seoul Searching* offers important commentary on racial, ethnic, and national difference—commentary that puts a progressive spin on the genre—but in the arena of gender and sex the film falls woefully short."[30] Jia tracks the film's misogyny and toxic masculinity, which is epitomized by the handling of an attempted sexual assault with the "'boys will be boys' mentality that has tainted teen comedies of years past (including Hughes's *Sixteen Candles,* where our 'hero' Jake lets nerdy Ted drive his girlfriend home—implying that they'll have sex—joking that she's so drunk she 'won't know the difference')."[31] The difference between the Hughes vehicles from the 1980s and *Seoul Searching* is nearly three decades, but the sexualization of young women persists across time.

In post-#MeToo times, what may have only been discomfort when watching John Hughes films has taken on a different meaning when it comes to grappling with their representation of young women and girlhood. As actress Molly Ringwald notes, before his films, the representation of women was limited and one-dimensional, and most of "the successful teen comedies of the period . . . were written by men for boys," with Amy Heckerling's *Fast Times at Ridgemont High* (1982) an outlier. Hughes's films stood out, according to

Ringwald, because "no one in Hollywood was writing about the minutiae of high school, and certainly not from a female point of view."[32] Nonetheless, even for Ringwald, whose career was launched by her appearance in three Hughes films, situating the treatment of young women alongside the transformative effect of the films on the lives of so many teenagers is difficult. Discussing *Sixteen Candles* (1984) and *The Breakfast Club,* she writes, "If I sound overly critical, it's only with hindsight. Back then, I was only vaguely aware of how inappropriate much of John's writing was, given my limited experience and what was considered normal at the time." What is significant about Ringwald's reflections is her raising the important question of what to do with "art that we both love and oppose," recognizing that "erasing history is a dangerous road when it comes to art—change is essential, but so, too, is remembering the past, in all of its transgression and barbarism, so that we may properly gauge how far we have come, and also how far we still need to go."[33] Hughes died in 2009, nearly a decade before the #MeToo movement went viral in 2017. While Tarana Burke coined the term in 2006, only the viral nature of the hashtag propelled a change in discourse about sexual violence.

If *Seoul Searching* desires to pay homage to Hughes, it must confront the racism and sexism of his films. Instead of Long Duk Dong, viewers see anti-Blackness in a variety of forms, and instead of the sexual assault of white women, viewers experience the near sexual assault of Grace Park (Jessika Van) and a male-centered plot. The latter also accounts for the film's introduction of Kris Schultz—the camera pans across her buttocks before we see her face—and of Sara Han—the camera swiftly moving from her face to her backside. We also witness Grace Park provocatively dance in an outfit revealing a lacy bralette, reminiscent of Madonna in *Desperately Seeking Susan* (1985). Accounting for Lee's treatment of women and anti-Blackness, as well as the racialized caricature of the only Latino character, is critical to understanding the significance of the impact of Asian American cultural productions. Through their relationship with the young men in the film, the young women come into being. Their storylines exist only in relationship to those to whom they are attached at the film's end. Kris's adoption storyline unfolds alongside heteronormative conventions, and she ends up with Korean German Klaus Kim in a classic romantic comedy setup. To engage with the film's representation of adoption requires confronting racism and misogyny writ large. Reclaiming Asian American masculinity should not come at the expense of Asian American girlhood. A film can both make a significant contribution to representation and be critiqued. We must engage the reproduction of these systemic inequities regardless of nostalgia or a desire for a "feel good" Asian American coming-of-age tale. Fantasies require disruption.

ADOPTEES RETURN AS MEMBERS OF
THE KOREAN DIASPORA

Seoul Searching offers an opportunity to scrutinize what returning to Korea meant to adoptees prior to their inclusion as "overseas Koreans" in 1998, which resulted in their eligibility for the F-4 visa and access to dual citizenship beginning in January 2011.[34] Writing about the first international gathering of adopted Koreans held in 1999 and a 2001 return trip sponsored by the Overseas Koreans Foundation, Eleana J. Kim comments, "Adult adopted Koreans negotiate a complex relationship to Korea in a globalized economy that has made it possible for them to recognize their own ethnic identity in new ways, both individually and collectively."[35] The industry catering to returning adoptees was in its nascent stages in 1986. Tobias Hübinette traces the earliest return of adoptees to "the second half of the 1970s, either as individuals or as participators in tours organized by friendship associations and adoption agencies like Holt (from 1975), the Norwegian Children of the World (*Verdens barn*) (from 1982) or the Adoption Centre (*Adoptionscentrum*) of Sweden (from 1983) as part of their so-called post-adoption or post-placement services."[36] The return trips started by Holt may also date later to 1983, when the Holt International Summer School informally launched. It was formally established in 1991.[37] These return trips aligned with sporadic reporting on adoptees in Korean newspapers by foreign correspondents and the placement of advertisements by adoptees seeking their birth parents in Korean media in the late 1980s.[38] Kim Park Nelson notes, "The South Korean government's Overseas Koreans Foundation (OKF) reports that 38,712 Korean adoptees visited South Korea between 1982 and 2005, although it is unlikely that this is accurate. . . . Many more adoptees are likely to have visited the country without contacting their adoption agencies."[39] Nonetheless, South Korean society and those returned adoptees were in uncharted waters, as the children cast off by the nation came back when everyone thought they had embarked on a one-way journey to a new life.

The inclusion of the character Kris Schultz is thus significant given the limited avenues for adoptees to return to South Korea at the time. It is revealed that Kris grew up in Fairborn, Ohio, a suburb of Dayton, which is also home to the Wright-Patterson Air Force Base. Perhaps it is a coincidence; however, the location could signify that one of Kris's parents was part of the US military. This would align with many early adoptees having familial ties to the US military, since many of those families were early adopters. Her ability to connect with other Koreans or Asian Americans would have been limited. The Census Tract for Dayton reveals that only 429 Asians and Pacific Islanders lived in the city of Fairborn in 1980, and an even smaller percentage were of Korean ethnic background.[40] To connect with one another in the US, adoptees were limited to heritage-based culture camps, frequently operated by adoptive parents or adoption agencies. The earliest US-based culture camp for Korean adoptees, Korean Culture Camp in Minneapolis, Minnesota, was established in 1977.[41] The earliest adult adoptee organizations in the US were not formed until the 1990s, and the oldest European adopted Korean organization was founded in 1986 in Sweden, with organizations in the Netherlands, Denmark, and Norway following in 1990.[42] While it could be easy to dismiss this piece of information about her hometown as a throwaway line, I suggest that situating Kris within broader US military and adoption histories is crucial to thinking about her as a three-dimensional character.

Given the limited opportunities for adoptees to connect with one another and the negligible numbers of Asian Americans, let alone Korean Americans, in Fairborn when Kris arrives at Gimpo Airport for the start of the summer program, it is no surprise that she seems slightly disoriented as she takes in her surroundings. Viewers see a young woman who tentatively looks around at the Koreans greeting the summer program arrivals in the airport. Her apprehensive demeanor reflects Korean adoptees' positioning within the Korean diaspora in the mid-1980s, when adoptees of that era recount negligible positive representations of Koreans and Asian Americans in popular culture.[43] Those few seconds when we are introduced to the unnamed Kris Schultz are significant, then, as they provide a glimpse into adoptee reticence and what it means to arrive in Korea for the first time. Discussing adoptees' return trips to Korea, Kim writes, "First trips to Korea could be complex and potent emotional and psychological experiences that unmoored identity and dislodged narratives of coherent selves. . . . Korea as a place and nation holds specific meaning for adoptees as they locate their particular origins and the places of their prior presences."[44] The sensorial experience can be overwhelming and intoxicating, as everyone looks like you and you look like everyone else. Despite showing markers of "Westernness," you have a desire to "blend in" with the surroundings, which for many adoptees was impossible in the countries of their adoption.

The revelation that Kris is an adoptee challenges the summer school teachers' and participants' understanding of the Korean diaspora. While the others can find common ground in their immigrant parents' experiences, or at least a particular shared history in their families' departures from Korea following the end of the Korean War, Kris represents the failure of a nation to provide adequate social welfare supports and monies to economically precarious families in the shadow of Park Chung Hee's industrialization mobilization.

Adoptees' returns and existence within the Korean diaspora are stark reminders that South Korea's prosperity relied on the adoption economy. As Korean
adoptees returned to South Korea, memoirs, documentaries, and scholarly
writings demonstrated the South Korean government's lack of preparedness,
as it had not anticipated the return of these children. The government, similar to Korean adoption agencies and orphanages, believed adoption was the
best option in the wake of constrained choices that would have allowed them
to remain in the country. In an exchange between Kris and her calligraphy
teacher, Mr. Chae (Choi Gwi-hwa), it becomes evident that the idea of an
adoptee taking part in this program was not at the forefront of his mind. Mr.
Chae stops at her desk, where she is writing "Kris" repeatedly on the page.

> MR. CHAE: Wow. Very good. Now try writing your name in Korean.
>
> KRIS: Um. I don't know how to write in Korean.
>
> MR. CHAE: That's okay. Then just tell me your Korean name, and I will write
> it for you.
>
> KRIS: I don't remember my Korean name.
>
> MR. CHAE: Don't remember? Let's try writing your English name in Korean.
> What is your last name?
>
> KRIS: Schultz.
>
> MR. CHAE: Schultz . . . Shirt?

This exchange may seem benign; however, its inclusion in the film demonstrates how limited notions of "Koreanness" shape interactions among ethnic
Koreans. While Mr. Chae aims to be inclusive by the end of this short conversation by teaching Kris how to write her last name in Korean, this emphasis on Korean names is complicated, especially since many adoptees' Korean
names are fabricated by adoption agencies. Or, in some more complex cases,
children may have even been switched.[45] More importantly, this scene raises
the probability that Kris's adoptive parents withheld her adoption file from
her. The documents in their possession should have included her Korean
name, her case number, and the social study report conducted on her while
she was in the orphanage. A lack of disclosure of those documents would be
the reason she would not know her Korean name. In denying Kris access to
those documents, her parents participate in the erasure of their daughter's
Korean identity.

The calligraphy class serves as a site for viewers to get to know Kris and
watch her relationship with Klaus unfold. Working side by side in a subsequent scene, Kris writes her English first name in Korean. In the dialogue
below, she asks whether Klaus speaks Korean or German to his parents.

KLAUS: What about you? Do you speak any Korean to your parents?

KRIS: No, I can't speak Korean at all.

KLAUS: Your parents must speak English very well.

KRIS: I hope so, since they're white.

KLAUS: Excuse me?

KRIS: I'm adopted.

KLAUS: Oh. When were you adopted?

KRIS: When I was about four?

KLAUS: And do you have any memories of your natural parents?

KRIS: I have memories of my biological mother, but I haven't seen her since she gave me up for adoption.

KLAUS: Have you ever thought about finding her?

KRIS: Not really. I mean, I wouldn't even know where to begin. Besides I don't even speak Korean.

KLAUS: I could help you as a translator if you needed one.

These two exchanges offer insight into the complexities of return for adoptees. The film captures the myriad cultural losses that adoptees undergo upon adoption. Addressing these intangible injuries, Eleana J. Kim writes, "For many adoptees who go to South Korea, the past weighs heavily, whether as something to actively explore through birth family searches or as something to defer. Many confront their individual histories and understandings of cultural identity and belonging in ways that they may never have done before. This sense of belonging is, in some ways, connected to 'Korea' as nation-state and ethnic-cultural paradigm, but it is also produced out of a disjuncture from 'Korea.'"[46] As Kris negotiates her belonging alongside her peers, it becomes clear that for some in Korea—as evidenced in a scene involving Sid, Sergio, Klaus, and Gangster Song (Choi Sung Guk) at a nightclub—speaking the language is key to authentic Korean identity. Gangster Song says to the three youths, "Koreans must be able to speak Korean, or it will bring shame to their family." This type of comment is echoed in other exchanges we see between Sid and Mr. Kim (Cha In-Pyo) as well as in assumptions about the cultural Korean identities these diasporic returnees should embody.

The inclusion of Kris mirrors the film's incorporation of mixed-race Black or nonnative English-speaking diasporic returnees in that these characters destabilize the Korean transnational subject identity. While Klaus adheres to normative understandings of an acculturated Western Korean subject, Sergio is racialized vis-à-vis his Mexican cultural identity. At the same time, Jamie is Othered and reduced to a flat, one-dimensional storyline alongside the anti-Black hip-hop Blaccent trio who leave the school midway through the program. Zainichi Koreans (Korean Japanese) even make an appearance as high school students also visiting Korea, but they are set up as adversaries to the main characters of the film. Lee fails to contextualize Koreans' presence in Japan, including Japan's colonialization of Korea and the racism behind it. The film clumsily attempts to demonstrate the heterogeneity of the diaspora through reductive tropes and an investment in highlighting the multiple countries Koreans emigrated to throughout the twentieth century. Lee's lack of nuance or self-awareness about the film's stereotyping undermines his attempt to challenge what the Korean diaspora looks like.

SEARCHING FOR KOREA, SEARCHING FOR ONE'S MOTHER

It should not come as a surprise that the birth family search, initiated more than halfway into the film, ends up successful. In an interview with *Hyphen*, when asked what elements of the film were based on his experiences, Lee says, "Yes, the fight with the Japanese kids actually took place in the summer camp I attended. The adoptee character did not exist. I decided to include an adoptee in the story because they're an important part of the Korean diaspora who are quite often overlooked."[47] The reunion thus operates as a fantastical element not only because Lee had never met adoptees while participating in the summer program on which the film is based but also given the low success rate of reunions.

Adoptees report that Korean adoption agencies fail to provide all the pertinent details of their adoption cases when they make appointments to view their files. Park Nelson notes, "For those who search, the process can be fairly straightforward, or very complicated and difficult; some adoptees have enough identifying information in their adoption records to find birth family quickly, while others must follow up on a few clues that may or may not lead to family identity. Most adoptees who search do so through their adoption agencies, through soliciting information about themselves in the Korean media (in newspapers or on television), or both."[48] The forthcomingness of the adoption agencies also varies based on the social worker. On this, Kim comments, "Social workers stand as unpredictable gatekeepers to valuable knowledge about the adoptee's identity as represented by her past life and genealogical origins. . . . The wide-ranging inconsistencies in treatment by agencies suggest to many adoptees that unethical and possibly illegal adoptions are being covered up."[49] Viewers of *Seoul Searching* most likely will not have this knowledge about the complexities and disingenuous nature of the file review process. The film, which takes license to ensure that the story line is complete, should be interrogated for overlooking the documented ways Korean agencies obscure important details of adoptees' identities and operate, at times, as barriers to recovering the truths of their adoptions. Although fictionalized, such portrayals of adoption should not be dismissed, as these cultural productions help shape public perceptions.

When Klaus and Kris enter the Korean adoption agency, there is limited staff, and it is clear that they do not have an appointment. This differs from how these types of visits to agencies have operated in the last two to three decades as agencies have established post-adoption services. Based on the photographs of Harry and Bertha Holt and their adopted children on the bulletin board where they wait for the social worker, it appears as if Kris was adopted through Holt Korea. Given the Holts' oversized role in shaping Korean transnational adoption as well as their notoriety, it is only to be expected that Holt is featured, even if it goes unnamed. When the social worker speaks to Klaus and Kris, she reveals that not much has been updated in Kris's adoption file but that there is a letter from her birth mother.

With Klaus as her interpreter, Kris translates the letter without support from the agency. This type of emotional labor is significant because there is always a concern that not all information will be adequately translated if one uses a translator provided by the agency. This apprehension is rooted in the information shared in adoptees' whisper networks, where they disclose a lack of transparency in the process and instances of mistranslation or moments when translation falls short not because of language lost in translation but rather because the interpreter exercises control over what is translated. As they leave the agency in a taxi, Klaus opens the letter and asks Kris if she is ready. He reads,

> August 20, 1980. Dear Joo-eun, I am writing this letter to you on your birthday. You are thirteen years old today. Ever since I left you at the orphanage, I've always wondered about you and where you are in the world. You are probably angry with me, but please try to understand that my situation was very complicated. The most important thing I wanted for you was a better life. One that I could not provide for you. Jong-Ok Han.

Hearing the longing Jong-Ok has for her daughter humanizes the birth mother. This rendering of birth mothers as sympathetic figures aligns with the broader public perception of birth mothers as selfless. Jong-Ok relinquished her daughter to ensure she had a "better life." Even as the notion of birth mothers as selfless is reductive, I caution against dismissing this portrayal of birth mothers. Birth mothers and birth families by extension are not inherently "bad"; the placement of Kris/Joo-eun into an orphanage was fueled by Jong-Ok's precarious existence. This exchange mirrors the experiences of many adoptees and their birth families.[50]

The letter propels Kris's story line, and viewers watch Klaus at a pay phone later that day calling Jong-Ok Han (Park Ji-Ah). Their exchange results in a meeting between the birth mother and Kris being scheduled for the next day. It is clear that the cinematic investment in the birth search and reunion take center stage, as these processes rarely occur so quickly and with such ease. When we see the mother and daughter meet over Korean food, the chasms produced by adoption are visible. Both women rely on Klaus to painstakingly translate what the other desires to share, and viewers become privy to Klaus's discretion in his translations in what I argue is a misguided attempt to protect Kris and Jong-Ok from additional hurt. The brief conversation reveals that Jong-Ok has since remarried and has a ten-year-old daughter. Her family does not know about her prior daughter—Kris/Joo-eun. Tearful, Jong-Ok plainly states, "They don't know I have daughter. This has to be hidden. If they know about this . . ." As her voice trails off, it becomes clear that if Kris's identity is revealed to Jong-Ok's family, she could potentially lose everything. This concern is not unfounded or uncommon given the complexity of reunion and the secrecy within adoption. Yet Kris experiences this disclosure—when Klaus says, "I don't know how to say this, but I think she never told her family about you"—as a secondary rejection, the first being her adoption. Kris angrily says, "So I'm a secret. Well, tell her it doesn't matter. I don't need to meet her family. I have one already and she will never have to see me again," and leaves the private room in the restaurant.

It is significant that *Seoul Searching* depicts the emotional labor involved in reunion, as it is not as simplistic a happy ending as people would love to believe—that a resolution with a bow tied around it occurs once parent and child find one another. Instead, the film makes palpable how silence figures into feelings of rejection and articulates the contours of reunion that are often only apparent to adoptees and whispered to one another in the corners of a room or online. Viewers gain a new perspective on birth mothers when Kris meets Jong-Ok for a second time, without Klaus. Her monologue to her mother in English demonstrates not only Kris's ability to disentangle her adoption from a singular experience but also her sympathy for a woman who had limited choices.

> You, know, before I met you . . . I had no idea what to expect. Deep inside, I secretly hoped we would have this instant bond and connection that mothers and daughters should have. I hoped that it would be this wonderful

reunion that turned into a discovery of an unknown past. I never expected that . . . I would be denied that again. The first year I went to America . . . I remember crying every night wondering when I was going back home to see you. But, as the years went by, I eventually stopped crying and my feelings for you got buried deep inside of me. Now that I finally met you all those emotions have resurfaced. When you told me I had to remain a secret, it made me angry. But Klaus told me about your circumstances and the suffering that you went through, and I realized it was much more complicated than I imagined. I don't understand everything, but I trust you did what you had to do out of love. So, I want you to know that I'm not sad anymore. Just seeing your face and finding the answers to questions I have always wanted to ask is all I need. Anyway, I'm glad we met. And knowing that you are happy with your family makes me happy. I had a . . . really good life with my adopted family and I love them very much. There's no need to feel any guilt or shame about what happened. I know you don't understand what I'm saying, but . . . maybe I can study Korean in college and we can have a real conversation someday. Who knows? Maybe someday you wouldn't mind if I called you "Omma."

Even as *Seoul Searching* offers a three-dimensional portrayal of birth mothers through Jong-Ok, the film is complicit in shaping discourse that portrays adoption as a humanitarian act. The palpable losses of adoption cannot be forgotten, even if Kris's comments that she had a "really good life" and there is "no need to feel any guilt or shame" are true. These words frame the positives of adoption with minimal consideration of what it means for a child to be crying wondering where their mother is during the first year of their adoption.

In film review after review that I encountered, the writers seemed to be enamored with the reunion between birth mother and daughter. Lee is commended for handling the reunion beautifully.[51] Nick Allen, writing for *RogerEbert.com*, comments, "Lee's story often hits emotional climaxes with over-zealous waterworks, but his best story involves a young woman (whose 'type' is that she's adopted), who meets her biological Korean mother. In their two scenes, they can't communicate with language, only through intense emotion—the daughter's calm, mournful tone, responded to with a mother's billowing, muted shame—creating an extraordinary and tender parent-child moment that is the best John Hughes–like quality of Lee's film."[52] These reviews fetishize the reunion as spectacle. There is something endearing about watching two people separated reunite. However, little thought is given to the trauma endured by hundreds of thousands of children separated from their parents because of the nation's institutionalization of adoption as a form of child welfare.

The notion of adoption as humanitarian act must be centered within main-stream white America's investment in adoption as child rescue. These motivations fueled domestic adoption as evidenced by the orphan train movement in the nineteenth century, the Indian Boarding School Project and Indian Adoption Project, and the language concerning the transracial adoption of Black and Latinx children. This rhetoric comes to the fore in discussions of transnational adoption. The white American fantasy of adoption as rescue endures in US popular media, and Korean adoptees themselves disclose their adoptive parents' investment in thinking about the adoption of their children through this lens. *Seoul Searching* upholds this understanding of adoption, even as adult adoptees continue to counter the claim that adoption is the better option.

Recognizing the discrepancies between the film and adoptees' real-life interactions with agencies, the main one being that Kris's efforts are fruitful, is vital to situating Asian American fantasies of adoption within white American society's romanticization of adoption. Similar to the dangers that Kim warned of concerning the South Korean government's co-optation of adoptees and their experiences, Asian American cultural producers risk reducing adoptees' "complex histories . . . to spectacles of national and cultural alterity, thus denying a history of violence and displacement in favor of homecoming and national reunion."[53] Here we see the ways in which the nexus of objectification manifests itself in Asian American fantasies of adoption, especially when accounting for the Asian American male gaze in the lives of Asian American women.

ASIAN AMERICAN FANTASIES OF ADOPTION

Seoul Searching cleaves open the intricacies and contradictions of what it means to be a transnational Korean subject. Even though non-adopted overseas Koreans may not speak Korean, the perception persists that they are somehow *more* Korean than their adopted counterparts. Perhaps it is linked to Mr. Chae's question about Kris's Korean name. Perhaps it is the power of having tangible ties to Korea that transfixes a sense of Korean identity. As Kim demonstrates, there are limits to the inclusion of adoptees as diasporic Koreans: "Going back is not always experienced as a warm homecoming; in fact, it can be a disorienting journey through space and time, and it often results in the disruption of idealized expectations and longings."[54] The film's ability to facilitate conversations about the realities of reunion ensures that it departs from other portrayals of adoption, including documentaries that may celebrate reunion with little consideration of its ramifications in the lives of adoptees. Nevertheless, the film reinforces the notion that adoption leads to a better life, because it overlooks the losses and struggles adoptees experience in favor of a flattened perception that absolves the South Korean government, orphanages, and adoption agencies of the conditions that made those adoptions possible.

More importantly, the film's anti-Blackness and sexualization of Korean women should not be ignored, even as the film depicts adoptees as Koreans. Attending to the racism and misogyny makes apparent the rifts within the Korean diaspora and the operationalization of anti-Blackness within adoption. The latter informs the patterns of adoption of mixed-race Black children from Korea and calls attention to the anti-Blackness within adoptee communities similar to other communities of color. What does it mean to hold Asian American cultural producers accountable, then? Why can't Asian Americans do better and move beyond reductive adoption portrayals that emphasize melancholia, self-loathing, or inauthenticity while also not trafficking in anti-Blackness? This question requires us to consider the stakes involved in holding Asian American men accountable at a moment when the Asian American community must contend with Men's Rights Activist Asian men (MRAsians) and expose the ways toxic (white) hegemonic masculinity operates in *Seoul Searching* and in Asian America on a greater scale.[55]

As Asian Americans strive for narrative plentitude, so too do adoptees. There is a desire to move beyond search and reunion narratives to allow for complexity and nuance. Asian American fantasies of adoption must reckon with how the specter of adoption as rescue casts a shadow over the fulfillment and betterment seen in adoption plots in Asian American cinema. Even as *Seoul Searching* elucidates the commonalities that link members of the transnational Korean diaspora to one another, including adoptees, its characterization of adoption as an inherent good propagates mainstream adoption discourse. To simply be transgressive in humanizing birth mothers is not sufficient, even if it is significant.

An urgency exists to see ourselves represented in mainstream Asian American and white media as subjects with agency rather than objects and spectacles. I am reminded of Viet Thanh Nguyen, who writes, "The real test of narrative plentitude is when we have the luxury of making mediocre movies. And after having made mediocre movies, we would be rewarded with the opportunity to make even more mediocre movies, just as Hollywood continues to make enormous numbers of mediocre movies about white people, and specifically white men."[56] This notion feeds into the idea that adoptees should not be excited for narrative scraps in which their stories are co-opted to fulfill Asian American or white desires for adoption fairy tales or in which they are continually spoken for with little regard to their lived experiences. The desire for narrative plenitude is why in 2023 adoptees waited with trepidation mixed with excitement for *Joy Ride* (2023), an unapologetic, sex-positive feminist comedy featuring an all Asian American cast of women and gender-nonbinary actors who star as four unlikely friends. The film depicts a birth mother search as part of one of its main storylines. And while the film falls outside the scope of this monograph's time frame, it's worth mentioning because it marks the first time a mainstream film incorporates an Asian adopted woman character in a meaningful lead role, since as I noted in chapter 2, Stephanie from *Better Luck Tomorrow* plays a supporting role in the character development of the male leads. In the next chapter, I turn to the ways in which the adopted woman maintains her access to the adoptive family. Adoptees must demonstrate their happiness and acceptance of mainstream adoption narratives to maintain their acceptance within the adoptive family and not be seen as a threat to celebrations of adoption.

CHAPTER 5

Twinsters and Adoptee Negotiations of the Desire for an Adoption Fairy Tale

The 2010s saw Korean adoptees leading the charge to #FlipTheScript on staid adoption narratives and imploring US society to recognize their expertise on the realities of adoption in the lives of adoptees.[1] The phrase "flip the script" emerged from white domestic adoptee Amanda Transue-Woolston's use of the language in a video for *Dear Wonderful You: Letters to Adopted and Fostered Youth*. At the start of National Adoption Month in November 2014, Korean adoptee Rosita González led the Twitter hashtag movement. Both Transue-Woolston and González were active members of the blog *Lost Daughters,* which began in 2011. In documenting the history of the #FlipTheScript hashtag, the *Lost Daughters* website notes: "#flipthescript sought to address social media's inundation with messages about adoption in which adoption professionals and adoptive parents are overwhelmingly represented during the month of November, National Adoption Month. Whenever education is taking place about an issue or community, all voices of that community must be included. The world needs to hear adoptee voices included in the dialogue about adoption."[2] The hashtag along with other kindred examples of adoptee activism illustrates social media's ability to facilitate rapid connections between adoptees across deterritorialized communities, more democratic dissemination of cultural productions, and access to new spaces to reimagine adoptee narratives.

These connections build on adoptee efforts to counter notions about adoption's benefits, exposing its contradictions and in some cases documenting unethical practices that have led to adoptions or placements in families in which physical, sexual, or emotional abuse was the norm.[3] Notably, the 2006 publication of *Outsiders Within: Writing on Transracial Adoption,* edited by Jane Jeong Trenka, Julia Chinyere Oparah, and Sun Yung Shin—three transracial adoptee-activist writers—features the voices of transracial adoptees and allies and employs a systemic lens to move beyond singular adoptee stories to consider the systems and institutions that undergird the adoption marketplace.[4] *Outsiders Within* contributes to the critiques made by same-race, white domestic adoptees about adoption and the voices of activist birth mothers such as Concerned United Birthparents.

By articulating the multidimensional aspects of the adoption experience, adoptee counterstories reveal "alternative standpoints" and produce new insights into multiple knowledges that "reveal omissions, distortions, and deficiencies in particular accounts."[5] Counterstories facilitate adoptees' entry into critical adoption studies discourse, moving adoptees beyond the reductive notion of adoption as the best option and reflecting their political engagement to shift conversations concerning the rights of adoptees and birth parents (e.g., adoptees' contributions to the 2012 revisions to South Korea's Special Adoption Law).[6] The authors of the earliest counterstories were *adoptee killjoys*—those who disrupt fantasies of adoption as a humanitarian act and who are often seen as angry in their demand for accountability.[7] Their narratives required members of the adoption constellation to critically consider the legacies and implications of transnational adoption in the lives of birth parents and adoptees. These counterstories facilitated a new iteration of cultural production by adoptees, who created quick and easy bites for viewers to consume through Web 2.0 media about their framing of adoption and return to South Korea.

This chapter analyzes the documentary *Twinsters* (2015), which follows the story of Korean adoptee twins Samantha Futerman and Anaïs Bordier, who were separated upon adoption and reunited in adulthood, and the companion memoir, *Separated @ Birth: A True Love Story of Twin Sisters Reunited* (2014). Futerman entered an American family and Bordier entered a French family. Only in adulthood did the events that led to their reunion transpire, when Bordier's friend informed her that he had seen a girl who looked exactly like her in a YouTube video. Their documentary gained popularity in the US mainstream and within the Korean adoptee community. News outlets featured the pair as a special interest story because they were one of the few known pairs of twins adopted to different families in South Korea's more than sixty years of participation in adoption.[8]

Twinsters provides adoptees an opportunity to explore adoption in an accessible, nonthreatening manner. Moving beyond niche releases as an "adoption film" and "adoption book," the documentary and memoir represent adoptees' entrance into twenty-first-century US middlebrow culture. The cinematic narrative offers a palatable adoption tale—carefully crafted for societal acceptance. *Twinsters* markets reunion as a success story, and thus it chooses not to critically engage with the institutional deception that caused the twins' separation. The documentary mediates their separation, adoption, and reunion through a Hollywood arc, glamorized and dramatic. Futerman and Bordier's joint memoir, *Separated @ Birth,* echoes this narrative, paying scant attention to the institutional and systemic conditions that separated them from one another and from their birth mother. When more serious topics are mentioned, they occur within conversations that focus on making the adoptee relatable to other adoptees, Asian Americans, and the broader public. A layer of levity is woven in to make the content more accessible to those who may find the adoptee killjoy ethos too confrontational, too much, too willful.[9]

The buoyant narrative of reunion as a happy object proffered in *Twinsters* and the accompanying memoir exist in contrast to the incisive critiques and counterstories offered by directors Tammy Chu and Deann Borshay Liem in their respective documentaries. Tammy Chu directed *Searching for Go-Hyang* (1998), about her own adoption, and *Resilience* (2009), which centers on Korean adoptee Brent Beesley and his reunion with his Korean mother. Deann Borshay Liem directed *First Person Plural* (2000) and *In the Matter of Cha Jung Hee* (2010) about her adoption and the fabrication of her identity as Cha Jung Hee, while *Geographies of Kinship* (2019) traces the journey of four adult Korean adoptees. *Twinsters* reached a broader public audience as the first Korean adoption documentary written and directed by an adoptee released on a major streaming platform.[10] Most Asian adoptee documentaries prior to *Twinsters* were distributed on PBS or screened at film festivals or adoption-related conferences. The sanitized portrayal of adoption found in *Twinsters* and its accompanying memoir ensures that both are marketable to a broad audience, which, being mostly composed of non-adopted people, resists grappling with hard adoption truths that destabilize their notion of adoption as the best option.

Twinsters relies on the sentimental appeal of adoptee reunion stories, promoting an image that reflects the happiness so often associated with adoption and reunion.[11] In this *every adoptee* experience, adoption is not examined as a system or institution but is instead reduced to discrete events (e.g., the day of arrival in the "receiving" country or "firsts" such as returning to Korea or meeting other adoptees). The "every adoptee" seemingly complies with fairy-tale narratives and holds gratitude for their adoption. Yet this positioning is precarious. Their neutrality in adoption discourse exists until their disappointment is registered. In doing so, "[they] create a rhetorical space for adoptees to complicate binary logics of what it means to be *good* and *grateful*."[12] Locating adoption as individualized moments offers feel-good opportunities for the audience, who are not required to consider the conditions that generated these moments of firsts or to question the conditions that made one adoptable.

Such fantasies of adoption elide the violence wrought by the systemic and institutional inequities and imbalances of adoption. Whether it's the fantasies of adoption that involve rescuing the infant adoptee and rendering the adoptive parent as savior, as seen in chapters 1 and 3, or how the Asian American fantasy of adoption is invested in creating a tidy narrative of reunion as the happy object, these combined fantasies obscure adoption's realities. Adoptees are acutely familiar with this particular bind of representation given the nexus of objectification's role in their lives. This bind is different from yet similar to the hypersexualization that Asian American girls and women encounter. These constraints result in the calculations we see in *Better Luck Tomorrow* (2002) as Stephanie shares bits and pieces of being adopted with Ben. To recognize adoption as an analytic, we must attend to and acknowledge the demands of adoption's racist love—adoptees' minor feelings must comport with the *right* ways to satisfy non-adoptees' investments in adoption as a social good.

Consequently, even as Futerman's and Bordier's adoptions appear to have happy endings, we can scrutinize the institutional practices and the role of reunion narratives in shaping public perceptions of adoption. The tale of the dissolution of the familial bond is rarely given the spotlight, which is why I trace the silences within the texts. I read the film and memoir against the grain with a focus on adoptee interiority in an effort to recognize their affective resistance to one-dimensional understandings of adoption. Central to this analysis is the influence of *biographic mediation*—demands for personal disclosures that affect public perceptions of adoption and adoptees' reflections of their adoption experiences—on the documentary's arc and what information is disclosed in the memoir. The emphasis on individual adoptee stories facilitates seeing adoption as a specific act and moment in time whereby one is adopted versus locating adoption as an integral component of identity that exists throughout one's lifetime. To divorce adoption from the system of adoption and the various assemblages involved encourages an isolated view of adoption that fails to account for how all the individual examples demonstrate patterns of violence, misinformation, and obfuscation. After all, operating simultaneously are adoption agencies and institutions, which mediate adoption records and the information that is disclosed to adoptees in adulthood and adoptive parents during the adoption process.

CRAFTING A MEDIA-FRIENDLY NARRATIVE

Western society's notion of adoption as a humanitarian act that provides homes for pitiful orphans frames how we interpret nonwhite adoptees' reflections on racism and xenophobia. Any discussion of adoptee marginalization or encounters with racism and xenophobia renders the adoptee ungrateful for the benefits of adoption and is accompanied by accusations like "Don't they understand their life is much better adopted to Country X versus remaining in Country Y?" *Twinsters* and the accompanying memoir are cognizant of these implicit norms as they retell the twins' reunion and reflect on what life was like growing up in North America and Europe. These narratives seek to present the fantasy that adoption was not *too* bad, relative to other options such as remaining in Korea or being adopted by a different family and minimize the disclosures of racist love within the adoptive family. Both texts sell the fantasy that not only were their adoptions successful (i.e., Futerman and Bordier are happy adoptees overall) but that their reunion supersedes discovering the inconsistencies that resulted in their adoptions by two separate families.

In considering the biographic mediation of Futerman and Bordier's reunion narrative, I use a feminist approach to reflect on what is present and what is absent in the film and memoir. Biographic mediation captures the institutional demands for the personal disclosures of Futerman and Bordier concerning their adoptions. At the same time, feminist standpoint theory elucidates the intricacies of the varied, contrasting, and sometimes contradictory experiences of Korean adoptees.[13] This interdisciplinary approach facilitates a deeper examination of Futerman's and Bordier's stories within the tension between satisfying a public audience and asserting control over their adoption narratives in the mediation of their own truths. The pair's disclosures about their upbringings and reunion are constrained to biographical details that make their experiences as adoptees legible and appealing to satisfy assumptions about what adoption and adoption reunions look like.

My analysis emphasizes the bureaucratic obfuscations that facilitated their separation and the crafting of a media-friendly reunion. Media producers who demand happiness and gratitude from adoptees for their adoptions, adoptive parents who want their reasons for adoption validated, and the broader public, who lack intimate ties with adoption, also influence what information is shared. Adoptees are encouraged to disclose biographical details that reinforce the trope of adoption as rescue and to not question orphanages' and adoption agencies' roles in mediating their information. Fragments of explicit dissent are silenced as the joyous occasion of reunion is centered. It is only through reading against the grain that one can tease out moments of resistance.

While Futerman and Bordier do not criticize the ethics of adoption, they raise important questions concerning adoptee identity formation. I draw on Sianne Ngai's discussion of the minor registers of affect, specifically the "minor and generally prestigious feelings [that] are deliberatively favored over grander passions like anger and fear."[14] Ngai explores how "emotion might be recuperated for critical praxis in general, shedding new light on the intimate relationship between negative affect and 'negative thinking.'"[15] In the case of adoptees' lived realities, it is imperative that these minor feelings are centered to take into account the experiences of adoptees who are not necessarily seen as adoptee killjoys and to critique normative adoption discourse that celebrates adoption as a humanitarian act.

When read against the grain, Futerman's and Bordier's narratives contribute to broader shifts in expectations of adoptees' affective behavior. *Twinsters* explores their reunion as a joyous occasion with little investigation into the factors that fueled their separate placements in two different countries and families. Their biographies are packaged for public consumption to center the "happy reunion" over other possible narratives. US popular media and mainstream society reify narratives that adhere to a particular respectability politics of adoption, wherein adoptees embody an affect of gratefulness while distancing themselves from stories that expose adoption's limitations as a form of kin-making. They move away from reductive and pathological notions that previously rendered adoptee narratives as "cautionary tales."[16] Nevertheless, *Twinsters* is transgressive, as it subtly underscores what was lost in these women's lives when they were adopted and separated from one another. If one is not careful, these moments may be overlooked. Futerman and Bordier challenge expectations of what reunion with a biological family member should look like as they reunite with one another and *not* their biological parents, carving out a new space to consider adoptees' return to Korea. The minor affects of Futerman and Bordier reveal how *Twinsters* and *Separated @ Birth* are potential sites of resistance. Combined, the film and memoir provide space to hold the complexities of adoption by simultaneously providing a heartwarming narrative—reunion as a happy occasion—and a public narrative that cannot help but raise questions about the choice that separated the twins and enabled their respective adoptions.

Futerman and Bordier cultivate an adoptee identity that is playful, cute, and nonthreatening while also appearing compliant with the promises of adoption by not explicitly challenging its ethics or raising questions about whether their adoptive parents were prepared to raise nonwhite children. The memoir and film situate the young women within the broader adoptee movement of the last decade which moves beyond stories of birth family search and reunion to consider the *everydayness*—and arguably the mundane-ness—of adoptee experiences. The inclusion of adoptees' everyday realities illustrates their autonomy over what adoption details are disclosed to various audiences—family, friends, intrusive strangers, and in the case of the docu-mentary and memoir, viewers and readers.

ADOPTEES AS CUTE AND
ADOPTION AS CELEBRATORY

The stylization and tone of the Korean cutesy aesthetic associated with *hallyu* (the Korean Wave) frames Futerman and Bordier's first digital encounter as well as the overall documentary narrative. This cute aesthetic supports the positioning of adoptees' adoption and reunion as celebratory events while fetishizing their stories. The aesthetic is reminiscent of Korean *aegyo* (per-formed winsomeness), a style and performance found in Korean dramas like *Hello, My Twenties* (2016–17), KakaoTalk Friends, Line Friends, hyperfemi-nine Korean girl group idols, and the uniformity associated with mainstream Korean beauty culture.[17]

The reliance on cuteness is akin to Japanese cute-cool culture (e.g., Hello Kitty). In her discussion of Japanese cute-cool, Christine R. Yano argues that pink globalization—"the transnational spread of goods and images labeled *kawaii* (glossed in English as 'cute,' but with different cultural nuances)"—pro-vides soft power to the Japanese government to influence public discourse.[18] Situating kawaii in an US context, Leslie Bow writes, "The cute anthropo-morphic orientalized object may avoid touching the third rail of American racial politics because it seems to counter the Asian stereotype of 'threatening competence' by inscribing its opposite: the Asian as endearing, amusing, lov-able."[19] In the case of adoptees and Korean cultural products, the cute aes-thetic functions similarly. Adoptees are the cute objects, as kawaii is not only attached to anthropomorphic objects. On this point, Ngai notes, "Cuteness is a way of sexualizing beings and simultaneously rendering them unthreaten-ing."[20] Hyperfeminization provides an opportunity to shape public discourse on Korea's adoption participation and understandings of adoptee affect. The cute aesthetic also lets viewers know what *Twinsters* is not—an adoption film that critiques the system or raises explicit ethical concerns.

Cute packaging conveys adoption and reunion as happy objects, even if, as Sara Ahmed notes, "we are made happy by different things, then we are affected by things differently."[21] We cannot assume that all adoptees experi-ence adoption in the same way. Yet there is a desire to consume the happiness that adoption (and reunion) allegedly holds. The cute aesthetic is a strategy of biographic mediation to hyperfocus on how the "happiness" of adoption can recuperate separation as an opportunity for reunion. Biographic mediation, tracked through the separate itinerary of each sister, offers narrative material for the "happiness" of sibling reunion without investigating the institutional means of separation. Chasing the object of happiness eliminates the potential for other affects—happiness is the only possibility. As Bow asserts, "Cuteness veils pleasure in domination; the cute object's extreme passivity incites a desire for control."[22] Biographic mediation manifests control through cuteness. The construction of cuteness within the documentary reflects the use of adoptees' affective labor to satisfy the public's desire to see their reunion as only a joyous occasion and not one that is potentially mixed with loss.

The cute imagery throughout the documentary makes the adoption deception—not notifying the adoptive parents that their daughters had a biological sibling also available for adoption—palatable for the viewer. Cuteness signifies the sentimentality of adoption; specifically, it calls attention to the ways the adoptee is commodified as both object and subject—the adoptable purchase and the adopted child deserving of rescue. Moreover, the cute discourse in which the film operates positions the twins as girls, not as women. This distinction is important, especially considering that Asian, Asian European, and Asian American women's bodies are fetishized as hyperfeminine and that women of color are hypersexualized in contrast to white girlhood or womanhood.

The language used by the twins to discuss their reunion is complicit in the manufacturing of adoptee affect. Anticipating the wondrous reunion, Futerman comments, "I'm super excited. I am a little nervous to be honest. This is like a crazy fucking thing that could happen." As she travels to London to meet Bordier for the first time, she declares in amazement, "I can't complain about anything ever again. I'm the luckiest person in the world." Futerman's sentiments highlight the surreal nature of the twins' reunion. Not only was adoption supposed to be a one-way journey to a new life away from Korea (and result in the adoptee's social death); connecting with a biological sibling in adulthood was supposed to be only a fantasy. This is why there is an undercurrent of the gratefulness trope when the twins connect. Upon their physical reunion, Bordier pokes Futerman to see if she is truly real and not just a figment of her imagination. Absent from this celebratory narrative is an intentional examination of their unmaking as twins on paper and how this led to two separate adoptions. This absence is amplified when Futerman exclaims, "Oh my god, this is so weird, like *The Parent Trap!*" While both the 1961 and 1998 versions of the film inspire laughter as the protagonists discover one another and antics ensue, the real-life experiences of Futerman and Bordier are no Disney fairy tale. The allusion to Disney films minimizes what actually happened and focuses on the amusing shenanigans one can get into with one's identical twin. Sibling reunions of this sort are romanticized to obscure the deceit of the initial separation.

While I critique the presentation of the twins and their story as complicit in the manufacture of a consumable cute adoption tale, the documentary offers opportunities to think more critically about the production of adoptees' biographies. Its slivers of criticism must be read against the grain to ensure that the resistance they present is not lost. For example, Nancy Segal, director of the Twin Study Center at California State University, Fullerton, raises the possibility of other separations of identical siblings when she says in the film, "It makes me wonder how many of these are out there." Segal works with the pair as they undergo genetic testing to confirm whether they are related, let alone twins. She delivers the results to them via Skype as the pair are together in London for the first time following Futerman's transatlantic flight to visit Bordier. The question Segal raises continues to be answered with the almost annual occurrence of adoptee twins being reunited in the news.

Perhaps the absence of critique is the most transgressive feature of the film. The fetishizing of adoptee affect through the use of cuteness allows this story to be told. The subtext throughout the documentary is that they were separated to begin with. I read the silences on this topic as evidence of the lack of language available to process the traumatic realization that they could have been raised together. After all, ruminating on *what if* and *what could have been* scenarios does not make for an engaging narrative nor one that aligns with happy reunion tropes. Instead, the silences percolate underneath the surface, bubbling up occasionally in the twins' interactions with the adoption agencies and orphanages in the documentary. The memoir makes these silences palpable as they intercede in a narrative of what *should be* a joyous occasion—reunion with one's sister.

CELEBRATING WHAT?
REUNION OR DECEPTION?

For many adoptees, the date that holds the most significance in the transformation of their lives as adopted persons is the day of their arrival in their adopted countries and their entry into their adopted families. Representing their social death, this arrival day finds itself commemorated in adoptive families, celebrated annually similar to birthdays, and marked by colloquial names such as Airplane Day or Gotcha Day. Exemplifying the impact of arrival in the adopted country, Bordier reflects, "When I was fifteen, I wanted to change my birth date from November 19, 1987, to March 5, 1988, the day that I first arrived in France and my life started."[23] Aspiring to be born the day one arrives in their adopted country reveals the role of social death in shaping the adoptee's sense of self and their (re)birth as a Western subject.

Other adoption-related days that may hold meaning for adoptees include their first engagement with the broader adult adoptee community, their first return trip to Korea, their first time at an International Korean Adoptee Associations (IKAA) gathering and/or IKAA annual convention (previously known as mini-gatherings), and birth search and/or reunion. For many adoptees, beyond these important firsts, the idea that they could potentially meet a birth sibling may never cross their mind, but this type of reunion, alongside meetings with other extended family kin, is becoming more of a reality with the popularization of DNA testing and genealogy.[24] The emphasis on the parent-child relationship creates a dynamic that obscures the existence of potential siblings or extended kin.

The start of the twins' reunion can be traced back to December 15, 2012, when a friend of Bordier alerted her that someone who looked exactly like her was in a video on YouTube. For Bordier, the experience of watching the video on her mobile phone was surreal. Bordier notes, "The girl grinning back at me on my Samsung Galaxy looked so much like me that I thought one of my artistic friends might be pranking me."[25] She shared her suspicions that she could have a cousin or half-sister, or even a twin, with her parents during her winter break from Central Saint Martins, a London-based art and design university. Nonetheless, Bordier did not pursue connecting with Futerman until February, when she saw a clip of Futerman in *21 & Over* (2013). After researching Futerman's acting career and discovering they shared the same birthday, November 19, 1987, Bordier reached out to Futerman over social media. In their memoir, both women recount how they scoured one another's Facebook profiles for more information. Their first face-to-face online encounter would occur at the end of February on Skype.

Upon discovering one another, Bordier and Futerman contacted their respective adoption agencies, Holt International Children's Services and Spence-Chapin Services to Families and Children. They were fostered by two separate women in Korea, and it is unclear how their orphanage placements differed. Bordier was placed with Holt Korea and Futerman with Social Welfare Services. One of the only moments in which viewers hear about an agency raising a question about their potential separation is within the first fifteen minutes of the film as Bordier reads an email to Futerman from Holt. The unnamed social worker who examines her record acknowledges the similarities in birth date and birth city, stating, "So it's true that we can ask ourselves why." Unfortunately, this acknowledgment by an adoption agency or orphanage is an isolated instance. When Futerman had visited Social Welfare Society the year prior on her motherland tour, she had viewed her file, but there had been no mention of a biological sister. Her adoption paperwork lists her as a single birth.

This fact is significant to the creation of adoptable children in that there is a template for biographical details: seemingly unique details (e.g., infant/toddler personality type, facial features, affect) that come from stock language or stories of children's arrival at the orphanage (e.g., foundling at a police station, Korean War orphan). For example, Deann Borshay Liem challenges the fraudulent repurposing of the orphan Cha Jung Hee's narrative to facilitate her own adoption in the documentary *In the Matter of Cha Jung Hee* (2010).[26] Discussing the impact of this type of biographic mediation—the fabrication of details about an adoptee's birth and origins—legal scholar David Smolin highlights transnational adoption's reliance on "official processes of the adoption and legal systems to 'launder' them as 'legally' adopted children."[27] Here, I distinguish between Futerman's and Bordier's adoptions and cases of child kidnapping and trafficking, as well as other forms of documented corruption, that may result in countries terminating adoption programs or barring particular orphanages or adoption agencies from operation. Rather, I am interested in the official processes of adoption and the requisite paperwork that transform children through a manufactured adoptee identity.

What is significant about Futerman's disclosure is that she was *not* furnished a copy of the file. Instead, she has photographs of her documents. This detail may seem minor; however, it speaks to the deception involved not only in Futerman's and Bordier's adoptions but in the routine denial of access to their full documents. Korean adoption agencies act as gatekeepers, with adoptees disclosing that sometimes they are able to physically touch their files but that other times the documents rest on a table between them and their social worker. Korean adoptees often recount being told different information in multiple interactions with their orphanages or only seeing an excerpt from their file and not the entire contents.[28] The revelation that Futerman was not furnished copies of her file may be the sole time in the documentary that viewers learn adoptees lack full access to their adoption paperwork. The orphanages' and adoption agencies' mediation of access to adoption documents reflects the existence of their file rooms as spaces of containment, cordoning off adoption as a happy object by only providing preselected information that renders adoptees as blank slates. This is particularly true in cases of domestic

adoption in the US and other countries that maintain sealed records. Historically, US domestic adoption also relied on race- and religion-matching.[29]
Even as the orphanages and adoption agencies seek to support the twins and
determine their biological ties, viewers ought to remain skeptical because the
retroactive support is always mediated.

And yet, the failure to examine the root causes of not only adoption but
also the falsified documents is what makes Futerman and Bordier *accessible*
adoptees. In an effort to craft a narrative that appeals to a broad audience
invested in happy narratives of adoption, the film's producers elide opportunities to critically interrogate the multiple systemic deceptions and failures that led to the twins' separation or even the factors that led to their
adoption. These failures are linked to an industry that is more interested in
fulfilling the needs of its consumers, the adoptive parents, than in protecting the rights of adoptees, orphans, and birth families.[30] Underscoring this
investment in promoting a happy reunion narrative is Futerman's discussion at the end of the documentary in which she describes the new inquiry
both women receive. Instead of questions that interrogate their separation,
she says, "People keep asking us, if you could have been raised together if
we would have." Her response is noteworthy: "I say no. I wouldn't change
anything because I wouldn't be here. I wouldn't be who I am. And neither
would Anaïs. . . . It's comforting to know that life unfolds in a way that it's
supposed to." Futerman looks forward to the new relationship she can forge
with her sister.

This outlook rejects what it would mean for orphanages to be held
accountable for separating biological siblings who could have been raised
in an intact adoptive family unit. Additionally, unless they read the memoir,
viewers will be unaware of the nuances of the twins' adoption. Bordier reveals
what is notable about the twins' separation:

> My mother explained that she had addressed the option of adopting twins
> when she first signed on with Holt International Children's Services. . . . She
> had told them that if twins became available, she would happily adopt both
> of them. That was even a question on her application: *Would you take twins?*
> She told me that there would have been no reason to separate me from a
> twin sister, if I had been part of a pair. They had a copy of my birth record,
> too. It said "single birth," and my parents had full faith that it was correct.[31]

The engineering of Bordier as a single birth aligns with Futerman's paperwork, which notes that she, too, was a singleton. The single birth renders a
child more adoptable, even as *Twinsters* advertises the cuteness of the reunion
and their being identical twins. Adoption is mediated and marketed as a

humanitarian, child-saving act to produce a happy object—the single-birth orphan ready for a new family.

Biographic mediation in the film and in the paperwork advertises possibilities for family formations (e.g., the orphan as a blank slate) and uses the tension of the reunion unfolding on screen to generate appeal despite complications. In trying to make sense of the deception and falsified documents, Futerman writes in the memoir, "Who knew what, if anything, was true?"[32] Their skepticism is warranted, as the two compared their adoption documents and found that they featured two different surnames and origin stories. Yet this explicit interrogation of the fraudulent documents only occurs in the memoir, in which Futerman places the onus of these untruths on their birth mother, who may have provided inaccurate information to avoid being found, and on the translation of Korean into English and French. Futerman consciously mediates what aspects of her adoption journey are told and in what venue by inserting this line of inquiry into the memoir versus the documentary. In doing so, she controls how her affect concerning reunion, and arguably the birth search, is experienced by both viewer and reader.

THE MINOR AFFECTS OF ADOPTEES

As the documentary and memoir circle around the issues of fraudulent paperwork and access to adoption documents, both works make evident that adoptees do not have identical experiences within adoptive families. The happiness and gratitude of Futerman is contrasted with the sadness of Bordier as the two describe their upbringings in the US and France. I am hesitant to label Bordier melancholic, for we risk entertaining reductive notions of what it means to confront the multiple, compounding losses, contradictions, and complications wrought by adoption. This is why the work of Ayla McCullough and Jieun Lee, as referenced in chapter 4, is useful for sifting through the ways the residues of adoption inform adoptees' minor feelings and the reluctance of non-adopted people to disentangle their investments in fantasies of adoption from the lived experiences of adoptees.

Bordier speaks of a particular type of displacement in which she felt betwixt and between growing up ethnically Korean in Europe. Implicit in these disclosures is the assumption that adoptees in the US might encounter less racism; however, this is not a unique phenomenon, as many Korean adoptees in the US, among other countries, have similar experiences.[33] At the same time, it is important to recognize that Futerman asserts personal agency and mediates her adoption experience to construct a legible experience for viewers and readers whereby adoption is a happy object.

Bordier acknowledges the teasing and harassment she experienced for being Korean and that she "always hoped to find someone who looked like [her]."[34] She also encountered racial microaggressions when she visited friends' homes in Belgium, where her family lived for a time. Her friends' mothers served her white rice as a way of "accommodating" her. This perpetual foreignness continued into adulthood as Bordier discloses instances where she is assumed to be a maid or housecleaner and not French.[35] The perpetual foreigner stereotype exists in the US too, so viewers and readers should not assume Futerman and other Korean adoptees in the US are immune to such racism.[36] Racial difference resulted in a sense of displacement for Bordier, as it signified her membership in a nonwhite ethnic group. Describing her sister's adoption, Futerman notes, "[Anaïs] felt that she didn't choose to be adopted. She was just thrown in it." It is through Bordier's character development in the film that we see glimpses of her struggle negotiating what it means to be Korean in France and the other European countries where she lived.

Commonalities exist among adoptees across continents. Not only does anti-Asian racism operate on a global scale, the arbitrariness of Korean adoption placement and the interchangeability of adoptees means Futerman easily could have been adopted to France and Bordier to the US. The explicit nature of the contradictions and complexities of adoptee identity become clear to readers of the co-authored memoir. There is something to be said for Bordier's candor in discussing her upbringing. Love does not triumph over an adoptee's sense of isolation or discomfort. Adoption has produced unease in Bordier's racial, ethnic, and cultural identities, subverting the norm of adoption as the best option. She exposes the fault lines in the positioning of adoption as a happy object. Those who contradict adoption as a route to happiness find themselves critiqued for not being happy "in the right way" because they fail to "feel pleasure and pain where appropriate, in relation to the right objects . . . [or] experience the right amount of such feeling, where the right amount is the 'mean,' which means not too much or too little."[37] There is a vulnerability in Bordier's disclosures, as she is not performing a particular type of affect for the camera to encourage a specific viewer response or to confirm viewers' assumptions about the alleged happiness brought about by adoption.

In contrast to the consistency in Bordier's framing of her experience with her multiple identities, Futerman's admissions in the film and memoir about her lived reality as an adoptee lack the same clear alignment. *Twinsters* presents Futerman as an adoptee who easily assimilated into her adoptive family, with her noting that adoption "was never an issue" and one of her brothers commenting, "I never thought of Sam as an adopted sister. Just as a sister." Futerman says, "From that day on [her Arrival Day] these people were my family." This depiction of her childhood shifts in the book. Futerman wrestles with her ethnic and racial identity like her twin sister, even if its manifestation is different. Similar to other Asian adopted women, Futerman recalls, "As a kid, I remember thinking about my reflection. When I looked in the mirror, I didn't see a small Asian girl. I saw a small white girl. I aspired to have the blue eyes and blond hair like seemingly everyone else in Verona, New Jersey."[38] And yet, she wants to make clear to the reader that being adopted was *not* a problem for her, writing, "My mom was my mom, my dad was my dad, and my brothers were my brothers."[39] Futerman's reflections demonstrate Ahmed's observation: "If we arrive at objects with an expectation of how we will be affected by them, this affects how they affect us, even in the moment they fail to live up to our expectations. Happiness is an expectation of what follows, where the expectation differentiates between things, whether or not they exist as objects in the present."[40] The inclusion of these memories from her childhood reveals the tension between what it means to be adopted and the desire to perform a particular affect that reflects an image of the *good* adoptee—the grateful, easily assimilable adopted child.

Even as Futerman presents her entry into her adoptive family as smooth, albeit with some contradictions given the dysphoric feelings about her racial identity, an anecdote from the memoir stands out for its exposure of the present absence of adoptee status in adoptive families. Futerman recalls a comment that her brother Matt made about adoption: "I don't understand why you would adopt kids, if you can have your own."[41] Upset and angry with her brother, Futerman turns to her parents. Their response is noteworthy as they smile at one another. Her dad states, "Sam, it's a compliment. Matt doesn't even think of you as being adopted."[42] Her father's answer invokes the color-blind rhetoric of adoptive parents that they do not see color or racial difference and, by extension, that they fail to see how race affects an individual's lived realities. Futerman appears to have internalized this messaging, writing, "He considered me his biological sister, as much as he and Andrew were biological brothers. Wow. Dad was right. I changed from outraged to honored. It was a moment I'll never forget." Being ethnically Korean is thus tangential in this scenario. This flattening of racial difference in order to cement Futerman's inclusion in her adoptive family reflects the operationalization of banal multiculturalism—the denial and silencing of racial inequality under the guise that equality has been achieved in neoliberal society.[43]

The minor affects of happiness, discomfort, sadness, and pain elucidate the paradox of adoption. To be adopted does not mean achieving wholeness—where wholeness is equivalent to being a grateful, happy adoptee. By presenting their reunion through a happy, heartfelt tale, *Twinsters* splices in moments of contestation without risking being seen as another "angry" adoptee production. Crystal Mun-hye Baik reads the scenes that disrupt adoption as a fairy tale as "subtle cues rather than as explicit critiques of Korean transnational adoption."[44] There is no room for the minor feelings produced by adoption in the lives of adoptees. The producers of the documentary and the twins recognize the affective life of adoption and reunion as presumed objects of happiness. As a result, the publicly disseminated biographies of Futerman's and Bordier's adoption experiences and collective reunion with one another exist within the expected parameters of the happy adoption.

REUNION AS A HAPPY OBJECT

Twinsters and *Separated @ Birth* present viewers and readers with tangible objects of happiness onto which they can project their desires and perceptions of adoption. Emphasizing adoption and reunion as happy objects is not limited to the texts' consumers; orphanages, adoption agencies, adoptive parents, and even some adoptees invest in this notion because viewing the biographic trajectories of the twins as a cute story of reunion furthers the positive associations of adoption. Both texts illustrate the bind of representation offered by the nexus of objectification in that adoptees' use of biographic mediation occurs within the frameworks of fantasies of adoption. The documentary and memoir offer imperfect biographies—mediated to tell one strand of the adoption and reunion narrative—given the moments of resistance by the twins. The creation of their public narrative is edited to ensure that happiness is not absent from the story while raising questions about the way power is operationalized in adoption.

It is easy to reduce *Twinsters* as a superficial, cute representation of Korean adoption that fails to deliberately engage with the politics of the twins' separation; however, the documentary as well as the memoir allow for resistance in their exploration of the minor affects of Futerman and Bordier. The texts join adoptee counterstories in the public imaginary to alter what narratives are produced about adoptees. The personal disclosures by Futerman and Bordier may be mediated through the cinematic production and publishing processes, but these women claim authorship of the story being told. In doing so, both engage in biographic mediation, asserting autonomy over what, how, and when details of their adoption are disclosed. This chapter's analysis reveals the impact of adoption records on adoptees' life trajectories and the storytelling adoptees participate in as they generate alternative truths about what it means to be adopted. *Twinsters* and *Separated @ Birth,* as well as other adoptee-created content, make evident the various ways adoptees generate alternative narratives or rewrite existing narratives to explain and remedy the documents that underpin and authorize their adoptions, which are authored by orphanages and adoption agencies.

To dismiss their lack of unequivocal critique overlooks the impact of this documentary and memoir on adopted and non-adopted persons alike. To assume all counterstories must be radical or issued by adoptee killjoys overlooks the significant role of adoptees like Futerman and Bordier in subverting normative adoption discourse. In fact, to some, the protagonists of *Twinsters* may represent the adoptee killjoy in that these women reconnected, returned to Korea, and are exploring their identities as adoptees in ways that make visible institutional and state failures to preserve their biological ties. Both the present absence of critique and the emotional impact of the twins' reunion cement adoptees' entry into twenty-first-century American, and by extension Asian American, middlebrow culture, beyond niche releases.[45] While Bordier is European, I locate *Twinsters* within the Asian American canon of adoptee-produced texts to examine how the US, as the largest receiving country of Korean children, incorporates these adoptees into broader conceptions of the Korean American and Asian American experiences.

CODA

Disrupting Fantasies of Adoption

Multiculturalism has failed us. The promises of adoption have gone unfulfilled. Every "successful" adoption narrative and "happy" adoptee in the media, we know, is not the full story. It is the story of contingent kinship. Not only do I consider how Kathryn Mariner deploys this term to discuss the precarities of the act of adoption from the perspective of the prospective adoptive parent, I also address the ways adoptive parents' demands for a particular adoptee affect cast a shadow over these relationships.[1] Mia Farrow's castigation of Soon-Yi Previn, and arguably of Moses Farrow, made these contingencies visible to the world. *Twinsters* depicts how adoptees mediate their narratives to ensure a positive reception. Potential opportunities to critique the adoption industry that facilitated the separation of siblings are minimized to produce a happier story of reunion for public consumption. Fictional portrayals of adoption in US television and film demonstrate the limits of multicultural rhetorics. Asian adopted girl infants and toddlers grow up to become Asian American adult women and experience the world similarly to their non-adopted counterparts. *Seoul Searching* demonstrates that even when an Asian American filmmaker is at the helm, the heterosexual male gaze can still operate, resulting in depictions of Asian American women and girls as objects of racialization and hypersexualization. The film also reveals how Asian American fantasies of adoption run parallel to white, mainstream popular culture notions of adoption.

Adoption Fantasies elucidates what's at stake when adoptees are embraced under a banner of diverse families yet rendered outside the US familial imaginary in adulthood by the protections of whiteness. In disassembling and disentangling the racialization and sexualization of adopted women and girls, *Adoption Fantasies* demands an attentiveness to what happens when popular media circulates unquestioned. What does it mean when adoptee and adoption storylines are included if we are not invited to shape those narratives? Recognizing Asian adopted women and girls as subjects necessitates acknowledging them as nonwhite and the ways white supremacy, settler colonialism, imperialism, and militarism shape their interactions with the world. After all, whiteness will not save us. White supremacy never does; rather, white adoptive parents have a possessive investment in adoptees' infantilization as adoptees of color alleviate their concerns of being racist.[2] As perpetual children—or adoptable objects—the adoptee of color fulfills white fantasies of adoption.

Because I desire to disrupt these fantasies, I implore folks to center the voices of adult Asian adoptees and to see us as agents to tell those stories. To think about who has control of those narratives and what is being distributed. What does it mean when adoptees are behind the camera as opposed to a non-adopted Asian American cultural producer or a white adoptive parent or extended family member? A new generation of adopted Asian girls is entering adulthood. A shift in whose stories are told, uplifted, and heard will coincide with this generational unfolding as more Chinese adoptees speak up and speak out. What will their stories tell us? Will they echo the narratives of Asian adopted women who openly disclose the abuse, fraud, and malfeasance of adoption and raise questions regarding what it means to be reared in white households?

Adoption Fantasies explores the daily violence adoptees endure as their stories are told and written over, whereby they are not seen as the legitimate authors of such *feelings*. Their truths are erased because Asian adopted women and girls' minor feelings are seen as disposable, or as not worthy subjects of interest. These elisions require interrogation to confront the disavowal of adoption as an analytic. *Adoption Fantasies* brings that disavowal to the fore to explore what it means to exist in that silence as I sift through the residues and detritus produced by those artifacts.

This is not to say that same-race white adoptees are not critiquing adoption practices, nor to imply that other adoptees of color and Indigenous adoptees are not participating in conversations concerning the limits of adoption. Rather, the deployment of technology since the turn of the twenty-first century has facilitated adoptee connections in far greater ways than those participating in the early email discussion groups could have imagined. It is through the connections made via email, the blogosphere, online magazines (e.g., the now-defunct *Gazillion Voices*), and social media that adoptees have found a range of platforms to push back against dominant discourse.[3] Asian adoptees alongside Black, Indigenous, Latinx, and multiracial adoptees have constructed both in-person and online communities, joining the voices of same-race white adoptees and other allies seeking reforms in adoption.

Adoptee-authored and/or -produced content alters who controls the narrative, allowing possibilities for ethnographic refusal and agency over how—when and to whom—biographical details of one's adoption are disclosed. Perhaps what I have learned since embarking on this project is that we will write our way out. Whether through crafting documentary narratives, sharing our stories on digital platforms, engaging in creative fiction, writing memoirs and essays, or authoring solo performances, we continue to reclaim our subjecthood. For example, the poetry and prose of Jennifer Kwon Dobbs, Sun Yung Shin, and Ansley Moon should be seen in conversation with the writings of Mi Oak Song Bruining and Susan Ito.[4] These interventions in who tells our stories and what is disclosed are also mediated by ethnographic refusal as we comb through the attendant effects of adoption on all facets of our lives.

Underscoring what it means when adoptees are at the helm in telling our stories is the anthology *When We Become Ours: A YA Adoptee Anthology*, edited by Shannon Gibney and Nicole Chung. That collection brings together fifteen BIPOC adoptees who write provocative and compelling stories featuring adoptee protagonists that grapple with adoption's complexities without rendering the adoptee subject as one-dimensional. The stories reveal the intimacies of adoption and disrupt adoption fantasies as the fictionalized adoptee lives demonstrate the dissonance produced by transracial and/or transnational adoption. Perhaps the book's publication will spark a broader conversation of what it means when non-adopted people write adoption and tell adoptee stories.

This coda is my invitation to you, dear reader, to consider your own positionality to adoption. As we confront the end of *Roe* and renewed interest in how adoptees are commodified in the US, it's imperative that the voices of adoptees, birth parents (especially birth mothers), and scholars of critical adoption studies who have been engaged in this work are not overshadowed by folks just joining the conversation. Listen to the voices of Black women leading the calls for reproductive justice. This requires that we collectively hold ourselves—as feminists—accountable to one another and call each other into these vital conversations. To reflect on what it means to find ourselves complicit in the very economies we seek to challenge and dismantle.

At the same time, when deconstructing Asian American fantasies of adoption, we must remember that adoptees are not merely a fetishistic object to enact a gaze on because you find us "interesting." To render us melancholic without deeper intrinsic exploration means that you fail to recognize how the layers of obfuscation and violence within adoption inform our realities. In other words, melancholia fails to account for the combined effects that orphan record fabrications, limited access to our full adoption files through orphanages and/or adoption agencies, and the racial (dis)identification many experience due to our upbringings circumscribe our existence as adopted people. An overemphasis on melancholia constructs adoptees as existing with an inherent lack, whereby adoptees are missing a piece of themselves. And even if adoptees may invoke this metaphor, this does not mean that we're in a constant state of mourning. We must move past this circular reductive logic that fails to account for the racist love of adoption that results in fractures to our existence. Instead, we must employ a holistic approach to bridge the profound dissonance adoption produces and sit with those tensions.

As I complete this coda, I have recently viewed an early screening of *Joy Ride* (2023). The film offers narrative plentitude for not only its portrayal of Asian American women as holding agency over their sexuality as assertive, funny, multidimensional people, including Deadeye (Sabrina Wu) asserting sex work is real work. *Joy Ride* also provides a layered portrayal of adoption. The latter still is imperfect, for it constructs a narrative undergirded by birth search and reunion with a dose of a quest for authenticity in its adoptee character, Audrey Sullivan (Ashley Park), thus trafficking in tropes of Asian American fantasies of adoption. Nevertheless, the film depicts the racism and microaggressions around one's "real family" and relinquishment, as seen in the film's early scene of Audrey completing a family tree assignment in elementary school, as well as calling attention to her internalized racism. While some may disagree with the way the birth search and reunion resolves itself in the film, *Joy Ride* marks one of the few, if not the only, times I have watched a portrayal of adoption in a feature length film and did not cringe at the lack of nuance around our identities. Yet the imperfect storyline should not be discounted; rather, it must be troubled and interrogated to continue to critique Asian American adoption fantasies and adoption as a plot device.[5] *Joy Ride* engenders a new conversation as we see Asian American women who are unabashedly themselves, which may at times be messy and complicated. I wonder, then, what it might look like if we consider futures of adoption storytelling that are unapologetic, where *When We Become Ours* and *Joy Ride* meet to form a new era of adoptee characters.

Adoption Fantasies lays bare the misrecognition and discomfort produced by the multiple fantasies of adoption in the lives of Asian adopted women and girls. It's a call to action to tell our truths and to reckon with the real damage of these fantasies as they circulate in the middlebrow imaginary. It's about considering the systemic nature of a system that renders adoptees commodities and not subjects with agency. *Adoption Fantasies* troubles how fantasies of adoption and Asian women are intertwined and read onto our bodies. In foregrounding the implications of letting fantasies circulate unchecked, I recuperate the subjugated knowledges of adoptees to create a new adoptee epistemology—a new way of knowing that recognizes we are experts on what it means to be adopted and that we do not have to adhere to anyone's fantasy of adoption.

NOTES

NOTES TO INTRODUCTION

1. Kanesaka, "Yellow Peril, Oriental Plaything," 97.
2. Melamed, "Spirit of Neoliberalism," 7.
3. While it is estimated that two-thirds of the roughly 200,000 Korean adoptees adopted by families in Western nations reside in the US, Korean adoptees recount living isolated and away from other adoptees. See Meier, "Cultural Identity and Place"; and Park Nelson, *Invisible Asians.*
4. The emergence of these organizations is documented at the end of Choy, *Global Families.* For a discussion of Korean adult adoptee organizations, see Hübinette, *Comforting an Orphaned Nation*; Eleana Kim, *Adopted Territory*; and Park Nelson, *Invisible Asians.*
5. McKee, "Gendered Adoptee Identities."
6. For a deeper discussion of how these Oriental fantasies operate in the lives of those who do not identify as cisgender, heterosexual Asian or Asian American women, please see Eng and Hom, *Q & A*; Eng, *Racial Castration*; Masequesmay and Metzger, *Embodying Asian/American Sexualities*; Shimizu, *Straitjacket Sexualities*; and Manalansan, Hom, and Fajardo, *Q & A.*
7. Ishii, "Diversity Times Three," 44.
8. McKee, *Disrupting Kinship*, 10. Please see *Disrupting Kinship* for a deeper discussion of adoptee gratitude and how I engage erin Khuê Ninh's discussion of ingratitude and her work discussing the debtor-creditor relationship between parent and child. Ninh, *Ingratitude.*
9. Please see *Disrupting Kinship* for my initial discussion of the adoptee killjoy, which builds on Sara Ahmed's notion of the feminist killjoy and discussion of happy objects; Ahmed, *Promise of Happiness*, 21.
10. Mariner, *Contingent Kinship*, 125.

11. An assumption exists that transnational adoption will ensure that reunification between birth family and child is not feasible and that the biological parents will not try to retrieve them. Such a belief ignores the voices of adult adoptees and movements to secure rights for birth parents and adopted people.

12. Sisson, "'I Want In'"; Briggs, *How All Politics*; McKee, "Adoption as Reproductive Justice Issue"; and Wexler et al., "Understanding Adoption."

13. Lowe, "Heterogeneity, Hybridity, Multiplicity."

14. Pate, *From Orphan to Adoptee*; and Woo, *Framed by War*.

15. McKee, "More than an Outcome."

16. Volkman, *Cultures of Transnational Adoption*; Dorow, *Transnational Adoption*; Hübinette, *Comforting an Orphaned Nation*; Bergquist et al., *International Korean Adoption*; Jacobson, *Culture Keeping*; Song and Lee, "Past and Present Cultural Experiences"; Eleana Kim, *Adopted Territory*; Yngvesson, *Belonging in an Adopted World*; Briggs, *Somebody's Children*; Choy, *Global Families*; Kim, Reichwald, and Lee, "Cultural Socialization"; Pate, *From Orphan to Adoptee*; Louie, *How Chinese Are You?*; Oh, *To Save the Children*; Joyce Lee et al., "Ethnic Identity"; Park Nelson, *Invisible Asians*; Varzally, *Children of Reunion*; Graves, *War Born Family*; McKee, *Disrupting Kinship*; and Woo, *Framed by War*.

17. Novy, *Reading Adoption*; Jerng, *Claiming Others*; C. Callahan, *Kin of Another Kind*; and Askeland, "Adoption and Orphan Tropes."

18. Birnbaum, "Kinship Roots"; C. Callahan, "Bad Seeds"; Morey and Nelson, "Cross-Species Kinship Dilemmas"; Satz, "Introduction"; Bartz, "'I Can Turn Into Anything'"; Fedosik, "Power to 'Make Live'"; Donnell, "Orphan, Adoptee, Nation"; Fedosik, "Adoption in Stephen Spielberg's *AI*"; and Wills, "Formulating Kinship."

19. Anagnost, "Scenes of Misrecognition"; Eng, *Feeling of Kinship*; Pate, *From Orphan to Adoptee*; Raleigh, *Selling Transracial Adoption*; Woo, *Framed by War*; and Mariner, *Contingent Kinship*.

20. McKee, *Disrupting Kinship*.

21. Bow, *Betrayal*, 39. Bow continues, "Emphasis on gender and sexuality as criteria for entry into the United States does not minimize the significance of Asian immigrant women as wage laborers given the largely economic rationale underlying the exclusion laws. Nevertheless, their immigration was clearly determined relationally—by what effect it would have on male labor"; Bow, *Betrayal*, 39.

22. Style, "Curriculum as Window."

23. This is a common phrase deployed by white adoptive parents. The erasure of racial difference implicitly demonstrates adoptive parents' inability to comprehend how racism informs the lived experiences of adoptees of color.

24. Melamed, "Spirit of Neoliberalism," 6. Even as contemporary adoptive families embrace the multicultural nature of their kinship, transnational and transracial adoption illustrate the transgression of the color line. Kathryn Joyce notes that some white evangelical churches found themselves becoming racially diverse not because they intentionally engaged communities of color; rather, the transracial adoption of children from countries in Africa led to their previously white congregations finding themselves integrated; Joyce, *Child Catchers*, 68–69.

25. These children include adoptees from Hong Kong, Japan, South Korea, China, Vietnam, and India, among other Asian nations.

26. The act included immigrant quotas restricting the number of individuals migrating from Asia to a mere 2,990 people. Chan, *Asian Americans*, 146.

27. Krieder and Raleigh, "Residential Racial Diversity," 1202.

28. Dorow, *Transnational Adoption*; Jacobson, *Culture Keeping*; and Raleigh, *Selling Transracial Adoption*.

29. For a deeper discussion of adoptions of mixed-race Black Asian children, see Hamilton, *Children of the Occupation*; Varzally, *Children of Reunion*; and Graves, *War Born Family*.

30. C. Kim et al., *Mixed Korean*; Cannon et al., *Together at Last*; Quaites, *Faith & Favor*; and Windom, *Orchestration*.

31. Hatzipanagos, "I Know My Parents Love Me." Recently, former NFL quarterback Colin Kaepernick encountered criticism after disclosing incidents of anti-Blackness within his adoptive family. Blanco, "Colin Kaepernick"; Foster, "Colin."

32. Wyver, "'More Beautiful.'"

33. Hong, *Minor Feelings*, 55.

34. Thomas, *Multicultural Girlhood*.

35. Derickson, "Racial Politics of Neoliberal Regulation," 895.

36. Wills, Hübinette, and Willing, *Adoption and Multiculturalism*; and Wyver, "'More Beautiful.'"

37. Melamed, "Spirit of Neoliberalism," 1.

38. James Lee, *Urban Triage*, 148.

39. Chin and Chan, "Racist Love."

40. Tang, *Repetition and Race*, 6.

41. Bow, *Racist Love*, 18.

42. Bow, 6.

43. Bow, 162.

44. The underlying belief that once they are adopted, these children will find permanence and love is why adoptive families are commonly referred to as "forever families." Nonetheless, the murders and abuse experienced by adoptees within these families and the practice of rehoming adopted children demonstrate the spuriousness of such language.

45. Hong, *Minor Feelings*, 57.

46. Hong.

47. Hong, 56; and Ngai, *Ugly Feelings*.

48. Ngai, *Ugly Feelings*, 8.

49. Myers, "'Real Families,'" 176.

50. Hong, *Minor Feelings*, 55.

51. Hong, 57.

52. The consumption of the middlebrow by members of the middle class offers them cultural capital and access to imagining the possibilities of upward, social mobility. Radway, *Feeling for Books*.

53. Thomas, *Multicultural Girlhood*, 16. For a deeper examination of racial innocence and the childhoods of white and Black children, please see Bernstein, *Racial Innocence*.

54. Restrepo, "Pathologizing Latinas."

55. Ho, *Consumption and Identity*.

56. Reddy, *Fashioning Diaspora*.

57. Epstein, Blake, and González, *Girlhood Interrupted*; Toliver, "Alterity and Innocence"; and Morris, "Countering the Adultification."

58. Breslow, *Ambivalent Childhoods*.

59. This is evident in discourse around Dylann Roof and Kyle Rittenhouse, two white young adults who murdered civilians, versus the US media's portrayal of Michael Brown, Trayvon Martin, Tamir Rice, and other Black youth murdered by police officers.

60. Bernstein, *Racial Innocence*; and N. Wright, *Black Girlhood*.

61. Projansky, *Spectacular Girls*, 37.

62. In their discussions of the deployment of hegemonic masculinity and the gendered nature of boy children, Eleana J. Kim, Arissa Oh, SooJin Pate, and Susie Woo recognize the military mascot and houseboy as figures preceding the adoptable boy orphan. Kim, *Adopted Territory*; Oh, *To Save the Children*; Pate, *From Orphan to Adoptee*; and Woo, *Framed by War*. Recognizing how these male children became part of the first generation of adoptees from Korea, Oh writes, "The bonds of affection that developed between servicemen and their mascots led to some of the first intercountry adoptions from Korea. . . . [Military

newspaper] *Stars and Stripes* presented mascot adoptions in ways that foregrounded the boys' metamorphosis from orphans to Americans, an approach picked up by mainstream magazines like *Life*." Oh, *To Save the Children*, 35–36. For a discussion of how this gendered notion of masculinity found itself transmitted in television, see Donnell, "Orphan, Adoptee, Nation."

63. Pate, *From Orphan to Adoptee*, 47.

64. Pate, 57.

65. Pate, 57.

66. Woo, *Framed by War*. The connective tissues woven together by Woo exemplify what David Eng gestures toward when he contends, "Dissociating transnational adoption from the historical and economic legacy of war brides, mail-order brides, comfort women, and sex workers thus obscures an understanding of this practice as one of the more recent embodiments of gendered commodification . . . emerging under the shadows of colonialism and now sustained through practices of global capitalism." Eng, *Feeling of Kinship*, 105.

67. L. Kang, *Traffic in Asian Women*.

68. K. Moon, *Sex among Allies*; Höhn and Moon, *Over There*; and Jin-Kyung Lee, *Service Economies*.

69. Merish, "Cuteness and Commodity Aesthetics," 189.

70. Woo, *Framed by War*.

71. Ngai, *Our Aesthetic Categories*, 85; and Kanesaka, "Yellow Peril, Oriental Plaything," 99.

72. Hong, *Minor Feelings*, 94.

73. Patton, *Birth Marks*; and Simon and Roorda, *In Their Own Voices*. Black and mixed-Black transracial adoptee memoirs also offer an opportunity to interrogate how adoptees negotiate racialized and gendered stereotypes; Carroll, *Surviving the White Gaze*; and Gibney, *The Girl I Am*.

74. See Ty, *Politics of the Visible*; Leong, *China Mystique*; and Shimizu, *Hypersexuality of Race*.

75. Mulvey, "Visual Pleasure and Narrative Cinema," 838.

76. White, "Gaze," 75.

77. Please note that all of these films were produced by Korean adopted women filmmakers. Other documentaries chronicling the journeys of Korean adopted men by adoptee filmmakers were also released during this period, including *Passing Through* (1998), *Going Home* (2009), *Resilience* (2009), and *Finding Seoul* (2011). These cinematic representations have been joined by memoirs and essay collections engaging in narrative pushback, including Tonya Bishoff and Jo Rankin's *Seeds from a Silent Tree: An Anthology by Korean Adoptees*; Susan Soon-Keum Cox's *Voices from Another Place: A Collection of Works from a Generation Born in Korea and Adopted to Other Countries*; Katy Robinson's *A Single Square Picture: A Korean Adoptee's Search for Her Roots*; Jane Jeong Trenka's *The Language of Blood* and *Fugitive Visions: An Adoptee's Return to Korea*; Jeannine Joy Vance's *Twins Found in a Box: Adapting to Adoption*; Jane Jeong Trenka, Julia Chinyere Oparah, and Sun Yung Shin's *Outsiders Within: Writing on Transracial Adoption*; and Indigo Willing et al.'s *Vietnamese.Adopted: A Collection of Voices*. Korean adoptee artists kimura byol-nathalie lemoine, Jane Jin Kaisen, and kate-hers RHEE intervened in adoption discourse beginning in the 1990s through their use of visual media and mixed media. Hübinette, *Comforting an Orphaned Nation*; Eleana Kim, *Adopted Territory*; and Baik, *Reencounters*. Vietnamese adoptee photographer Anh Đào Kolbe offers an opportunity to rethink Vietnamese adoption and diaspora. Theater also provides adoptees a medium to reshape narratives of adoption. Katie Hae Leo's adoption satire *Four Destinies* premiered at Theatre Mu (St. Paul, MN) in October 2011. Marissa Lichwick's *The Yellow Dress* first previewed in 2011 at the University of Washington's School of Drama. Sun Mee Chomet's *How to Be a Korean Woman* premiered at Dreamland Arts (St. Paul, MN) in 2012. Deb Sivigny's installation *Hello, My Name Is . . .* opened in Washington, DC, in 2017. For a deeper discussion of

adoption portrayals in theater, please see Jieun Lee, "Representing Korean Orphans"; Kim and Ginther, "'I Am Who I Am—'"; and Jieun Lee, *Performing Transnational Adoption.* Asian adopted men also have contributed to reshaping adoption narratives, as seen in the work of Kevin Vollmers, Adam Chau, Thomas Park Clement, Glenn Morey, Eric Sharp, Lee Herrick, Matthew Salesses, Bryan Thao Worra, and Kev Minh Allen, among others.

78. Gregory Paul Choy and Catherine Ceniza Choy critique *Daughter from Danang* for perpetuating violence by silencing the adoptee voice. Choy and Choy, "What Lies Beneath."

79. McKee, "Anti-Asian Racism at Home."

NOTES TO CHAPTER 1

1. Donnell, "Orphan, Adoptee, Nation," 72.
2. Asian adopted boys were represented on screen in *Trophy Wife* (2013), in the character of Bert Harrison, and in 2015–16 episodes of *Fresh Off the Boat* (2015–20), in the character of Phillip Goldstein. Perhaps underscoring the interchangeability of adoptees is the fact that both, distinctly different, characters were played by Albert Tsai. The lawyer-focused drama *Harry's Law* (2011–12) featured a story about Chinese parents attempting to regain custody of their daughter who was relinquished as a result of the Chinese government's one-child policy; this story took center stage in episode 7 of season 2, "American Girl." Viewers of *House* also learned that the character Lawrence Kutner (Kal Penn) was adopted by a foster family during his childhood. These examples coincide with adoption storylines in television series on the major networks (ABC, NBC, CBS, and Fox), such as *Glee, Smash,* and *Grey's Anatomy.*
3. Pate, *From Orphan to Adoptee,* 94.
4. Pate, 94.
5. Kanesaka, "Yellow Peril, Oriental Plaything," 95.
6. Louie, *How Chinese Are You?,* 52.
7. Leslie Wang, *Outsourced Children,* 54.
8. Dorow, *Transnational Adoption,* 250–51.
9. Jacobson, *Culture Keeping,* 42–43.
10. Gailey, *Blue-Ribbon Babies,* 96–97.
11. Anagnost, "Scenes of Misrecognition," 391; and Louie, *How Chinese Are You?,* 35.
12. Twin sisters Alexandra and Parker Fong played Lily York Goldenblatt in the *Sex and the City* films, and Cathy Ang stars as Lily York Goldenblatt in *And Just Like That.*
13. The actresses cast as Lily Tucker-Pritchett are not Vietnamese. It is reported that the mother of the Hiller twins is from the Philippines. Aubrey Anderson-Emmons, who replaced the Hiller twins, is the daughter of comedian Amy Anderson, a Korean adoptee from Minnesota.
14. McRobbie, *Aftermath of Feminism,* 12. See also Gill, *Gender and the Media*; and Genz and Brabon, *Postfeminism.*
15. Molina-Guzmán, "'Latina Wisdom,'" 73; and Cavalcante, "Anxious Displacements."
16. Ishii, "Diversity Times Three," 37.
17. For more information about the priceless child, see Zelizer, *Pricing the Priceless Child.*
18. Louie, *How Chinese Are You?,* 35.
19. Myers, "Complicating Birth-Culture Pedagogy," 68–69.
20. Myers, 75–76; and McGinnis et al., *Beyond Culture Camp.*
21. It is important to also recognize the establishment of Pact: An Adoption Alliance in 1991. This organization primarily serves transracial domestic adoptees and adoptive families.
22. Although I briefly had a relationship with a chapter near my graduate school, it is unclear how different chapters of Families with Children from China fostered meaningful connections with adult adoptees at the turn of the twenty-first century. This is not to say that

this did not occur; however, I am not aware of intentional outreach conducted during this period to create connections with adult adoptees. As the children of those families entered adulthood, their programming most likely has shifted. Recently, Chinese Adoptee Alliance evolved from FCCNY (Families with Children from China New York) in August 2022. Prior to the change in organization name, other steps for more adoptee inclusion were "the creation of the Adoptee Board (2017), the election of adoptees as President and Vice President (2021), the election of additional adoptees as Board members (2021), the revision of [the] Mission Statement . . . (2021), and the departure of adoptive parent Board members (2022)." Chinese Adoptee Alliance, "Transition FAQs."

23. McKee, "Public Intimacy and Kinship."

24. McGinnis, "Adult Korean Adoptee Groups."

25. Choy, *Global Families*, 168–69; Myers, Baden, and Ferguson, "Going Back 'Home'"; and "Filipino Adoptees Network."

26. Hübinette, *Comforting an Orphaned Nation*; Eleana Kim, *Adopted Territory*; and McGinnis, "Adult Korean Adoptee Groups."

27. Meier, "Loss and Reclaimed Lives"; and Eleana Kim, *Adopted Territory*.

28. In *Disrupting Kinship*, I discuss adoptee erasure in mainstream conversations of adoption. Reporting by Maggie Jones has offered an opportunity to hear adult adoptee voices. Jones, "Why a Generation of Adoptees"; and Jones, "Adam Crapser's Bizarre Deportation Odyssey." Examples of adoptee advocacy can be evidenced by the work of adoptee organizations concerning adoptees' access to retroactive citizenship; Kim and Park Nelson, "'Natural Born Aliens'"; and McKee, *Disrupting Kinship*.

29. In the wake of the majority opinion of the US Supreme Court *Dobbs v. Jackson Women's Health Organization* (2022) decision, adoptees encounter continued criticism as they resist the use of adoption as an abortion alternative. *Adoption & Culture*'s special issue (2023) focused on the *Dobbs v. Jackson Women's Health Organization* (2022) US Supreme Court decision makes the weaponization of adoption clear in the discourse concerning the bodily autonomy of people who can become pregnant.

30. Edelman, *No Future*. Kelly Condit-Shrestha discusses the reformulation of adoptees' labor from physical labor (e.g., the Orphan Train movement and use of children in farming families in the Midwest) to affective labor reliant on the sentimentality of childhood and adoption; Condit-Shrestha, "Post-WWII Regimes." Condit-Shrestha echoes David Eng's discussion of how "the exploitation of the transnational adoptee is largely an emotional affair. She helps to consolidate the *affective* boundaries of the white, heteronormative middle-class nuclear family"; Eng, *Feeling of Kinship*, 108–9.

31. Muñoz, *Cruising Utopia*; and McKee, *Disrupting Kinship*.

32. *Sex and the City*, season 6, episode 1, "To Market, To Market."

33. *Sex and the City*, season 4, episode 12, "Just Say Yes."

34. *Sex and the City*, season 4, episode 12, "Just Say Yes."

35. Douglas and Michaels, *Mommy Myth*, 5.

36. *Sex and the City*, season 4, episode 11, "Coulda, Woulda, Shoulda."

37. Joyce, *Child Catchers*, 61–63.

38. Joyce, 62.

39. Joyce, 61–64. See also Marre and Briggs, *International Adoption*; Briggs, *Somebody's Children*; and Stein, "Privileging God the Father."

40. Raleigh, *Selling Transracial Adoption*, 2.

41. As a reminder, I am interested in the ways that Mimi Thi Nguyen's discussion of the "gift of freedom" concerning refugees can be translated to think through demands for adoptees' gratitude; M. Nguyen, *Gift of Freedom*.

42. Raleigh, *Selling Transracial Adoption*, 26.

43. Raleigh, 79.

44. Gailey, *Blue-Ribbon Babies*, 88.

45. Raleigh, *Selling Transracial Adoption*, 80; and Quiroz, *Adoption in a Color-Blind Society*.

46. McRobbie, *Aftermath of Feminism*, 19.

47. Hays, *Cultural Contradictions of Motherhood*, x.

48. Hays, 8.

49. Hays, 9.

50. Jacobson, *Culture Keeping*; and Raleigh, *Selling Transracial Adoption*.

51. Tuan and Shiao, *Choosing Ethnicity*.

52. Leslie Wang, *Outsourced Children*, 53.

53. *Sex and the City*, season 6, episode 20, "An American Girl in Paris (Part Deux)."

54. Stacey, *In the Name of the Family*, 38; Modell, *Kinship with Strangers*; and Terrell and Modell, "Anthropology and Adoption."

55. Eng, *Feeling of Kinship*, 24.

56. Eng, 45.

57. Ishii, "Diversity Times Three," 44.

58. Eng, *Feeling of Kinship*, 101.

59. Eng, 99.

60. Please note that in season 3, the producers replaced the twins with actress Aubrey Anderson-Emmons.

61. *Modern Family*, season 1, episode 1, "Pilot."

62. For a more comprehensive discussion of adoptees' (re)birth upon their entry into their adoptive countries and families, please see McKee, *Disrupting Kinship*.

63. I draw from Orlando Patterson's discussion of social death in the context of slavery, a process that renders the slave a social nonperson; Patterson, *Slavery and Social Death*. Lisa Marie Cacho furthers this discussion of social death in her examination of those whose personhood is negated and devalued; Cacho, *Social Death*. By deploying the term *social death*, I do not mean to imply a direct comparison between enslaved people and adoptees. Rather, I am invested in how the concepts of social death and natal alienation offer an avenue for sufficiently addressing the loss in sovereignty that adoptees experience, similar to Jodi Kim's deployment of social death in her examination of Korean adoptees and Hosu Kim's discussion of social death and natal alienation to locate the experiences of Korean birth mothers; Jodi Kim, *Ends of Empire*, 281n56; and H. Kim, *Birth Mothers*.

64. *Modern Family*, season 1, episode 1, "Pilot."

65. Choy, *Global Families*; and Oh, *To Save the Children*.

66. *Modern Family*, season 1, episode 1, "Pilot."

67. Uchida, "Orientalization of Asian Women."

68. Uchida, 167.

69. *Modern Family*, season 1, episode 1, "Pilot"; and *Modern Family*, season 1, episode 5, "Coal Digger." In her discussion of the series, Molina-Guzmán discusses Sofia Vergara's Latina identity as a comedic prop of racial difference. Molina-Guzmán, "'Latina Wisdom.'"

70. *Modern Family*, season 1, episode 12, "Not in My House."

71. Mannur, *Intimate Eating*.

72. *Smash*, season 1, episode 1, "Pilot"; and *Smash*, season 1, episode 2, "The Callback."

73. Mariner, *Contingent Kinship*, 19.

74. Mariner, 19.

75. Mariner, 62.

76. Raleigh, *Selling Transracial Adoption*; and Gailey, *Blue-Ribbon Babies*. In the case of African American families in the mid-twentieth century, prospective adoptive parents and foster parents found themselves subject to narrow constructions of heterosexual gender roles; Potter, *Everybody Else*; Graves, *A War Born Family*.

77. McKee and Gibney, "'It Came.'"

NOTES TO CHAPTER 2

1. Tajima, "Lotus Blossoms Don't Bleed," 308.

2. Ho, "To Be an Asian Woman."

3. Ho; M. Kang, "Why Are Perpetrators' Motives?"; Mitra, Kang, and Clutario, "It's Time to Reckon"; and *All Things Considered*, "Sociologist's View."

4. McKee, "Do You See Me?"; Westerman, "'Am I Asian Enough?'"; and Clements and Consing, "Awakening."

5. These sexualized remarks are only one form of harassment. As the COVID-19 pandemic demonstrates, anti-Asian violence, racism, and xenophobia target persons of Asian descent regardless of adoptee status, immigrant status, or nationality. Stop AAPI Hate, "Reports."

6. Cho, "Asian Pacific American Women," 165–66.

7. While there are many languages spoken in Asia, the most common "hellos" seem to be in Mandarin or Japanese; it is always surprising when someone says hello in Korean or Vietnamese, let alone another Asian language. This may be changing given the popularity of the Korean wave.

8. Documenting the way adoptees may fall vulnerable to predatory behavior is the fictional story "Sexy" by Jenny Heijun Wills, which chronicles high school-age Asian Canadian teenager Hannah Russo-Hartman, whose French teacher preyed upon her loneliness and inexperience.

9. Merskin, "Reviving Lolita?"; and Levin and Kilbourne, *So Sexy So Soon*.

10. Mila, "Hey Mom, They Don't See"; and Newton, "I Am Not My Dad's Girlfriend."

11. Lim, "Alt-Right's Asian Fetish"; and Five Alive, "No Conflicts."

12. Quinn, "'Sideways' Logic."

13. Peck, *Prohibition Hangover*, 127.

14. Lavin, "Young, Well-to-Do, Intelligent"; Donnelly, "Honor Roll Murder"; and N. Kim, "Too Smart."

15. Thrupkaew, "Filmic Face-Lift," 41. See also Feng, "Asian American Media Studies," 125.

16. Hu and Pham, "In Focus," 115.

17. McCabe, *Feminist Film Studies*, 29.

18. hooks, *Black Looks*.

19. L. Kang, "Desiring of Asian Female Bodies," 76. See also Shimizu, *Hypersexuality of Race*, 12.

20. Public writings by Anne Anlin Cheng, Cathy Park Hong, and Elaine Hsieh Chou capture the ways Asian American women recognize the discourses surrounding our bodies and the role of this gaze in rendering our bodies as objects, erasing our autonomy, agency, and subjecthood. Cheng, "Dilemma of Intimacy"; Hong, *Minor Feelings*; and Chou, "What White Men Say."

21. hooks, *Black Looks*.

22. Shimizu, *Hypersexuality of Race*, 16.

23. Tammy Chu, *Searching for Go-Hyang* (1998); Deann Borshay Liem, *First Person Plural* (Mu Films, 2000); and Vicente Franco and Gail Dolgin, *Daughter from Danang* (2002; Alexandria, VA: PBS, 2003), DVD. Also debuting in 1998 were Jennifer Arndt-Johns's *Crossing Chasms* and Nathan Adolfson's *Passing Through*. In 2000 *Passing Through* premiered on PBS as part of its Independent Lens programming. These documentaries are available for purchase as DVDs except for *Crossing Chasms*, which is only available on VHS.

24. Bishoff and Rankin, *Seeds from a Silent Tree*; Ito, "Hambun-Hambun"; Cox, *Voices from Another Place*; Wilkinson and Fox, *After the Morning Calm*; Elizabeth Kim, *Ten Thousand Sorrows*; and Vance, *Twins Found in a Box*.

25. Trenka, *Language of Blood*, 92. The reproduction of the full quote from *The Language of Blood* with the racial slurs that Trenka endured underscores how as Sun Yung Shin asserts, "We'd prefer a world without sexualized racism BUT HERE WE ARE"; Sun Yung Shin, text message to author, April 21, 2023. The erasure of the vitriol would only mean that we do not confront the racism on the page even though we encounter such racism in real life.

26. Trenka, 83.

27. Trenka, 65.

28. Trenka, 79.
29. Trenka, 98.
30. Trenka, 99.
31. Kearly, "I'm Iwish," 64–65.
32. Smalkoski, "China," 80.
33. Ninh, "Without Enhancements."
34. Ninh and Roshanravan, "#WeToo," 4.
35. Wong, "Big Bad Prank"; and Seethaler, "'Big Bad Chinese Mama.'"
36. Trenka, *Language of Blood,* 82–84.
37. Trenka, 86, 90.
38. Ho, *Racial Ambiguity,* 62.
39. US Census Bureau, "California, 2000: Census 2000 Profile"; and "Population of Santa Barbara County."
40. Peck, *Prohibition Hangover,* 106.
41. Peck, 106.
42. Peck, 123–25.
43. US Census Bureau, "California, 2000: Summary Population," 100.
44. Park Nelson, *Invisible Asians.*
45. Gross, "Winding Career of Sandra Oh."
46. In reflecting on the casting decision, Sandra Oh comments: "It's never talked about in the film. It's never dealt with. It's a very short scene where it's a visual thing, but I think it's strong because whatever you get from it, it tells a deeper story about Stephanie." Gross, "Winding Career of Sandra Oh."
47. US Census Bureau, "California, 2000: Summary Population," 189.
48. Cox, Navarro-Rivera, and Jones, "Race, Religion, and Political Affiliation"; PRRI, "PRRI Survey"; and Stearns, Buchmann, and Bonneau, "Interracial Friendships."
49. Shimizu, *Hypersexuality of Race,* 268.
50. Feng, "Recuperating Suzie Wong," 48.
51. Hong, *Minor Feelings,* 174–75.
52. Shimizu, *Hypersexuality of Race,* 274.
53. Harris, *All about the Girl,* xx.
54. Ho, *Consumption and Identity,* 6.
55. One film capturing Asian North American adolescent life in a family-friendly manner is Pixar's *Turning Red* (2022).
56. Dahlen and Thomas, *Harry Potter and the Other.*
57. Ninh, *Passing for Perfect,* 152.
58. Okada, *Making Asian American Film,* 120.
59. For a discussion of Asian American masculinities in relation to Asian American independent cinema, please see Jun, *Race for Citizenship*; Shimizu, *Straitjacket Sexualities*; and Ju Yon Kim, *Racial Mundane.*
60. Ninh, *Passing for Perfect,* 158.
61. Ninh, 158.
62. Shimizu, *Straitjacket Sexualities,* 131.
63. Shimizu, 156.
64. Mulvey, "Visual Pleasure and Narrative Cinema," 837–38.
65. Lee is also the author of a middle-grade novel focused on the life of an adoptee. See M. Lee, *If It Hadn't Been.* For a discussion of Lee's work on telling adoption-themed narratives, see Dahlen, "'It Is Part.'"
66. Fuchs, "'It's Three-Dimensional.'"
67. K. Fang, "Globalization, Masculinity," 102.
68. Perkins, "How to Hit On an Asian Girl." I first came across the site via Phil Yu's *Angry Asian Man.* Yu, "How to Hit On an Asian Girl."

69. Drenka, "Grieving as an Asian Adoptee."
70. Newton, "Stop Centering Whiteness."
71. Chung, "My White Adoptive Parents."
72. Townsend, "Asian Fetishism, Consent, and Adoption."

NOTES TO CHAPTER 3

1. Soon-Yi was initially taken to live with the Previn family in England, but after Farrow's divorce from André Previn, the youngest four children (Fletcher, Lark, Daisy, and Soon-Yi) moved to the US, and her eldest sons—twins Sascha and Matthew—remained with their father.

2. Maureen Orth, "Momma Mia!" Allen acknowledges that his paternity has been questioned, noting, "Despite her suggesting [Ronan] was Frank Sinatra's child, I think he's mine, though I'll never really know. She may have still been sleeping with Frank, as she hinted, and may have had any number of outside affairs, for all I know. As I said, we lived apart." W. Allen, *Apropos of Nothing,* 228.

3. Fischer, "Oedipus Wrecked?," 106.

4. The *Allen v. Farrow* miniseries features interviews with then Connecticut district attorney Frank S. Maco, New York City Child Welfare Administration supervisor Sheryl Harden, and others in combination with notes and other documentation from NYC Child Welfare Administration veteran caseworker Paul Williams and other child welfare professionals and doctors to demonstrate Allen's guilt, even as he was never indicted for molestation. *Allen v. Farrow,* episode 3, directed by Kirby Dick and Amy Ziering, aired February 2021, on HBO. In presenting its evidence, the miniseries relies on the court of public opinion.

5. Mia and Ronan Farrow publicly criticized Allen on social media and labeled him a child predator. On January 12, 2014, Ronan commented, "Missed the Woody Allen tribute—did they put the part where a woman publicly confirmed he molested her at age seven before or after Annie Hall?"; Selby, "Ronan Farrow Blasts Dad Woody." A day later, Mia tweeted: "A woman has publicly detailed Woody Allen's molestation of her at age 7. GoldenGlobe [*sic*] tribute showed contempt for her & all abuse survivors." Mia Farrow (@MiaFarrow), "A Woman." Dylan publicly addressed the accusations in a February 2014 open letter featured in the *New York Times* confirming Allen's sexual abuse and the long-standing impact the abuse has had on her life. D. Farrow, "An Open Letter." Dylan addressed her sexual abuse in the context of the #MeToo movement in December 2017. D. Farrow, "Op-Ed." The 2021 HBO miniseries *Allen v. Farrow* ensured that these allegations remain percolating in popular culture.

6. Please note that because of my examination of the Farrow-Allen-Previn scandal, I am only looking at father-daughter incest as opposed to other forms of incest (e.g., mother-son, brother-sister). "The 'Phaedra Complex,'" which describes the attraction between stepparent and stepchild, expands the definition of incest to include nonnormative families. Messer, "'Phaedra Complex.'"

7. *Allen v. Farrow,* episode 2.

8. Merkin, "After Decades of Silence."

9. Complicating this understanding of her age is the fact that in her memoir, Farrow asserts that not until 1980 was Soon-Yi's "true" age confirmed to be seven, going on eight, as a result of "the standard method of X-raying her wrists." Mia Farrow, *What Falls Away,* 179. At the time, bone measurements were frequently used to estimate the age of individuals who lacked official documentation for their year of birth.

10. H.R. 1552, Private Law 95-37 (1978).

11. H.R. 12508, Public Law 95-417 (1978).

12. Kim and Park Nelson, "'Natural Born Aliens'"; and McKee, *Disrupting Kinship.*

13. Mia Farrow, *What Falls Away*, 163.
14. Merkin, "After Decades of Silence."
15. Mia Farrow, *What Falls Away*, 178.
16. W. Allen, *Apropos of Nothing*, 217.
17. W. Allen, 217.
18. *Allen v. Farrow*, episode 1.
19. *Allen v. Farrow*, episode 1.
20. Moses Farrow, "A Son Speaks Out."
21. *Allen v. Farrow*, episode 1.
22. Mia Farrow, *What Falls Away*, 179.
23. Mia Farrow, 182.
24. W. Allen, *Apropos of Nothing*, 220.
25. Merkin, "After Decades of Silence."
26. Mia Farrow, *What Falls Away*, 188.
27. W. Allen, *Apropos of Nothing*, 231.
28. Mia Farrow, *What Falls Away*, 219.
29. Macintyre, "Farrow Bitter Winner."
30. Macintyre.
31. Strathern, "What Is a Parent?," 255.
32. Strathern, 256.
33. N. Callahan, "Why Dylan Farrow's Adoption Matters."
34. Herman and Hirschman, *Father-Daughter Incest*, 70. See also Harkins, *Everybody's Family Romance*.
35. Herman and Hirschman, 27.
36. Sacco, *Unspeakable*; Valenti, "Acting Older Isn't Being Older"; Beusman, "Judge Decides It Was 'Illegal'"; and Connolly, *Domestic Intimacies*.
37. For a more expansive Foucauldian analysis of incest and power dynamics, please see Bell, *Interrogating Incest*.
38. The illicit nature of the father-daughter incest taboo, often written about in literary fiction, rarely enters popular culture in the same manner as sibling incest in the public American imaginary, which is often treated as an amusing fiction. Contemporary examples of incest include *Arrested Development*'s (2003–2019) flirtation with a relationship between George Michael and Maeby, Richie and Margot in *The Royal Tenenbaums* (2001), and the incestuous nature of Cersei and Jamie Lannister's relationship in *Game of Thrones* (2011–19). One of the most notable examples of potential incest that evokes laughter is Luke and Leia from the original *Star Wars* trilogy (*Star Wars* [1977]; *The Empire Strikes Back* [1980]; and *Return of the Jedi* [1983]).
39. Macintyre, "Farrow Wins Custody Battle."
40. Polhemus, *Lot's Daughters*, 325.
41. Lax, *Woody Allen*, 387.
42. *Allen v. Farrow*, episode 4.
43. Farrow's own relationships with men are rooted in age differences not unlike the gap in age between Soon-Yi and Allen. Her marriage to Sinatra in 1966 occurred when she was twenty-one and he was fifty. They had met two years prior as she filmed the television show *Peyton Place*. Farrow's relationship, at age twenty-four, with André Previn began as an affair when the then forty-one-year-old composer was married to singer-songwriter Dory Previn. These formative relationships and interactions with men, in addition to witnessing her father's womanizing, including his relationship with Ava Gardner, who at the time was married to Sinatra, may have shaped her perception that all men are predators. Note that while Farrow advocates on behalf of her daughter Dylan in an effort to seek justice against Allen, she is notably silent about her brother John Charles Villiers-Farrow, who was sentenced for child sexual abuse. NBC4 Washington, "Mia Farrow's Brother"; and Williams,

"Mia Farrow's Sex Abuse Silence." She also defended director Roman Polanski as recently as 2005, when she served as a character witness as part of a libel suit in England. Flanagan, "I Actually Read Woody Allen's Memoir." Polanski, for the uninitiated, raped a thirteen-year-old girl in 1977 and fled the US for Europe after pleading to a lesser crime—sex with a minor. Grady, "Roman Polanski." Polanski directed Farrow in her groundbreaking *Rosemary's Baby* (1968) performance. Interviewed in 2018, Farrow appears ambivalent about Polanski, noting, "It's not in the cards, but I don't think I would" on whether she would work again with the director, while also reflecting that *Rosemary's Baby* was "the film project she found most creatively engaging" and that "it's wonderful working with Roman Polanski." Langmuir, "Mia Farrow."

44. Herman and Hirschman, *Father-Daughter Incest*, 39.

45. Herman and Hirschman, 39.

46. Angelides, "Feminism, Child Sexual Abuse," 144.

47. Adegoke, "Counting Down."

48. Fischer, "Oedipus Wrecked?," 106.

49. For a more detailed discussion of the Polaroids and the discovery of the photos by Farrow, see Mia Farrow, *What Falls Away*; and *Allen v. Farrow*, episode 2.

50. This public discussion of Soon-Yi occurred as part of efforts to demonstrate her incompetence. Meade, *Unruly Life of Woody Allen*, 207. The focus on her intelligence traffics in ableist rhetoric that dismisses effects of what it must have been like to be adopted as an older child into a home without continuity of care because of her mother's acting schedule and divorce from André Previn.

51. *Allen v. Farrow*, episode 4.

52. Mia Farrow, *What Falls Away*, 259.

53. Mia Farrow, 263.

54. Mia Farrow, *What Falls Away*, 233–34.

55. *Allen v. Farrow*, episode 1; *Allen v. Farrow*, episode 3; and *Allen v. Farrow*, episode 4.

56. Weide, "Woody Allen Allegations."

57. Lewis, "Very Last Lover."

58. Hevesi, "Woody Allen Tells His Side."

59. Meade, *Unruly Life of Woody Allen*, 207. Subini Annamma and Maisha Winn document how IQ tests are infused with racism and ableism. Annamma and Winn, "Transforming Our Mission."

60. Groteke, *Mia & Woody*, 80.

61. Groteke, 80.

62. As discussions of Soon-Yi's cognitive abilities occur, it is important to recognize how any developmental delays recounted in public discourse may directly relate to the psychological effects of institutional care. Weitzman and Albers, "Long-Term Developmental, Behavioral, and Attachment Outcomes"; Stryker, *Road to Evergreen*; and van den Dries et al., "Infants' Physical and Cognitive Development." Post-adoption services were limited, and Farrow may have been ill equipped to understand intellectual disabilities and/or posttraumatic stress disorder related to institutional care. This stands in contrast to how physically disabled children's needs are discussed within adoption processes.

63. Carlson, *Faces of Intellectual Disability*, 29–30.

64. Although this chapter does not draw conclusions regarding whether Soon-Yi identifies as someone with intellectual disabilities, Soon-Yi has publicly stated that she does have a "little learning disability," noting, "I've never spoken about it, because Mia drummed it into me to be ashamed about it. It comes out in spelling, and I had to work much harder in school. But I was driven and interested, and I wish I'd had a tutor the way some kids do for homework." Merkin, "After Decades of Silence." The term *learning disability* is broad, and Previn has not disclosed what specific disability affects her beyond indicating "trouble with homonyms, in particular, and spelling." Merkin. This is not to overlook how women

with disabilities, broadly defined, find themselves vulnerable to sexual abuse, including incest. During the same period that Soon-Yi embarked on a relationship with Allen, these women often did not report assault and were considered to be at increased risk for abuse. Sobsey and Doe, "Patterns of Sexual Abuse"; Womendez and Schneiderman, "Escaping from Abuse"; Allen and Borgen, "Multimodal Therapy Treatment"; and McCabe, Cummins, and Reid, "Empirical Study."

65. *Allen v. Farrow,* episode 2.

66. *Allen v. Farrow,* episode 2.

67. *Allen v. Farrow,* episode 2.

68. Merkin, "After Decades of Silence."

69. Groteke, *Mia & Woody,* 87.

70. Meade, *Unruly Life of Woody Allen,* 205.

71. Carlson, *Faces of Intellectual Disability,* 68.

72. Carlson, 69; and Trent, *Inventing the Feeble Mind.*

73. I use the phrase "mythic prostitute birth mother" purposefully here because of the ways adoptive parents and society-at-large often denigrate sex work pejoratively to prostitution and employ this specific language, "prostitute birth mother," as a tool to pathologize birth families.

74. Macintyre, "Farrow Bitter Winner."

75. NYDN, AP, "Lark Previn."

76. Merkin, "After Decades of Silence."

77. Merkin.

78. Merkin.

79. *Newsweek* staff, "Soon-Yi Speaks."

80. Dennis, "Dylan Farrow's Brother."

81. Moses Farrow, "A Son Speaks Out."

82. Hansen, "Minnesota Politics"; and Elizabeth Kim, *Ten Thousand Sorrows.*

83. *Chosun Ilbo,* "Four Korean Adoptees Murdered"; and K. Wright, "Md. Father Charged."

84. Merkin, "After Decades of Silence."

85. R. Farrow, "From Aggressive Overtures."

NOTES TO CHAPTER 4

1. McKee and Gibney, "'It Came.'"

2. Adoption and the experiences of adoptees have been appropriated by white authors in children's, young adult, and adult literature; Dahlen, "How to Evaluate"; and Yi, "Memoirs or Myths?" There are limited fictional portrayals of adoption and adoptee protagonists written by adoptees. This makes the fictional works of adoptee authors such as Mariama J. Lockington, Shannon Gibney, Meredith Ireland, Eric Smith, Alice Stephens, Kosoko Jackson, and Matthew Salesses stand out. Such a paucity of adoptee-authored fiction writing underscores the groundbreaking nature of Shannon Gibney and Nicole Chung's edited volume, *When We Become Ours: A YA Adoptee Anthology,* for it features stories written by fifteen adoptee authors.

3. It was unsurprising, yet disconcerting, to discover that *The Blind Side* (2009) is Netflix's most popular movie in the streaming services history; Bologna, "Most Popular Movies."

4. Since the premiere of the Netflix-produced show *Beef* (2023) on April 6, 2023, David Choe's misogynoir and disclosure of sexual violence and rape on a 2014 podcast episode have resurfaced. When the *Ugly Delicious* episode aired, the podcast episode was not well-known, even as the question was raised by writers at feminist websites Reappropriate and XO Jane when it originally happened; J. Fang, "Did Korean American?"; Setten, "Did Facebook's Graffiti Artist?" Choe stars in *Beef* alongside Steven Yeun and Ali Wong, both

of whom stand in support of Choe, who asserts that these claims are fabricated; Abad-Santos, "Beef's Sexual Assault Controversy, Explained"; and Ford, "*Beef* Creators Respond." I agree with Soleil Ho, who comments: "To uncritically embrace 'Beef' for what it gives to the Asian American community shows that we're on board with rape culture and with misogyny, especially against Black women. To embrace it shows that we're willing to let others pay the price for our feelings of validation and belonging"; S. Ho, "We're in Asian America's."

5. Koo, "'We Deserve to Be Here.'"

6. Eng and Han, *Racial Melancholia*, 67, 77. This same distinction is drawn by Eng in *The Feeling of Kinship*, whereby he writes of "racial melancholia for Asian Americans and transnational adoptees" (121).

7. For a discussion of how the adoptive Korean family is Asian American, please see *Disrupting Kinship*, where I discuss the adoptive family as Asian American, even if they may not identify that way themselves.

8. Westerman, "'Am I Asian Enough?'"; Mitchell, "'I'm Not Allowed'"; and Clements and Consing, "Awakening."

9. For example, in January 2022 the #VeryAsian hashtag emerged following the racism experienced by Korean adoptee and St. Louis, Missouri, news anchor Michele Li. After reporting on New Year's Day traditions and reflecting on the Korean traditions she celebrates, Li received a racist and verbally abusive voicemail and was told to "keep her Korean to herself." This incident of anti-Asian racism resonated with the Asian American community and made evident how adoptees encounter the forever foreigner stereotype. Bellamy-Walker, "#VeryAsian Hashtag." Emerging from this racist incident is the Very Asian Foundation, which was initially partnered with the Asian American Journalists Association. Li was also interviewed by Asian American cultural critics Jeff Yang and Phil Yu. Yang and Yu, "They Call Us Very Asian."

10. McCullough, "Assemblaging Orphanhood"; and McCullough, "'You don't know when.'"

11. Jieun Lee, "Representing Korean Orphans"; and Jieun Lee, *Performing Transnational Adoption*.

12. Condit-Shrestha, "South Korea and Adoption's Ends," 390; Selman, "Intercountry Adoption"; and Hübinette, *Comforting an Orphaned Nation*.

13. Catsoulis, "Review."

14. Ford and McClintock, "Sundance."

15. This is not to overlook other films starring Asian Americans released in the last five years such as *The Farewell* (2019) or *Shang-Chi and the Legend of Ten Rings* (2021), which is part of the Marvel Cinematic Universe.

16. Jia, "Rumpus Review."

17. Catsoulis, "Review."

18. Catsoulis.

19. Chang, "Sundance Film Review."

20. V. Nguyen, *Nothing Ever Dies*, 203.

21. V. Nguyen, "Asian-Americans Need More Movies."

22. Jun, *Race for Citizenship*, 110.

23. Claire Kim, "Racial Triangulation."

24. Washington, *Blasian Invasion*, 10.

25. Jun, *Race for Citizenship*, 3.

26. Claire Kim, "Are Asians the New Blacks?," 238.

27. Bullock, "Seoul Searching."

28. Bullock.

29. Bullock. The treatment of Blackness, or at least the use of a Blaccent, did not improve with the premiere of *Crazy Rich Asians* three years later as actress Awkwafina (née Nora Lum) traffics in AAVE (African American Vernacular English) as Peik Lin, the best friend,

sidekick to Constance Wu's Rachel Chu. Jackson, "Who Really Owns the 'Blaccent'?" For a discussion of Awkwafina's cultural appropriation, please see Makalintal, "Awkwafina's Past"; Shotwell, "Awkwafina May Have Forgotten"; Levenson, "Awkwafina Issues Statement."

30. Jia, "Rumpus Review."

31. Jia.

32. Ringwald, "What about 'The Breakfast Club'?"

33. Ringwald.

34. Eleana Kim, "Wedding Citizenship and Culture"; and Global Overseas Adoptees' Link, "Dual Citizenship."

35. Eleana Kim, "Wedding Citizenship and Culture," 59–60.

36. Hübinette, *Comforting an Orphaned Nation*, 75. In her oral history collection with the first generation of adopted Koreans, Kim Park Nelson reports that one of her participants returned to Korea for the first time in 1977. Park Nelson, *Invisible Asians*, 177.

37. Prébin, *Meeting Once More*, 52. For example, Sun Yung Shin traveled to South Korea as part of a Holt Motherland Tour in 1987 at age thirteen. Her recollection is important to also contextualize that participants on these tours were similar to the high-school-age fictional protagonists of *Seoul Searching*; Sun Yung Shin, personal communication to author, March 21, 2023. According to Elise Prébin, the Holt program provided a set of prescriptive guidelines that not only regulated clothing attire (e.g., no provocative outfits including tank tops and miniskirts) but also stipulated that "participants could not smoke cigarettes in public or drink alcohol." Prébin, *Meeting Once More*, 53. Prébin notes that these regulations were said to have been implemented to prevent residents with disabilities from mimicking participants' behavior; nonetheless, it also follows that Holt believed that only a certain type of adoptee behavior was permitted in an effort to inculcate a particular type of "Korean" identity.

38. Hübinette, *Comforting an Orphaned Nation*, 75.

39. Park Nelson, *Invisible Asians*, 155. From personal experience, my husband returned to South Korea with his three other adopted siblings from Korea with his parents in 1992, when they were sixteen, thirteen, eleven, and eight. I mention this because in the early 1990s it was an anomaly for adoptees to encounter other adoptees who traveled to South Korea unaffiliated with motherland tours aimed at adoptive families (e.g., the Ties program based in Wisconsin or operated by adoption agencies). Situating this travel alongside the early returns made by adopted teens and adult adoptees on motherland tours sans families is significant when tracing the genealogy of waves of adoptees going back to Korea. To overlook these earliest returns risks erasing these histories from the broader historical adoptee memory.

40. US Department of Commerce and Bureau of the Census, "1980 Census of Population," 66, 71.

41. Myers, "Complicating Birth-Culture Pedagogy," 72.

42. Hübinette, *Comforting an Orphaned Nation*, 78n29. Eleana J. Kim notes, "Since the early 1990s, at least a dozen adult adoptee organizations and support groups have sprung up worldwide—in Europe, Australia, the United States, and South Korea." Eleana Kim, "Wedding Citizenship and Culture," 66.

43. Clement, *Unforgotten War*; Robinson, *Single Square Picture*; and Trenka, *Language of Blood*.

44. Eleana Kim, *Adopted Territory*, 185.

45. McKee, *Disrupting Kinship*.

46. Eleana Kim, "Wedding Citizenship and Culture," 61.

47. Tau, "Interview with 'Seoul Searching' Director."

48. Park Nelson, *Invisible Asians*, 157–58.

49. Eleana Kim, *Adopted Territory*, 219.

50. An example of this in film is Tammy Chu's *Resilience* (2009).
51. Catsoulis, "Review."
52. N. Allen, "Seoul Searching."
53. Eleana Kim, "Wedding Citizenship and Culture," 76.
54. Eleana Kim, *Adopted Territory*, 181.
55. Evelyn Kim, "Open Letter"; Liu, "MRAsians"; and Mak, "'Men's Rights Asians.'"
56. V. Nguyen, "Asian-Americans Need More Movies."

NOTES TO CHAPTER 5

1. Christian, Transue-Woolston, and González, *Flip the Script*.
2. "#flipthescript," *Lost Daughters*. Note that I capitalize the first letters of each word in the hashtag to adhere to best practices regarding accessibility and screen reader technology.
3. Bruining, "To Omoni, in Korea"; Bishoff and Rankin, *Seeds from a Silent Tree*; Clement, *Unforgotten War*; Robinson, *Single Square Picture*; Trenka, *Language of Blood*; Trenka, Oparah, and Shin, *Outsiders Within*; and Trenka, *Fugitive Visions*.
4. The book was reissued in a second edition in 2020 by University of Minnesota Press.
5. Hawkesworth, *Feminist Inquiry*, 176–77.
6. Homans et al., "Critical Adoption Studies"; and Bae, "Radical Imagination."
7. McKee, *Disrupting Kinship*.
8. In November 2017 the Korean adoptee community witnessed another public reunion story with identical twins Katey Bennett and Amanda Dunford meeting on *Megyn Kelly Today*. Eun Kyung Kim, "Identical Twins." The pair reunited after separately completing at-home DNA tests. Korean adoptee twins Molly Sinert and Emily Bushnell were reunited in April 2021 as a result of Bushnell's daughter asking to do a DNA test and matching with Sinert. Brutus, "Identical Twins."
9. Ahmed, *Willful Subjects*.
10. Futerman served as a director and writer of the documentary.
11. *Twinsters* and a collection of work featuring Korean adoptee rapper Dan Matthews (DAN-akaDAN; i.e., *akaDan* [2014], *asian-ish** [2016], and *akaSEOUL* [2016]) represent the first clear crossover of Korean adoption documentary/docuseries content into US popular media. McKee, "Gendered Adoptee Identities"; and McKee, *Disrupting Kinship*. The seven-installment *akaDan* (2014) and five-episode *asian-ish** (2016) were released on YouTube on the International Secret Agents (ISAtv) channel. ISA was founded by Wong Fu Productions and the Far East Movement. The seven-part *akaSEOUL* (2016) was released by NBC Asian America and documented the experiences of four Korean adoptees, including Matthews. This content is marketable for mainstream audiences because it offers "feel good" narratives and a layer of levity absent from other Asian adoption documentaries.
12. McKee, *Disrupting Kinship*, 12.
13. Harding, "Subjectivity, Experience, and Knowledge"; and Hennessy, "Subject, Knowledges."
14. Ngai, *Ugly Feelings*, 6.
15. Ngai, 8.
16. Jacobson, *Culture Keeping*.
17. Han, "Aesthetics of Cuteness"; Sharon Heijin Lee, "Beauty between Empires"; and Puzar and Hong, "Korean Cuties."
18. Yano, *Pink Globalization*, 6.
19. Bow, "Racist Cute," 44.
20. Ngai, *Our Aesthetic Categories*, 72.
21. Ahmed, *Promise of Happiness*, 27.
22. Bow, "Racist Cute," 40.
23. Bordier and Futerman, *Separated @ Birth*, 62.
24. Kopacz, "From Contingent Beginnings"; Cerissa Kim et al., *Mixed Korean*; and Cannon et al., *Together at Last*. Jieyi Cai, Adam Kim, and Richard M. Lee also have explored the use

of genetic testing by Korean adopted adolescents and noted, "Higher exploration of Korean ethnic identity strengthened the positive association between birth family thoughts and interest in genetic testing for adolescents"; Cai, Kim, and Lee, "Psychological Correlates," 467.

25. Bordier and Futerman, *Separated @ Birth,* 2.

26. Park Nelson, "'Loss Is More than Sadness'"; Choy, *Global Families;* and McKee, "Locating Adoptees in Asian America." For a further discussion of the use of transferrable language in marketing children and facilitating the construction of adoptees as interchangeable, see Riben, *Stork Market;* Raleigh, *Selling Transracial Adoption;* and McKee, *Disrupting Kinship.*

27. Smolin, "Child Laundering," 115.

28. Eleana Kim, *Adopted Territory,* 219. See also Park Nelson, *Invisible Asians,* 157–62.

29. Berebitsky, *Like Our Very Own;* and Herman, *Kinship by Design.*

30. Briggs, *Somebody's Children;* and Raleigh, *Selling Transracial Adoption.*

31. Bordier and Futerman, *Separated @ Birth,* 7.

32. Bordier and Futerman, 21.

33. Freundlich and Lieberthal, "Survey of Adult Korean Adoptees"; Meier, "Cultural Identity and Place"; Robinson, *Single Square Picture;* Trenka, *Language of Blood;* Shiao and Tuan, "Sociological Approach"; Shiao and Tuan, "Korean Adoptees"; Song and Lee, "Past and Present Cultural Experiences."

34. Bordier and Futerman, *Separated @ Birth,* 4.

35. Bordier and Futerman, 47.

36. Tuan, *Forever Foreigners or Honorary Whites?*

37. Ahmed, *Promise of Happiness,* 36.

38. Bordier and Futerman, *Separated @ Birth,* 67; and Bishoff and Rankin, *Seeds from a Silent Tree.*

39. Bordier and Futerman, *Separated @ Birth,* 67.

40. Ahmed, *Promise of Happiness,* 29.

41. Bordier and Futerman, *Separated @ Birth,* 85.

42. Bordier and Futerman, 85.

43. Thomas, *Multicultural Girlhood;* and Derickson, "Racial Politics of Neoliberal Regulation."

44. Baik, *Reencounters,* 126.

45. Asian adoptee writings found limited venues for publication outside of memoirs, with only a handful published in Asian American or feminist edited collections. Bruining, "Politics of Intercountry Adoption"; Bruining, "To Omoni, in Korea"; Ito, "Hambun-Hambun"; McKee, "Other Sister"; Dobbs, "Cure for Swedish Fever"; and Kinney, "Seoul Searching."

NOTES TO CODA

1. Mariner, *Contingent Kinship.*

2. Gerloff, "How We Got Here."

3. Eleana Kim, *Adopted Territory;* Ho, *Racial Ambiguity;* and McKee, *Disrupting Kinship.*

4. Bruining, "To Omoni, in Korea"; Bruining, "Politics of Intercountry Adoption"; Bruining, "Whose Daughter Are You?"; Ito, "Hambun-Hambun"; Dobbs, "Cure for Swedish Fever"; Shin, *Skirt Full of Black;* Shin, *Rough, and Savage;* Dobbs, *Paper Pavilion;* A. Moon, *How to Bury the Dead;* and Ito, *Mouse Room.* Dobbs and Shin have both released poetry after the period on which this book focuses (Shin, *Unbearable Splendor;* Dobbs, *Interrogation Room;* and Shin, *The Wet Hex*). Ito's memoir, *I Would Meet You Anywhere,* is scheduled for a November 2023 release. Other work by adopted Asian women poets released after 2015 include collections by Marci Calabretta Cancio-Bello (*Hour of the Ox*), Julayne Lee (*Not My White Savior*), and Tiana Nobile (*Cleave*); Nobile, Moon, and Cancio-Bello, "Three Asian Adoptee Poets."

5. McKee, "Complexities of Adoption."

BIBLIOGRAPHY

Abad-Santos, Alex. "Beef's Sexual Assault Controversy, Explained." *Vox,* April 18, 2023. https://www.vox.com/culture/23688007/david-choe-beef-netflix-rape-controversy-podcast.

Adegoke, Yomi. "Counting Down to Female Celebrities 'Turning Legal' Is More than Crass. It's Dangerous." *Medium,* June 7, 2019. https://medium.com/@yomiadegoke/counting-down-to-female-celebrities-turning-legal-is-more-than-crass-its-dangerous-94f8abbf4674.

Adolfson, Nathan, dir. *Passing Through.* 1999.

Ahmed, Sara. *The Promise of Happiness.* Durham, NC: Duke University Press, 2010.

———. *Willful Subjects.* Durham, NC: Duke University Press, 2014.

All Things Considered. "A Sociologist's View on the Hyper-Sexualization of Asian Women in American Society." NPR, March 19, 2021. https://www.npr.org/2021/03/19/979340013/a-sociologists-view-on-the-hyper-sexualization-of-asian-women-in-american-societ.

Allen, Brad, and Kathy Borgen. "Multimodal Therapy for Survivors of Sexual Abuse with Developmental Disabilities: An Evaluation of Treatment Effectiveness." *Sexuality and Disability* 12, no. 3 (September 1994): 201–6. https://doi.org/10.1007/BF02547906.

Allen, Nick. "Seoul Searching." *RogerEbert.com,* June 17, 2016. https://www.rogerebert.com/reviews/seoul-searching-2016.

Allen v. Farrow. Episodes 1–4. Directed by Kirby Dick and Amy Ziering. Aired February 2021, on HBO.

Allen, Woody. *Apropos of Nothing.* New York: Arcade Publishing, 2020.

Anagnost, Ann. "Scenes of Misrecognition: Maternal Citizenship in the Age of Transnational Adoption." *Positions: East Asia Cultures Critique* 8, no. 2 (2000): 389–421.

Anderson, Wes, dir. *The Royal Tenenbaums.* Walt Disney Studios Motion Pictures, 2001.

Angelides, Steven. "Feminism, Child Sexual Abuse, and the Erasure of Child Sexuality." *GLQ: A Journal of Lesbian and Gay Studies* 10, no. 2 (January 1, 2004): 141–77.

Annamma, Subini Ancy, and Maisha Winn. "Transforming Our Mission: Animating Teacher Education through Intersectional Justice." *Theory Into Practice* 58, no. 4 (October 2, 2019): 318–27.

Arndt-Johns, Jennifer, dir. *Crossing Chasms.* 1998.

Askeland, Lori. "Adoption and Orphan Tropes in Literary Studies." *Adoption & Culture* 4, no. 1 (2014): 13–25.

Bae, Shannon. "Radical Imagination and the Solidarity Movement between Transnational Korean Adoptees and Unwed Mothers in South Korea." *Adoption & Culture* 6, no. 2 (2018): 301–16.

Baik, Crystal Mun-hye. *Reencounters: On the Korean War and Diasporic Memory Critique.* Philadelphia: Temple University Press, 2020.

Bartz, Emily N. "'I Can Turn Into Anything as Long as It's Me': The Adoptee God[dess] of Lies and Stories in *Loki: Agent of Asgard.*" *Adoption & Culture* 8, no. 1 (2020): 83–113.

Bell, Vikki. *Interrogating Incest: Feminism, Foucault and the Law.* London: Routledge, 1993.

Bellamy-Walker, Tat. "#VeryAsian Hashtag Goes Viral after Racist Criticism of Korean American News Anchor." *NBC News,* January 3, 2022. https://www.nbcnews.com/news/asian-america/veryasian-hashtag-goes-viral-racist-criticism-korean-american-news-anc-rcna10777.

Berebitsky, Julie. *Like Our Very Own: Adoption and the Changing Culture of Motherhood, 1851–1950.* Lawrence: University Press of Kansas, 2000.

Bergquist, Kathleen Ja Sook, M. Elizabeth Vonk, Dong Soo Kim, and Martin D. Feit, eds. *International Korean Adoption: A Fifty-Year History of Policy and Practice.* New York: Haworth Press, 2007.

Bernstein, Robin. *Racial Innocence: Performing American Childhood from Slavery to Civil Rights.* New York: New York University Press, 2011.

Beusman, Callie. "Judge Decides It Was 'Illegal' to Sentence Teacher to 30 Days for Rape." *Jezebel,* September 4, 2013. http://jezebel.com/judge-decides-it-was-illegal-to-sentence-teacher-to-3-1252318261.

Bicks, Jenny, writer. *Sex and the City.* Season 4, Episode 11. "Coulda, Woulda, Shoulda." Directed by David Frankel. Aired August 5, 2011, on HBO.

———, writer. *Sex and the City.* Season 6, Episode 16. "Out of the Frying Pan." Directed by Michael Engler. Aired January 25, 2004, on HBO.

Bicks, Jenny, and Cindy Chupack, writers. *Sex and the City.* Season 6, Episode 18. "Splat!" Directed by Julian Farino. Aired February 8, 2004, on HBO.

Birnbaum, Susanna. "The Kinship Roots (Adoption) Narrative in Documentary and Animated Fantasy: *Somewhere Between, Twinsters,* and *Kung Fu Panda.*" *Adoption & Culture* 9, no. 2 (July 2021): 178–202.

Bishoff, Tonya, and Jo Rankin, eds. *Seeds from a Silent Tree: An Anthology by Korean Adoptees.* San Diego: Pandal Press, 1997.

Black, Shane, dir. *Iron Man 3.* Walt Disney Studios Motion Pictures, 2013.

Blanco, Andrea. "Colin Kaepernick Calls Out White Adoptive Parents for 'Problematic' Comments." *The Independent,* March 12, 2023, sec. News. https://www.independent.co.uk/news/world/americas/colin-kaepernick-parents-problematic-comments-racism-b2299142.html.

Bologna, Caroline. April 4, 2022. "The Most Popular Movies on Netflix Right Now Besides 'The Blind Side.'" *The Huffington Post.* https://www.huffpost.com/entry/the-blind-side-popular-netflix-movies_l_624a6f4ee4bod8266aadebf8#:~:text=%E2%80%9CThe%20Blind%20Side%E2%80%9D%20is%20the,received%20a%20Best%20Picture%20nomination.

Bordier, Anaïs, and Samantha Futerman. *Separated @ Birth: A True Love Story of Twin Sisters Reunited.* New York: Berkley Books, 2015.

Bow, Leslie. *Betrayal and Other Acts of Subversion: Feminism, Sexual Politics, Asian American Women's Literature.* Princeton, NJ: Princeton University Press, 2001.

———. "Racist Cute: Caricature, Kawaii-Style, and the Asian Thing." *American Quarterly* 71, no. 1 (2019): 29–58.

———. *Racist Love: Asian Abstraction and the Pleasures of Fantasy.* Durham, NC: Duke University Press, 2022.

Breslow, Jacob. *Ambivalent Childhoods: Speculative Futures and the Psychic Life of the Child.* Minneapolis: University of Minnesota Press, 2021.

Briggs, Laura. *How All Politics Became Reproductive Politics: From Welfare Reform to Foreclosure to Trump.* Oakland: University of California Press, 2017.

———. *Somebody's Children: The Politics of Transracial and Transnational Adoption.* Durham, NC: Duke University Press, 2012.

Bruining, Mi Ok. "The Politics of Intercountry Adoption: Made in Korea." *Sojourner: The Women's Forum* 14, no. 9 (1989): 18.

———. "To Omoni, in Korea." In *Making Face, Making Soul / Haciendo Caras,* edited by Gloria Anzaldúa, 153–55. San Francisco: Aunt Lute Books, 1990.

———. "Whose Daughter Are You? Exploring Identity Issues of Lesbians Who Were Adopted." *Journal of Gay and Lesbian Social Services* 3, no. 2 (1995): 43–60.

Brutus, Wilkine. "Identical Twins, Separated at Birth in South Korea, Reunite 36 Later in South Florida," *WLRN,* April 30, 2021. https://www.wlrn.org/news/2021-04-30/identical-twins-separated-at-birth-in-south-korea-reunite-36-years-later-in-south-florida.

Bullock, Lauren. "Seoul Searching and the Anti-Blackness of Asian Excellence." *Black Nerd Problems* (blog), July 27, 2016. https://blacknerdproblems.com/seoul-searching-and-the-anti-blackness-of-asian-excellence/.

Cacho, Lisa Marie. *Social Death: Racialized Rightlessness and the Criminalization of the Unprotected.* New York: New York University Press, 2012.

Cai, Jieyi, Adam Kim, and Richard M. Lee. "Psychological Correlates of Interest in Genetic Testing among Korean American Adoptees and Their Parents." Special issue, "Minority and Health Disparities in Research and Practice in Genetic Counseling and Genomic Medicine Special Issue—Part 2," edited by Lila Aiyar, Nadine Channaoui, and Vivian Ota Wang, *Journal of Genetic Counseling* 29, no. 3 (2020): 460–70.

Callahan, Cynthia. "Bad Seeds and Wayward Boys in Postwar Adoption Fiction." *Twentieth Century Literature* 67, no. 1 (March 1, 2021): 75–100.

———. *Kin of Another Kind: Transracial Adoption in American Literature.* Ann Arbor: University of Michigan Press, 2011.

Callahan, Nicole Soojung. "Why Dylan Farrow's Adoption Matters." *Salon,* February 11, 2014. http://www.salon.com/2014/02/11/why_dylan_farrows_adoption_matters/.

Cancio-Bello, Marci Calabretta. *Hour of the Ox.* Pittsburgh: University of Pittsburgh Press, 2016.

Cannon, Paul Lee, Nancy Lee Blackman, Cerissa Kim, Katherine Kim, and Linda Papi Rounds, eds. *Together at Last: Stories of Adoption and Reunion in the Age of DNA.* Bloomington, IN: Thomas & Wonsook Foundation, 2020.

Carlson, Licia. *The Faces of Intellectual Disability: Philosophical Reflections.* Bloomington: Indiana University Press, 2010.

Carroll, Rebecca. *Surviving the White Gaze: A Memoir.* New York: Simon & Schuster, 2021.

Catsoulis, Jeannette. "Review: In 'Seoul Searching,' Teenagers Explore Their Korean Roots to an '80s Soundtrack." *New York Times,* June 16, 2016. https://www.nytimes.com/2016/06/17/movies/seoul-searching-review.html.

Cavalcante, Andre. "Anxious Displacements: The Representation of Gay Parenting on *Modern Family* and *The New Normal* and the Management of Cultural Anxiety." *Television & New Media* 16, no. 5 (July 1, 2015): 454–71.

Chadha, Gurinder, dir. *Bend it Like Beckham.* Searchlight Pictures, 2003.

Chan, Sucheng. *Asian Americans: An Interpretive History.* Boston: Twayne, 1991.

Chang, Justin. "Sundance Film Review: 'Seoul Searching.'" *Variety,* January 23, 2015. https://variety.com/2015/film/reviews/sundance-film-review-seoul-searching-1201413290/.

Cheng, Anne Anlin. "A Dilemma of Intimacy." *Nation,* October 21, 2020. https://www.thenation.com/article/culture/essay-interracial-love/.

Chin, Frank, and Jeffrey Paul Chan. "Racist Love." In *Seeing through Shuck,* edited by Richard Kostelanetz, 65–79. New York: Ballantine Books, 1972.

Chinese Adoptee Alliance. "Transition FAQs." October 2022. https://fccny.org/about.

Cho, Sumi K. "Asian Pacific American Women and Racialized Sexual Harassment." In *Making More Waves: New Writing by Asian American Women,* edited by Elaine H. Kim, Lilia V. Villanueva, and Asian Women United of California, 164–73. Boston: Beacon Press, 1997.

Chomet, SunMee. *How to Be a Korean Woman.* Directed by Zaraawar Mistry, Dreamland Arts, 2012, St. Paul, MN.

Chosun Ilbo. "Four Korean Adoptees Murdered in US." March 27, 2008. http://english.chosun.com/site/data/html_dir/2008/03/27/2008032761009.html.

Chou, Elaine Hsieh. "What White Men Say in Our Absence." *Cut,* March 24, 2022. https://www.thecut.com/2022/03/what-white-men-say-in-our-absence.html.

Choy, Catherine Ceniza. *Global Families: A History of Asian International Adoption in America.* New York: New York University Press, 2013.

Choy, Gregory Paul, and Catherine Ceniza Choy. "What Lies Beneath: Reframing Daughter from Danang." In *Outsiders Within: Writing on Transracial Adoption,* edited by Jane Jeong Trenka, Julia Chinyere Oparah, and Sun Yung Shin, 221–31. Cambridge: South End Press, 2006.

Christian, Diane René, Amanda Transue-Woolston, and Rosita González, eds. *Flip the Script: Adult Adoptee Anthology.* North Charleston, SC: CreateSpace, 2015.

Chu, Jon M., dir. *Crazy Rich Asians.* Warner Bros., 2018.

Chu, Tammy, dir. *Resilience.* 2009.

———, dir. *Searching for Go-Hyang.* 1998.

Chung, Nicole. "My White Adoptive Parents Struggled to See Me as Korean. Would They Have Understood My Anger at the Rise in Anti-Asian Violence?" *Time,* March 22, 2021. https://time.com/5948949/anti-asian-racism-white-adoptive-family/.

Chupack, Cindy, writer. *Sex and the City.* Season 4, Episode 12. "Just Say Yes." Directed by David Frankel. Aired August 12, 2001, on HBO.

Clement, Thomas Park. *The Unforgotten War: Dust of the Streets.* Bloomfield, IN: Truepeny Publishing, 1998.

Clements, Rhiannon, and Nash Consing. "Awakening: Asian American Adoptees Reflect on Identity." *Voices,* August 26, 2021. https://voices.aaja.org/index/2021/8/26/awakening-asian-american-adoptees-reflect-on-identity.

Columbus, Chris, dir. *Harry Potter and the Sorcerer's Stone.* Warner Bros., 2001.

———, dir. *Harry Potter and the Chamber of Secrets.* Warner Bros., 2002.

Condit-Shrestha, Kelly. "Post-WWII Regimes: The Separations and Placements of West German, Japanese, and Korean Children." Paper presented at the Alliance for the Study of Adoption and Culture conference, virtual, October 2021.

———. "South Korea and Adoption's Ends: Reexamining the Numbers and Historicizing Market Economies." *Adoption & Culture* 6, no. 2 (2018): 364–400.

Connolly, Brian. *Domestic Intimacies: Incest and the Liberal Subject in Nineteenth-Century America.* Philadelphia: University of Pennsylvania Press, 2014.

Cox, Daniel, Juhern Navarro-Rivera, and Robert P. Jones. "Race, Religion, and Political Affiliation of Americans' Core Social Networks." PRRI, April 3, 2016, accessed August 5, 2022. https://www.prri.org/research/poll-race-religion-politics-americans-social-networks/.

Cox, Susan Soon-Keum, ed. *Voices from Another Place: A Collection of Works from a Generation Born in Korea and Adopted to Other Countries.* St. Paul, MN: Yeong and Yeong Books, 1999.

Cretton, Destin Daniel, dir. *Shang Chi and the Legend of the Ten Rings.* Walt Disney Studios Motion Pictures, 2021.

Dahlen, Sarah Park. "How to Evaluate Children's and Young Adult Books about Transracial and Transnational Asian Adoption." In *Diversity in Youth Literature: Opening Doors through Reading,* edited by Jamie Campbell Naidoo and Sarah Park Dahlen, 149–63. Chicago: ALA Editions, 2013.

———. "'It Is Part of Our Adoption Life Journey': Birth Searching and Transnationally Adopted Koreans in Young Adult Fiction." In *Growing Up Asian American in Young Adult Fiction,* edited by Ymitri Mathison, 127–46. Jackson: University Press of Mississippi, 2017.

Dahlen, Sarah Park, and Ebony Elizabeth Thomas, eds. *Harry Potter and the Other: Race, Justice, and Difference in the Wizarding World.* Jackson: University of Mississippi Press, 2022.

Dennis, Alicia. "Dylan Farrow's Brother Moses Defends Woody Allen." *People,* February 5, 2014. http://www.people.com/people/article/0,,20783306,00.html.

Derickson, Kate Driscoll. "The Racial Politics of Neoliberal Regulation in Post-Katrina Mississippi." *Annals of the Association of American Geographers* 104, no. 4 (July 4, 2014): 889–902. https://doi.org/10.1080/00045608.2014.912542.

Dobbs, Jennifer Kwon. "Cure for Swedish Fever." In *Echoes upon Echoes: New Korean American Writings,* edited by Elaine Kim and Laura Hyun Yi Kang, 167–71. Philadelphia: Temple University Press, 2003.

———. *Interrogation Room.* Buffalo, NY: White Pine Press, 2018.

———. *Paper Pavilion.* Buffalo, NY: White Pine Press, 2007.

Donnell, Kira Ann. "Orphan, Adoptee, Nation: Tracing the Korean Orphan and Adoptee through South Korean and American National Narratives." PhD diss., University of California, Berkeley, 2019. https://portfolium.com/entry/dissertation-36.

Donnelly, Sally B. "The Honor Roll Murder." *Time,* June 24, 2001. http://content.time.com/time/magazine/article/0,9171,160910,00.html.

Donner, Richard, dir. *The Goonies.* Warner Bros., 1985.

Dorow, Sara K. *Transnational Adoption: A Cultural Economy of Race, Gender, and Kinship.* New York: New York University Press, 2006.

Douglas, Susan J., and Meredith W. Michaels. *The Mommy Myth: The Idealization of Motherhood and How It Has Undermined All Women.* New York: Free Press, 2005.

Drenka, Stephanie. "Grieving as an Asian Adoptee." *Stephanie Drenka* (blog), March 20, 2021. https://stephaniedrenka.com/adoptee-grief/.

Edelman, Lee. *No Future: Queer Theory and the Death Drive.* Durham, NC: Duke University Press, 2004.

Eng, David L. *The Feeling of Kinship: Queer Liberalism and the Racialization of Intimacy.* Durham, NC: Duke University Press, 2010.

———. *Racial Castration: Managing Masculinity in Asian America.* Durham, NC: Duke University Press, 2001.

Eng, David L. and Alice Y. Hom, eds. *Q & A: Queer in Asian America.* Philadelphia: Temple University Press, 1998.

Eng, David L., and Shinee Han. *Racial Melancholia, Racial Dissociation: On the Social and Psychic Lives of Asian Americans.* Durham, NC: Duke University Press, 2018.

Epstein, Rebecca, Jamilia Blake, and Thalia González. *Girlhood Interrupted: The Erasure of Black Girls' Childhood.* Washington, DC: Georgetown Law Center on Poverty and Inequality, June 27, 2017. https://doi.org/10.2139/ssrn.3000695.

Fang, Jenn. "Did Korean American Graffiti Artist David Choe Confess to Rape on Podcast?" *Reappropriate,* April 21, 2014. http://reappropriate.co/2014/04/did-korean-american-graffiti-artist-david-choe-confess-to-rape-on-podcast/.

Fang, Karen. "Globalization, Masculinity, and the Changing Stakes of Hollywood Cinema for Asian American Studies." In *Asian American Literary Studies,* edited by Guiyou Huang, 79–108. Edinburgh: Edinburgh University Press, 2005.

Farrow, Dylan. "Op-Ed: Dylan Farrow: Why Has the #MeToo Revolution Spared Woody Allen?" *Los Angeles Times,* December 7, 2017. https://www.latimes.com/opinion/op-ed/la-oe-farrow-woody-allen-me-too-20171207-story.html.

———. "An Open Letter from Dylan Farrow." *New York Times,* February 1, 2014. http://kristof.blogs.nytimes.com/2014/02/01/an-open-letter-from-dylan-farrow/.

Farrow, Mia. *What Falls Away.* New York: Bantam Books, 1997.

——— (@MiaFarrow). "A woman has publicly detailed Woody Allen's molestation of her at age 7. GoldenGlobe tribute showed contempt for her & all abuse survivors." Twitter, January 13, 2014. https://twitter.com/MiaFarrow/status/422753419137265664; https://web.archive.org/web/20140309090244/https://twitter.com/MiaFarrow/status/422753419137265664.

Farrow, Moses. "A Son Speaks Out." *Moses Farrow* (blog), May 23, 2018. http://mosesfarrow.blogspot.com/2018/05/a-son-speaks-out-by-moses-farrow.html.

Farrow, Ronan. "From Aggressive Overtures to Sexual Assault: Harvey Weinstein's Accusers Tell Their Stories." *New Yorker,* October 10, 2017. https://www.newyorker.com/news/news-desk/from-aggressive-overtures-to-sexual-assault-harvey-weinsteins-accusers-tell-their-stories.

Fedosik, Marina. "Adoption in Stephen Spielberg's *AI Artificial Intelligence*: Kinship in the Posthuman Context." *Adoption & Culture* 6, no. 1 (2018): 182–205.

———. "The Power to 'Make Live': Biopolitics and Reproduction in *Blade Runner 2049*." *Adoption & Culture* 7, no. 2 (July 2019): 169–75.

Feng, Peter X. "Asian American Media Studies and the Problem of Legibility." *Cinema Journal* 56, no. 3 (March 22, 2017): 125–30.

———. "Recuperating Suzie Wong: A Fan's Nancy Kwan-Dary." In *Countervisions: Asian American Film Criticism,* edited by Darrell Y. Hamamoto and Sandra Liu, 40–58. Philadelphia: Temple University Press, 2000.

"Filipino Adoptees Network." Accessed April 11, 2022. http://www.filipino-adoptees-network.org/.

Fischer, Nancy L. "Oedipus Wrecked? The Moral Boundaries of Incest." *Gender & Society* 17, no. 1 (February 1, 2003): 92–110.

Five Alive. "No Conflicts: The Alt-Right's Embrace of Asian Women." *Plan A Mag,* January 7, 2018. https://planamag.com/no-conflicts-the-alt-rights-embrace-of-asian-women/.

Flanagan, Caitlin. "I Actually Read Woody Allen's Memoir." *Atlantic,* June 7, 2020. https://www.theatlantic.com/ideas/archive/2020/06/i-read-woody-allen-memoir/612736/.

Ford, Rebecca. "*Beef* Creators Respond to David Choe Controversy." *Vanity Fair,* April 21, 2023. https://www.vanityfair.com/hollywood/2023/04/beef-creators-statement-about-david-choe-rape-controversy.

Ford, Rebecca, and Pamela McClintock. "Sundance: 'Seoul Searching' Director Met with Consultants Familiar with North Korea." *Hollywood Reporter,* January 26, 2015. https://www.hollywoodreporter.com/movies/movie-news/sundance-seoul-searching-director-met-766898/.

Foster, Matt. "Colin Kaepernick Calls Out Adoptive Parents' Racism as He Promotes New Graphic Novel." CNN, March 10, 2023. https://www.cnn.com/2023/03/10/sport/colin-kaepernick-adoptive-parents-spt-intl/index.html.

Franco, Vicente, and Gail Dolgin, dirs. *Daughter from Danang.* 2002; Alexandria, VA: PBS, 2003. DVD.

Freundlich, Madelyn, and Joy Kim Lieberthal. "Survey of Adult Korean Adoptees: Report on the Findings." New York: Evan B. Donaldson Adoption Institute, 1999.

Fuchs, Cynthia. "'It's Three-Dimensional': Interview with Justin Lin, *Better Luck Tomorrow.*" *Morphizm,* May 1, 2003. http://www.morphizm.com/recommends/interviews/lin_better.html.

Futerman, Samantha, and Ryan Miyamoto. *Twinsters.* Netflix, 2015.

Gailey, Christine Ward. *Blue-Ribbon Babies and Labors of Love: Race, Class, and Gender in US Adoption Practice.* Austin: University of Texas Press, 2010.

Genz, Stéphanie, and Benjamin A. Brabon. *Postfeminism: Cultural Texts and Theories.* Edinburgh: Edinburgh University Press, 2009.

Gerloff, Grace. "How We Got Here: Historicizing Transnational Asian Adoptee Racial Identity." Paper presented at the Annual Conference of the Association for Asian American Studies, virtual, 2022.

Gibney, Shannon. *The Girl I Am, I Was, and Never Will Be: A Speculative Memoir of Transracial Adoption.* New York: Dutton Books, 2023.

Gibney, Shannon, and Nicole Chung, eds. *When We Become Ours: A YA Adoptee Anthology.* New York: HarperCollins, 2023.

Gill, Rosalind. *Gender and the Media.* Cambridge: Polity, 2007.

Global Overseas Adoptees' Link. "Dual Citizenship." *G.O.A'.L.* (blog), 2020. https://goal.or.kr/dual-citizenship/.

Goddard, Caroline, writer. *Modern Family.* Season 1, Episode 12. "Not in My House." Directed by Chris Koch. Aired January 13, 2010, on ABC.

Grady, Constance. "Roman Polanski Is Now Facing a 5th Accusation of Sexual Assault against a Child." *Vox,* August 17, 2017. https://www.vox.com/culture/2017/8/17/16156902/roman-polanski-child-rape-charges-explained-samantha-geimer-robin-m.

Graves, Kori A. *A War Born Family: African American Adoption in the Wake of the Korean War.* New York: New York University Press, 2019.

Groteke, Kristi. *Mia & Woody: Love and Betrayal.* New York: Carroll & Graf, 1994.

Hamilton, Walter. *Children of the Occupation: Japan's Untold Story.* New Brunswick, NJ: Rutgers University Press, 2013.

Han, Ae Jin. "The Aesthetics of Cuteness in Korean Pop Music." PhD diss., University of Sussex, 2016.

Hancock, John Lee, dir. *Blind Side*. Warner Bros., 2009.

Hansen, Jayme. "Minnesota Politics." *Land of Gazillion Adoptees* (blog), February 20, 2012. http://landofgazillionadoptees.com/2012/02/20/minnesota-politics; https://web.archive.org/web/20161011191424/https://landofgazillionadoptees.com/2012/02/20/minnesota-politics/.

Harding, Sandra. "Subjectivity, Experience, and Knowledge: An Epistemology from/for Rainbow Coalition Politics." In *Who Can Speak? Authority and Critical Identity,* edited by Judith Roof and Robyn Wiegman, 120–36. Champaign: University of Illinois Press, 1995.

Harkins, Gillian. *Everybody's Family Romance: Reading Incest in Neoliberal America.* Minneapolis: University of Minnesota Press, 2009.

Harris, Anita, ed. *All about the Girl: Culture, Power, and Identity.* New York: Routledge, 2004.

Hatzipanagos, Rachel. "'I Know My Parents Love Me, but They Don't Love My People': Adoptees of Color with White Parents Struggle to Talk with Their Families about Race." *Washington Post,* December 13, 2021. https://www.washingtonpost.com/nation/interactive/2021/transracial-adoption-racial-reckoning/.

Hawkesworth, Mary. *Feminist Inquiry: From Political Conviction to Methodological Innovation.* New Brunswick, NJ: Rutgers University Press, 2006.

Hays, Sharon. *The Cultural Contradictions of Motherhood.* New Haven, CT: Yale University Press, 1996.

Heckerling, Amy, dir. *Fast Times at Ridgemont High.* Universal Pictures, 1982.

Hennessy, Rosemary. "Subject, Knowledges, . . . and All the Rest: Speaking for What?" In *Who Can Speak? Authority and Critical Identity,* edited by Judith Roof and Robyn Wiegman, 137–50. Champaign: University of Illinois Press, 1995.

Herman, Ellen. *Kinship by Design: A History of Adoption in the Modern United States.* Chicago: University of Chicago Press, 2008.

Herman, Judith Lewis, and Lisa Hirschman. *Father-Daughter Incest.* Cambridge, MA: Harvard University Press, 1981.

Hevesi, Dennis. "Woody Allen Tells His Side to a Magazine." *New York Times,* August 23, 1992. https://www.nytimes.com/1992/08/23/nyregion/woody-allen-tells-his-side-to-a-magazine.html.

Ho, Jennifer A. *Consumption and Identity in Asian American Coming-of-Age Novels.* New York: Routledge, 2013.

———. *Racial Ambiguity in Asian American Culture.* New Brunswick, NJ: Rutgers University Press, 2015.

———. "To Be an Asian Woman in America." *CNN,* March 17, 2021. https://www.cnn.com/2021/03/17/opinions/to-be-an-asian-woman-in-america-ho/index.html.

Ho, Soleil. "We're in Asian America's Peak Media Moment." *San Francisco Chronicle,* April 17, 2023. https://www.sfchronicle.com/opinion/article/beef-netflix-asian-american-media-17902085.php.

Hoffman, Jason, dir. *Going Home.* 2009.

Höhn, Maria, and Seungsook Moon, eds. *Over There: Living with the US Military Empire from World War Two to the Present.* Durham, NC: Duke University Press, 2010.

Homans, Margaret, Peggy Phelan, Janet Mason Ellerby, Eric Walker, Karen Balcom, Kit Myers, Kim Park Nelson, et al. "Critical Adoption Studies: Conversation in Progress." *Adoption & Culture* 6, no. 1 (2018): 1–49.

Hong, Cathy Park. *Minor Feelings: An Asian American Reckoning.* New York: One World, 2020.

hooks, bell. *Black Looks: Race and Representation*. Boston: South End Press, 1992.

H.R. 1552, Private Law 95-37 (1978). https://www.congress.gov/95/statute/STATUTE-92/STATUTE-92-Pg3806-2.pdf.

H.R. 12508, Public Law 95-417 (1978). https://www.congress.gov/bill/95th-congress/house-bill/12508/text.

Hu, Brian, and Vincent N. Pham. "In Focus: Asian American Film and Media." *Cinema Journal* 56, no. 3 (March 22, 2017): 115–18.

Hübinette, Tobias. *Comforting an Orphaned Nation: Representations of International Adoption and Adopted Koreans in Korean Popular Culture*. Seoul: Jimoondang, 2006.

Hughes, John, dir. *The Breakfast Club*. Universal Pictures, 1985.

———, dir. *Sixteen Candles*. Universal Pictures, 1984.

Ishii, Douglas S. "Diversity Times Three: The '*Modern Family* Effect' and the Privatization of Diversity." *Camera Obscura: Feminism, Culture, and Media Studies* 32, no. 3 (2017): 33–61.

Ito, Susan. "Hambun-Hambun." In *Making More Waves: New Writing by Asian American Women*, edited by Elaine H. Kim, Lilia V. Villanueva, and Asian Women United of California, 128–32. Boston: Beacon Press, 1997.

———. *The Mouse Room*. Tempe, AZ: SheBooks, 2014.

———. *I Would Meet You Anywhere*. Columbus, OH: Mad Creek Books, 2023.

Jackson, Lauren Michele. "Who Really Owns the 'Blaccent'?" *Vulture*, August 24, 2018. https://www.vulture.com/2018/08/awkwafina-blaccent-cultural-appropriation.html.

Jacobson, Heather. *Culture Keeping: White Mothers, International Adoption, and the Negotiation of Family Difference*. Nashville, TN: Vanderbilt University Press, 2008.

Jerng, Mark C. *Claiming Others: Transracial Adoption and National Belonging*. Minneapolis: University of Minnesota Press, 2010.

Jia, Claire. "The Rumpus Review of *Seoul Searching*." *Rumpus*, August 11, 2016. https://therumpus.net/2016/08/the-rumpus-review-of-seoul-searching/.

Johnson, Susan, dir. *To All the Boys I've Loved Before*. Netflix, 2018.

Jones, Maggie. "Adam Crapser's Bizarre Deportation Odyssey." *New York Times Magazine*, April 1, 2015. http://www.nytimes.com/2015/04/01/magazine/adam-crapsers-bizarre-deportation-odyssey.html.

———. "Why a Generation of Adoptees Is Returning to South Korea." *New York Times Magazine*, January 14, 2015. https://www.nytimes.com/2015/01/18/magazine/why-a-generation-of-adoptees-is-returning-to-south-korea.html.

Joyce, Kathryn. *The Child Catchers: Rescue, Trafficking, and the New Gospel of Adoption*. New York: PublicAffairs, 2013.

Jun, Helen Heran. *Race for Citizenship: Black Orientalism and Asian Uplift from Pre-Emancipation to Neoliberal America*. New York: New York University Press, 2011.

Kanesaka, Erica. "Yellow Peril, Oriental Plaything: Asian Exclusion and the 1927 US-Japan Doll Exchange." *Journal of Asian American Studies* 23, no. 1 (2020): 93–124.

Kang, Laura Hyun Yi. "The Desiring of Asian Female Bodies: Interracial Romance and Cinematic Subjection." In *Screening Asian Americans*, edited by Peter X. Feng, 71–98. New Brunswick, NJ: Rutgers University Press, 2002.

———. *Traffic in Asian Women*. Durham, NC: Duke University Press, 2020.

Kang, Miliann. "Why Are Perpetrators' Motives Given More Importance than the Lives They Take?" *Ms.*, March 22, 2021. https://msmagazine.com/2021/03/22/asian-women-atlanta-victims-names-violence-racism-massage-parlor/.

Kaplan, Deborah, and Harry Elfont, dirs. *Can't Hardly Wait*. Columbia Pictures, 1998.

Kearly, Peter. "I'm Iwish." In *After the Morning Calm: Reflections of Korean Adoptees*, edited by Sook Wilkinson and Nancy Fox, 60–66. Bloomfield Hills, MI: Sunrise Ventures, 2002.

Kelley, David E., Lawrence Broch, and Devon Greggory, writers. *Harry's Law*. Season 2, Episode 7. "American Girl." Directed by Ron Underwood. Aired November 9, 2011, on NBC.

Kershner, Irvin, dir. *The Empire Strikes Back*. Lucasfilm Ltd., 1980.

Khan, Nahnatchka, dir. *Always Be My Maybe*. Netflix, 2019.

Khokha, Sasha, dir. *Calcutta Calling*. PBS, 2004.

Kim, Cerissa, Sora Kim-Russell, Mary-Kim Arnold, and Katherine Kim, eds. *Mixed Korean: Our Stories: An Anthology*. Bloomfield, IN: Truepeny Publishing, 2018.

Kim, Claire Jean. "Are Asians the New Blacks?: Affirmative Action, Anti-Blackness, and the 'Sociometry' of Race." *Du Bois Review: Social Science Research on Race* 15, no. 2 (2018): 217–44.

———. "The Racial Triangulation of Asian Americans." *Politics & Society* 27, no. 1 (March 1, 1999): 105–38.

Kim, Eleana J. *Adopted Territory: Transnational Korean Adoptees and the Politics of Belonging*. Durham, NC: Duke University Press, 2010.

———. "Wedding Citizenship and Culture: Korean Adoptees and the Global Family of Korea." *Social Text* 21, no. 1 (March 1, 2003): 57–81. https://doi.org/10.1215/01642472-21-1_74-57.

Kim, Eleana, and Kim Park Nelson. "'Natural Born Aliens': Transnational Adoptees and US Citizenship." *Adoption & Culture* 7, no. 2 (2019): 257–79.

Kim, Elizabeth. *Ten Thousand Sorrows: The Extraordinary Journey of a Korean War Orphan*. London: Bantam, 2002.

Kim, Eun Kyung. "Identical Twins, Discovered through DNA Tests, Meet for the First Time on TODAY." *Today*, November 14, 2017. https://www.today.com/health/identical-twins-discover-each-other-thru-dna-tests-meet-first-t118798.

Kim, Evelyn. "An Open Letter to the Asian American Men's Rights Movement." *Reappropriate* (blog), September 15, 2016. http://reappropriate.co/2016/09/an-open-letter-to-the-asian-american-mens-rights-movement/.

Kim, Hosu. *Birth Mothers and Transnational Adoption Practice in South Korea: Virtual Mothering*. New York: Palgrave Macmillan, 2016.

Kim, Jodi. *Ends of Empire: Asian American Critique and the Cold War*. Minneapolis: University of Minnesota Press, 2010.

Kim, Ju Yon. *The Racial Mundane: Asian American Performance and the Embodied Everyday*. New York: New York University Press, 2015.

Kim, Nary. "Too Smart for His Own Good?: The Devolution of a 'Model' Asian American Student." *Asian American Law Journal* 20, no. 1 (2013): 83–106.

Kim, Oh Myo, and Amy Mihyang Ginther. "'I Am Who I Am—': Archetypal Drama Therapy Workshops for Asian American Adoptees." *Drama Therapy Review* 5, no. 2 (2019): 251–66.

Kim, Oh Myo, Reed Reichwald, and Richard Lee. "Cultural Socialization in Families with Adopted Korean Adolescents: A Mixed-Method, Multi-Informant Study." *Journal of Adolescent Research* 28, no. 1 (January 2013): 69–95.

King, Michael Patrick, writer. *Sex and the City*. Season 6, Episode 20. "An American Girl in Paris (Part Deux)." Directed by Tim Van Patten. Aired February 22, 2004, on HBO.

———, writer. *Sex and the City*. Season 6, Episode 19. "An American Girl in Paris (Part Une)." Directed by Tim Van Patten. Aired February 15, 2004, on HBO.

———, writer. *Sex and the City.* Season 6, Episode 1. "To Market, To Market." Directed by Michael Patrick King. Aired June 22, 2003, on HBO.

———, dir. *Sex and the City.* New Line Cinema, 2008.

———, dir. *Sex and the City 2.* New Line Cinema, 2010.

Kinney, Rebecca J. "Seoul Searching." In *Asian American X: An Intersection of Twenty-First-Century Asian American Voices,* edited by Arar Han and John Y. Hsu. Ann Arbor: University of Michigan Press, 2004.

Knowlton, Linda Goldstein, dir. *Somewhere Between.* Ladylike Films, 2011. https://somewherebetweenmovie.com/.

Koo, Youngeun. "'We Deserve to Be Here': The Development of Adoption Critiques by Transnational Korean Adoptees in Denmark." *Anthropology Matters* 19, no. 1 (June 7, 2019): 35–71.

Kopacz, Elizabeth. "From Contingent Beginnings to Multiple Ends: DNA Technologies and the Korean Adoptee 'Cousin.'" *Adoption & Culture* 6, no. 2 (2018): 336–52. https://doi.org/10.26818/adoptionculture.6.2.0336.

Krieder, Rose M., and Elizabeth Raleigh. "Residential Racial Diversity: Are Transracial Adoptive Families More Like Multiracial or White Families?" *Social Science Quarterly* 97, no. 5 (2016): 1189–207.

Kubrick, Stanley, dir. *Full Metal Jacket.* Warner Bros., 1987.

Kwan, Daniel, and Daniel Scheinert, dirs. *Everything Everywhere All at Once.* A24, 2022.

Laing, John, dir. *Wendy Wu: Homecoming Warrior.* Disney Channel, 2006.

Langmuir, Molly. "Mia Farrow Takes an Unflinching Look at Her Past in the Wake of the #MeToo Movement." *Elle,* October 10, 2018. https://www.elle.com/culture/movies-tv/a23653929/mia-farrow-women-in-hollywood-me-too/.

Lavin, Cheryl. "Young, Well-to-Do, Intelligent—and Charged with a Brutal Murder." *Chicago Tribune,* February 1, 1993. https://www.chicagotribune.com/news/ct-xpm-1993-02-01-9303174606-story.html.

Lax, Eric. *Woody Allen: A Biography.* Boston: Da Capo Press, 2000.

Lee, Ang, dir. *Crouching Tiger, Hidden Dragon.* Sony Pictures Classics, 2000.

Lee, Barb, dir. *Adopted.* 2009.

Lee, Benson, dir. *Seoul Searching.* Netflix, 2015.

Lee, James Kyung-Jin. *Urban Triage: Race and the Fictions of Multiculturalism.* Minneapolis: University of Minnesota Press, 2004.

Lee, Jieun. *Performing Transnational Adoption: Unsettling Scripts.* Columbus: The Ohio State University Press (under contract).

———. "Representing Korean Orphans and Adoptees on the Asian American Stage." Paper presented at the Annual Conference of the Association for Asian American Studies, virtual, 2021.

Lee, Jin-Kyung. *Service Economies: Militarism, Sex Work, and Migrant Labor in South Korea.* Minneapolis: University of Minnesota Press, 2010.

Lee, Joyce P., Richard M. Lee, Alison W. Hu, and Oh Myo Kim. "Ethnic Identity as a Moderator against Discrimination for Transracially and Transnationally Adopted Korean American Adolescents." *Asian American Journal of Psychology* 6, no. 2 (2015): 154–63.

Lee, Julayne. *Not My White Savior.* Los Angeles: Vireo Book / Rare Bird Books, 2018.

Lee, Marie Myong-Ok. *Finding My Voice.* Boston: Houghton Mifflin, 1992.

———. *If It Hadn't Been for Yoon Jun.* Boston: Houghton Mifflin, 1993.

——. *Saying Goodbye*. Boston: Houghton Mifflin, 1994.

——. *Somebody's Daughter*. Boston: Beacon Press, 2005.

——. "Summer of My Korean Soldier." In *Making More Waves: New Writing by Asian American Women,* edited by Elaine H. Kim, Lilia V. Villanueva, and Asian Women United of California, 55–61. Boston: Beacon Press, 1997.

Lee, Sharon Heijin. "Beauty between Empires: Global Feminism, Plastic Surgery, and the Trouble with Self-Esteem." *Frontiers: A Journal of Women Studies* 37, no. 1 (2016): 1–31.

Leo, Katie Hae. *Four Destinies*. Directed by Suzy Messerole, Theater Mu, October 2011, Mixed Blood Theatre, Minneapolis, MN.

Leong, Karen J. *The China Mystique: Pearl S. Buck, Anna May Wong, Mayling Soong, and the Transformation of American Orientalism.* Berkeley: University of California Press, 2005.

Levenson, Eric. "Awkwafina Issues Statement Addressing Accusations That She Has Used a 'Blaccent.'" CNN, February 6, 2022. https://www.cnn.com/2022/02/06/entertainment/awkwafina-blaccent/index.html.

Levin, Diane E., and Jean Kilbourne. *So Sexy So Soon: The New Sexualized Childhood, and What Parents Can Do to Protect Their Kids.* New York: Random House, 2008.

Levitan, Steven, writer. *Modern Family*. Season 1, Episode 16. "Fears." Directed by Reginald Hudlin. Aired March 3, 2010, on ABC.

Levitan, Steven, and Christopher Lloyd, writers. *Modern Family*. Season 1, Episode 1. "Pilot." Directed by Jason Winer. Aired September 22, 2009, on ABC.

Lewis, Michael. "The Very Last Lover." *New Republic,* September 28, 1992, 11–12.

Lichwick, Marissa. *The Yellow Dress*. University of Washington's School of Drama, 2011, Jones Playhouse, Seattle, WA.

Liem, Deann Borshay, dir. *First Person Plural*. Mu Films, 2000.

——, dir. *Geographies of Kinship*. Mu Films, 2019.

——, dir. *In the Matter of Cha Jung Hee*. Mu Films, 2010.

Lim, Adele, dir. *Joy Ride*. Lionsgate, 2023.

Lim, Audrea. "The Alt-Right's Asian Fetish." *New York Times,* January 6, 2018. https://www.nytimes.com/2018/01/06/opinion/sunday/alt-right-asian-fetish.html.

Lin, Justin, dir. *Better Luck Tomorrow*. Paramount Pictures, 2002.

——, dir. *The Fast and the Furious: Tokyo Drift*. Universal Pictures, 2006.

Liu, Angela. "MRAsians: A Convergence between Asian American Hypermasculine Ethnonationalism and the Manosphere." *Journal of Asian American Studies* 24, no. 1 (2021): 93–112.

Lloyd, Christopher, writer. *Modern Family*. Season 1, Episode 5. "Coal Digger." Directed by Jason Winer. Aired October 21, 2009, on ABC.

Louie, Andrea. *How Chinese Are You? Adopted Chinese Youth and Their Families Negotiate Identity and Culture.* New York: New York University Press, 2015.

Lost Daughters. "#flipthescript." Accessed February 5, 2023. http://www.thelostdaughters.com/p/flipthescript.html.

Lowe, Lisa. "Heterogeneity, Hybridity, Multiplicity: Marking Asian American Differences." *Diaspora: A Journal of Transnational Studies* 1, no. 1 (1991): 24–44.

Lucas, George, dir. *Star Wars*. Lucasfilm Ltd., 1977.

Macintyre, Ben. "Farrow Bitter Winner of Venomous Courtroom Drama." *The Times* (London, England), June 8, 1993, sec. Overseas News.

———. "Farrow Wins Custody Battle; Judge Condemns Woody Allen as an Untrustworthy Father." *The Times* (London, England), June 8, 1993, sec. Overseas News.

Maguire, Sharon, dir. *Bridget Jones's Diary.* Universal Pictures, 2001.

Mak, Aaron. "'Men's Rights Asians' Think This Is Their Moment." *Slate,* September 15, 2021. https://slate.com/technology/2021/09/mens-rights-asians-aznidentity-stop-asian-hate-reddit.html.

Makalintal, Bettina. "Awkwafina's Past Makes Her a Complicated Icon of Asian American Representation." *Vice* (blog), January 24, 2020. https://www.vice.com/en/article/pkeg9g/awkwafinas-past-makes-her-a-complicated-icon-of-asian-american-representation.

Manalansan, Martin F., IV, Alice Y. Hom, and Kale Bantigue Fajardo, eds. *Q & A: Voices from Queer Asian North America.* Philadelphia: Temple University Press, 2021.

Mannur, Anita. *Intimate Eating: Racialized Spaces and Radical Futures.* Durham, NC: Duke University Press, 2022.

Mariner, Kathryn A. *Contingent Kinship: The Flows and Futures of Adoption in the United States.* Oakland: University of California Press, 2019.

Marquand, Richard, dir. *Return of the Jedi.* Lucasfilm Ltd., 1983.

Marre, Diana, and Laura Briggs, eds. *International Adoption: Global Inequalities and the Circulation of Children.* New York: New York University Press, 2009.

Masequesmay, Gina, and Sean Metzger, eds. *Embodying Asian/American Sexualities.* Lanham, MD: Lexington Books, 2009.

Mayron, Melanie, dir. *The Baby-Sitters Club.* Columbia Pictures, 1995.

McCabe, Janet. *Feminist Film Studies: Writing the Woman into Cinema.* London: Wallflower, 2004.

McCabe, Marita P., Robert A. Cummins, and Shelley B. Reid. "An Empirical Study of the Sexual Abuse of People with Intellectual Disability." *Sexuality and Disability* 12, no. 4 (December 1994): 297–306.

McCullough, Ayla. "Assemblaging Orphanhood: Maiming, Pain, and Hypochondria." Paper presented at the biennial conference of the Alliance for the Study of Adoption and Culture, virtual, 2021.

———. "'You don't know when the next transition will arrive': Orphanness, Maiming, and Ephemeral Care in Hanya Yanagihara's *A Little Life.*" *Adoption & Culture* (accepted, forthcoming).

McGinnis, Hollee. "Adult Korean Adoptee Groups from the 1990s–2020s: Spaces of Mutual Aid, Empowerment, Belonging, and Change." Paper presented at the 10th Biennial Adoption Initiative Conference 2020/2022, virtual, 2022.

McGinnis, Hollee, Susan Livingston Smith, Scott D. Ryan, and Jeanne A. Howard. "Beyond Culture Camp: Promoting Health Identity Formation in Adoption." New York: Evan B. Donaldson Adoption Institute, 2009.

McKee, Kimberly D. "Adoption as Reproductive Justice Issue." *Adoption & Culture* 6, no. 1 (2018): 74–93.

———. "The Anti-Asian Racism at Home: Reckoning with the Experiences of Adoptees from Asia." In *Global Anti-Asian Racism,* edited by Jennifer A. Ho. Columbia University Press, forthcoming 2024.

———. "The Complexities of Adoption in *Joy Ride* (2023)," n.d.

———. *Disrupting Kinship: Transnational Politics of Korean Adoption in the United States.* Champaign: University of Illinois Press, 2019.

——. "Do You See Me? Us? Asian America?" *KAAN* (blog), March 26, 2021. https://www.wearekaan.org/post/do-you-see.

——. "Gendered Adoptee Identities: Performing Trans-Pacific Masculinity in the 21st Century." In *Gendering the Trans-Pacific World,* edited by Catherine Ceniza Choy and Judy Tzu-Chun Wu, 221–45. Leiden, NL: Brill, 2017.

——. "Locating Adoptees in Asian America: Jane Jeong Trenka and Deann Borshay Liem." In *Our Voices, Our Histories: Asian American and Pacific Islander Women,* edited by Shirley Hune and Gail M. Nomura, 357–72. New York: New York University Press, 2020.

——. "More than an Outcome of War: Adoptions from Asia to the United States." *Journal of Asian American Studies* 25, no. 2 (2022): 247–60.

——. "The Other Sister." In *YELL-Oh Girls! Emerging Voices Explore Culture, Identity, and Growing Up Asian American,* edited by Vickie Nam, 142–44. New York: HarperCollins, 2001.

——. "Public Intimacy and Kinship in the Korean Adoption Community." *Women, Gender, and Families of Color* 8, no. 1 (Spring 2020): 40–64, 112.

McKee, Kimberly D., and Shannon Gibney. "'It Came, Over and Over, Down to This: What Made Someone a Mother?': A Reproductive Justice Analysis of Little Fires Everywhere, the Novel and the TV Series." *Feminist Formations* 35, no. 2 (Summer 2023): 128–52.

McRobbie, Angela. *The Aftermath of Feminism: Gender, Culture and Social Change.* London: Sage Publications, 2009.

Meade, Marion. *The Unruly Life of Woody Allen: A Biography.* London: Weidenfeld & Nicolson, 1999.

Meier, Dani I. "Cultural Identity and Place in Adult Korean-American Intercountry Adoptees." *Adoption Quarterly* 3, no. 1 (1999): 15–48.

——. "Loss and Reclaimed Lives: Cultural Identity and Place in Korean-American Intercountry Adoptees." PhD diss., University of Minnesota, 1998.

Melamed, Jodi. "The Spirit of Neoliberalism: From Racial Liberalism to Neoliberal Multiculturalism." *Social Text* 24, no. 4 (Winter 2006): 1–24.

Merish, Lori. "Cuteness and Commodity Aesthetics: Tom Thumb and Shirley Temple." In *Freakery: Cultural Spectacles of the Extraordinary Body,* edited by Rosemarie Garland-Thomson, 185–203. New York: New York University Press, 1996.

Merkin, Daphne. "After Decades of Silence, Soon-Yi Previn Speaks." *Vulture,* September 16, 2018. https://www.vulture.com/2018/09/soon-yi-previn-speaks.html.

Merskin, Debra. "Reviving Lolita? A Media Literacy Examination of Sexual Portrayals of Girls in Fashion Advertising." *American Behavioral Scientist* 48, no. 1 (2004): 119–29.

Messer, Alfred A. "The 'Phaedra Complex.'" *Archives of General Psychiatry* 21, no. 2 (1969): 213–18.

Mila. "Hey Mom, They Don't See Your Little Girl, They See an Asian Woman . . ." *Lost Daughters* (blog), March 19, 2013. http://www.thelostdaughters.com/2013/03/hey-mom-they-dont-see-your-little-girl.html.

Mitchell, Russ. "'I'm Not Allowed to Feel Those Things': How Adoptees Experienced Anti-Asian Hate." *Los Angeles Times,* April 16, 2021. https://www.latimes.com/business/story/2021-04-16/asian-adoptees-and-their-experiences.

Mitra, Dubra, Sara Kang, and Genevieve Clutario. "It's Time to Reckon with the History of Asian Women in America." *Harper's Bazaar,* March 23, 2021. https://www.harpersbazaar.com/culture/features/a35913981/its-time-to-reckon-with-the-history-of-asian-women-in-america/.

Modell, Judith. *Kinship with Strangers: Adoption and Interpretations of Kinship in American Culture*. Berkeley: University of California Press, 1994.

Molina-Guzmán, Isabel. "'Latina Wisdom' in 'Postrace' Recession Media." In *Gendering the Recession*, edited by Diane Negra and Yvonne Tasker, 59–80. Durham, NC: Duke University Press, 2014. https://doi.org/10.2307/j.ctv1131fr9.6.

Moon, Ansley. *How to Bury the Dead*. Minneapolis, MN: Coffee House Press, 2011.

Moon, Katherine. *Sex among Allies: Military Prostitution in U.S.–Korea Relations*. New York: Columbia University Press, 1997.

Morey, Anne, and Claudia Nelson. "Cross-Species Kinship Dilemmas: Adoption and Dinosaurs in the Jurassic Park Franchise." *Adoption & Culture* 9, no. 2 (July 2021): 154–77.

Morris, Monique W. "Countering the Adultification of Black Girls." *Educational Leadership* 76, no. 7 (April 1, 2019): 44–48.

Mulvey, Laura. "Visual Pleasure and Narrative Cinema." In *Film Theory and Criticism: Introductory Readings*, edited by Leo Braudy and Marshall Cohen, 833–44. New York: Oxford University Press, 1999.

Muñoz, José Esteban. *Cruising Utopia: The Then and There for Queer Futurity*. New York: New York University Press, 2009.

Myers, Kit. "Complicating Birth-Culture Pedagogy at Asian Heritage Camps for Adoptees." *Adoption & Culture* 7, no. 1 (2019): 67–94.

———. "'Real Families': The Violence of Love in New Media Adoption Discourse." *Critical Discourse Studies* 11, no. 2 (April 3, 2014): 175–93.

Myers, Kit, Amanda L. Baden, and Alfonso Ferguson. "Going Back 'Home': Adoptees Share Their Experiences of Hong Kong Adoptee Gathering." *Adoption Quarterly* 23, no. 3 (July 2020): 187–218. https://doi.org/10.1080/10926755.2020.1790452.

NBC4 Washington. "Mia Farrow's Brother Sentenced for Child Sex Abuse," February 4, 2014. https://www.nbcwashington.com/news/local/mia-farrows-brother-to-be-sentenced-for-sex-abuse/1957532/.

Newsweek staff. "Soon-Yi Speaks: 'Let's Not Get Hysterical.'" August 31, 1992, US edition, sec. Back of the Book.

Newton, Grace. "I Am Not My Dad's Girlfriend." *Red Thread Broken* (blog), August 19, 2014. https://redthreadbroken.wordpress.com/2014/08/19/i-am-not-my-dads-girlfriend/.

———. "Stop Centering Whiteness in #StopAsianHate." *Red Thread Broken* (blog), March 23, 2021. https://redthreadbroken.wordpress.com/2021/03/23/3755/.

Ngai, Sianne. *Our Aesthetic Categories: Zany, Cute, Interesting*. Cambridge, MA: Harvard University Press, 2015.

———. *Ugly Feelings*. Cambridge, MA: Harvard University Press, 2007.

Nguyen, Mimi Thi. *The Gift of Freedom: War, Debt, and Other Refugee Passages*. Durham, NC: Duke University Press, 2012.

Nguyen, Viet Thanh. "Asian-Americans Need More Movies, Even Mediocre Ones." *New York Times*, August 21, 2018, Opinion. https://www.nytimes.com/2018/08/21/opinion/crazy-rich-asians-movie.html.

———. *Nothing Ever Dies: Vietnam and the Memory of War*. Cambridge, MA: Harvard University Press, 2016.

Ninh, erin Khuê. *Ingratitude: The Debt-Bound Daughter in Asian American Literature*. New York: New York University Press, 2011.

——. *Passing for Perfect: College Impostors and Other Model Minorities.* Philadelphia: Temple University Press, 2021.

——. "Without Enhancements: Sexual Violence in the Everyday Lives of Asian American Women." In *Asian American Feminisms and Women of Color Politics,* edited by Lynn Fujiwara and Shireen Roshanravan, 69–81. Seattle: University of Washington Press, 2018.

Ninh, erin Khuê, and Shireen Roshanravan. "#WeToo: A Convening." *Journal of Asian American Studies* 24, no. 1 (2021): 1–8. https://doi.org/10.1353/jaas.2021.0001.

Nobile, Tiana. *Cleave.* Spartanburg, SC: Hub City Press, 2021.

Nobile, Tiana, Ansley Moon, and Marci Calabretta Cancio-Bello. "Three Asian Adoptee Poets Reflect on Craft, Adoption, and Anti-Asian Violence." *Catapult,* August 9, 2021. https://catapult.co/stories/three-asian-adoptee-poets-reflect-on-craft-adoption-and-anti-asian-violence_tiana_nobile_marci_cancio_bello_ansley_moon.

Novy, Marianne Lucille. *Reading Adoption: Family and Difference in Fiction and Drama.* Ann Arbor: University of Michigan Press, 2007.

NYDN, AP. "Lark Previn, Mia Farrow's Daughter, Dies on Christmas—UPDATED, PHOTO." *Huffington Post,* January 30, 2009. http://www.huffingtonpost.com/2008/12/30/lark-previn-mia-farrows-d_n_154139.html.

Oh, Arissa H. *To Save the Children of Korea: The Cold War Origins of International Adoption.* Palo Alto, CA: Stanford University Press, 2015.

Okada, Jun. *Making Asian American Film and Video: Histories, Institutions, Movements.* New Brunswick, NJ: Rutgers University Press, 2015.

Orth, Maureen. "Momma Mia!" *Vanity Fair,* October 23, 2013. https://www.vanityfair.com/hollywood/2013/11/mia-farrow-frank-sinatra-ronan-farrow.

Park Nelson, Kim. *Invisible Asians: Korean American Adoptees, Asian American Experiences, and Racial Exceptionalism.* New Brunswick, NJ: Rutgers University Press, 2016.

——. "'Loss Is More than Sadness': Reading Dissent in Transracial Adoption Melodrama in 'The Language of Blood' and 'First Person Plural.'" *Adoption & Culture* 1, no. 1 (2007): 101–28.

Pate, SooJin. *From Orphan to Adoptee: U.S. Empire and Genealogies of Korean Adoption.* Minneapolis: University of Minnesota Press, 2014.

Patterson, Orlando. *Slavery and Social Death: A Comparative Study: With a New Preface.* Cambridge, MA: Harvard University Press, 2018.

Patton, Sandra. *Birth Marks: Transracial Adoption in Contemporary America.* New York: New York University Press, 2000.

Payne, Alexander, dir. *Sideways.* Searchlight Pictures, 2004.

Peck, Garrett. *The Prohibition Hangover: Alcohol in America from Demon Rum to Cult Cabernet.* New Brunswick, NJ: Rutgers University Press, 2009.

Perkins, Mark, dir., and Caitlin M. Boston, creator. "How to Hit On an Asian Girl." August 26, 2011. YouTube video, 5:24. https://www.youtube.com/watch?v=MXoiRHYTCkg.

Pickett, Rex. *Sideways.* New York: St. Martin's Griffin, 2004.

Polanski, Roman, dir. *Rosemary's Baby.* Paramount Pictures, 1968.

Polhemus, Robert M. *Lot's Daughters: Sex, Redemption, and Women's Quest for Authority.* Palo Alto, CA: Stanford University Press, 2005.

"Population of Santa Barbara County, CA—Census 2010 and 2000 Interactive Map, Demographics, Statistics, Quick Facts—CensusViewer." Accessed November 29, 2021. http://censusviewer.com/county/CA/Santa%20Barbara; http://web.archive.org/web/20220119105446/http://censusviewer.com/county/CA/Santa%20Barbara.

Potter, Sarah. *Everybody Else: Adoption and the Politics of Domestic Diversity in Postwar America.* Athens: University of Georgia Press, 2014.

Prébin, Elise. *Meeting Once More: The Korean Side of Transnational Adoption.* New York: New York University Press, 2013.

Projansky, Sarah. *Spectacular Girls: Media Fascination and Celebrity Culture.* New York: New York University Press, 2014.

PRRI. "PRRI Survey: Friendship Networks of White Americans Continue to be 90% White." May 24, 2022. https://www.prri.org/press-release/prri-survey-friendship-networks-of-white-americans-continue-to-be-90-white/.

Puzar, Aljosa, and Yewon Hong. "Korean Cuties: Understanding Performed Winsomeness (*Aegyo*) in South Korea." *The Asia Pacific Journal of Anthropology,* 19, no. 4 (2018): 333–49.

Quaites, Lisa A. *Faith & Favor: Discovering Family at Fifty.* Omaha, NE: Summer Solstice Publishing, 2020.

Quinn, Sally. "'Sideways' Logic: Please, Spare Us the Slob Story." *Washington Post,* February 26, 2005. https://www.washingtonpost.com/archive/lifestyle/2005/02/26/sideways-logic-please-spare-us-the-slob-story/9d67f4bf-ae4e-4235-8c5e-1d5adb0231d8/.

Quiroz, Pamela Anne. *Adoption in a Color-Blind Society.* Lanham, MD: Rowman & Littlefield, 2007.

Radway, Janice A. *A Feeling for Books: The Book-of-the-Month Club, Literary Taste, and Middle-Class Desire.* Chapel Hill: University of North Carolina Press, 1997.

Raleigh, Elizabeth. *Selling Transracial Adoption: Families, Markets, and the Color Line.* Philadelphia: Temple University Press, 2017.

Rebeck, Theresa, writer. *Smash.* Season 1, Episode 1. "Pilot." Directed by Michael Mayer. Aired February 6, 2012, on NBC.

———, writer. *Smash.* Season 1, Episode 2. "The Callback." Directed by Michael Mayer. Aired February 13, 2012, on NBC.

Reddy, Vanita. *Fashioning Diaspora: Beauty, Femininity, and South Asian American Culture.* Philadelphia: Temple University Press, 2016.

Restrepo, Isabella C. "Pathologizing Latinas: Racialized Girlhood, Behavioral Diagnosis, and California's Foster Care System." *Girlhood Studies* 12, no. 3 (Winter 2019): 1–17. https://doi.org/10.3167/ghs.2019.120303.

Riben, Mirah. *The Stork Market: America's Multi-Billion Dollar Unregulated Adoption Industry.* Dayton, OH: Advocate Publications, 2007.

Ringwald, Molly. "What about 'The Breakfast Club'?" *New Yorker,* April 6, 2018. https://www.newyorker.com/culture/personal-history/what-about-the-breakfast-club-molly-ringwald-metoo-john-hughes-pretty-in-pink.

Robbins, Brian, dir. *Varsity Blues.* MTV Productions, 1999.

Robinson, Katy. *A Single Square Picture: A Korean Adoptee's Search for Her Roots.* New York: Berkley Books, 2002.

Rowling, J. K. *Harry Potter and the Chamber of Secrets.* London: Bloomsbury, 1998.

———. *Harry Potter and the Goblet of Fire.* London: Bloomsbury, 2000.

———. *Harry Potter and the Philosopher's Stone.* London: Bloomsbury, 1997.

———. *Harry Potter and the Prisoner of Azkaban.* London: Bloomsbury, 1999.

Sacco, Lynn. *Unspeakable: Father-Daughter Incest in American History.* Baltimore, MD: Johns Hopkins University Press, 2009.

Sanvidge, John, dir. *Finding Seoul.* 2011.

Satz, Martha. "Introduction: The Portrayal of Adoption in Popular Culture." *Adoption & Culture* 9, no. 2 (July 2021): 149–53.

Seethaler, Ina. "'Big Bad Chinese Mama': How Internet Humor Subverts Stereotypes about Asian American Women." *Studies in American Humor,* no. 27 (2013): 117–38.

Seidelman, Susan, dir. *Desperately Seeking Susan.* Orion Pictures, 1985.

Selby, Jenn. "Ronan Farrow Blasts Dad Woody Allen during Golden Globes: 'Did They Put the Part Where a Woman Publicly Confirmed He Molested Her at Age 7 before or after Annie Hall?'" *Independent,* January 13, 2014. http://www.independent.co.uk/news/people/news/ronan-farrow-blasts-dad-woody-allen-during-golden-globes-did-they-put-the-part-where-a-woman-publicly-confirmed-he-molested-her-at-age-7-before-or-after-annie-hall-9055775.html.

Selman, Peter. "Intercountry Adoption in the New Millennium; the 'Quiet Migration' Revisited." *Population Research and Policy Review* 21 no. 3 (June 2002): 205–25.

Setten, Melissa. "Did Facebook's Graffiti Artist Admit to Sexual Assault on His Podcast?" XOJane, April 17, 2014. https://web.archive.org/web/20140419234731/http://www.xojane.com/sex/david-choe-alleged-rape-rapist.

Shi, Domee, dir. *Turning Red,* Walt Disney Studios Motion Pictures, 2022.

Shiao, Jiannbin Lee, and Mia H. Tuan. "Korean Adoptees and the Social Context of Ethnic Exploration." *American Journal of Sociology* 113, no. 4 (2008): 1023–66.

———. "A Sociological Approach to Race, Identity, and Asian Adoption." In *International Korean Adoption: A Fifty-Year History of Policy and Practice,* edited by Kathleen Ja Sook Bergquist, M. Elizabeth Vonk, Dong Soo Kim, and Marvin D. Feit, 155–70. New York: Haworth Press, 2007.

Shimizu, Celine Parreñas. *The Hypersexuality of Race: Performing Asian/American Women on Screen and Scene.* Durham, NC: Duke University Press, 2007.

———. *Straitjacket Sexualities: Unbinding Asian American Manhoods in the Movies.* Palo Alto, CA: Stanford University Press, 2012.

Shin, Sun Yung. *Rough, and Savage: Poems.* Minneapolis, MN: Coffee House Press, 2012.

———. *Skirt Full of Black: Poems.* Minneapolis, MN: Coffee House Press, 2006.

———. *Unbearable Splendor.* Minneapolis, MN: Coffee House Press, 2016.

———. *The Wet Hex.* Minneapolis, MN: Coffee House Press, 2022.

Shotwell, Alyssa. "Awkwafina May Have Forgotten Her 'Blaccent,' but We Didn't." *The Mary Sue,* September 22, 2021. https://www.themarysue.com/awkwafina-blaccent-aave/.

Simon, Rita J., and Rhonda M. Roorda. *In Their Own Voices: Transracial Adoptees Tell Their Stories.* New York: Columbia University Press, 2000.

Sisson, Gretchen. "'I Want In': Bringing Adoption into Reproductive Justice." *Spectrum,* April 30, 2014. https://web.archive.org/web/20140813132753/http://spectrum.yourbackline.org/adoption/i-want-in-bringing-adoption-into-reproductive-justice/.

Sivigny, Deb. *Hello, My Name Is . . .* Directed by Randy Baker, The Welders, October–November 2017, Rhizome DC, Washington, DC.

Smalkoski, Kara. "China." In *Seeds from a Silent Tree: An Anthology by Korean Adoptees,* edited by Tonya Bishoff and Jo Rankin, 73–83. San Diego: Pandal Press, 1997.

Smolin, David M. "Child Laundering: How the Intercountry Adoption System Legitimizes and Incentivizes the Practices of Buying, Trafficking, Kidnapping, and Stealing Children." *Wayne Law Review* 52, no. 1 (2006): 113–200.

Sobsey, Dick, and Tanis Doe. "Patterns of Sexual Abuse and Assault." *Sexuality and Disability* 9, no. 3 (1991): 243–59.

Song, Sueyoung L., and Richard M. Lee. "The Past and Present Cultural Experiences of Adopted Korean American Adults." *Adoption Quarterly* 12, no. 1 (2009): 19–36.

Spielberg, Steven, dir. *Hook*. TriStar Pictures, 1991.

———, dir. *Indiana Jones and the Temple of Doom*. Paramount Pictures, 1984.

Stacey, Judith. *In the Name of the Family: Rethinking Family Values in the Postmodern Age*. Boston: Beacon Press, 1996.

Stearns, Elizabeth, Claudia Buchmann, and Kara Bonneau. "Interracial Friendships in the Transition to College: Do Birds of a Feather Flock Together Once They Leave the Nest?" *Sociology of Education* 82, no. 2 (April 2009): 173–95.

Stein, Valerie A. "Privileging God the Father: The Neoliberal Theology of the Evangelical Orphan Care Movement." In *The Politics of Reproduction: Adoption, Abortion, and Surrogacy in the Age of Neoliberalism,* edited by Modhumita Roy and Mary Thompson, 42–60. Columbus: The Ohio State University Press, 2019.

Stop AAPI Hate. "Reports." Accessed April 18, 2022. https://stopaapihate.org/reports/.

Strathern, Marilyn. "What Is a Parent?" *HAU: Journal of Ethnographic Theory* 1, no. 1 (November 2011): 245–78.

Stryker, Rachael. *The Road to Evergreen: Adoption, Attachment Therapy, and the Promise of Family*. Ithaca, NY: Cornell University Press, 2010.

Style, Emily. "Curriculum as Window and Mirror." National SEED Project. Accessed March 28, 2022. https://nationalseedproject.org/Key-SEED-Texts/curriculum-as-window-and-mirror.

Tajima, Renee E. "Lotus Blossoms Don't Bleed Images of Asian Women." In *Making Waves: An Anthology of Writings by and about Asian American Women,* edited by Asian Women United of California, 308–17. Boston, MA: Beacon Press, 1989.

Tang, Amy Cynthia. *Repetition and Race: Asian American Literature after Multiculturalism*. New York: Oxford University Press, 2016.

Tau, Timothy. "Interview with 'Seoul Searching' Director Benson Lee." *Hyphen,* March 10, 2015. https://hyphenmagazine.com/blog/2015/03/interview-seoul-searching-director-benson-lee.

Terrell, John, and Judith Modell. "Anthropology and Adoption." *American Anthropologist* 96, no. 1 (1994): 155–61.

Thomas, Mary E. *Multicultural Girlhood: Racism, Sexuality, and the Conflicted Spaces of American Education*. Philadelphia: Temple University Press, 2011.

Thrupkaew, Noy. "Filmic Face-Lift: Better Luck Tomorrow Makes Over Asian American Cinema." *American Prospect,* 41–42. May 1, 2003.

Toliver, Stephanie R. "Alterity and Innocence: 'The Hunger Games,' Rue, and Black Girl Adultification." *Journal of Children's Literature* 44, no. 2 (January 1, 2018): 4–15.

Townsend, Midnite. "Asian Fetishism, Consent, and Adoption." *KAAN* (blog), April 6, 2021. https://www.wearekaan.org/post/asian-fetishism.

Trenka, Jane Jeong. *Fugitive Visions: An Adoptee's Return to Korea*. Saint Paul, MN: Graywolf Press, 2009.

———. *The Language of Blood*. Saint Paul, MN: Graywolf Press, 2003.

Trenka, Jane Jeong, Julia Chinyere Oparah, and Sun Yung Shin, eds. *Outsiders Within: Writing on Transracial Adoption*. Cambridge, MA: South End Press, 2006.

Trent, James W., Jr. *Inventing the Feeble Mind: A History of Mental Retardation in the United States*. Berkeley: University of California Press, 1994.

Tuan, Mia. *Forever Foreigners or Honorary Whites? The Asian Ethnic Experience Today*. New Brunswick, NJ: Rutgers University Press, 1998.

Tuan, Mia, and Jiannbin Lee Shiao. *Choosing Ethnicity, Negotiating Race: Korean Adoptees in America*. New York: Russell Sage Foundation, 2011.

Ty, Eleanor. *The Politics of the Visible in Asian North American Narratives*. Toronto: University of Toronto Press, 2004.

Uchida, Aki. "The Orientalization of Asian Women in America." *Women's Studies International Forum* 21, no. 2 (1998): 161–74.

Ugly Delicious. Season 1, Episode 5. "BBQ." Directed by Jason Zeldes. Aired February 23, 2018, on Netflix.

US Census Bureau. *California, 2000: Census 2000 Profile*. Washington, DC: US Department of Commerce, Economics and Statistics Administration, August 2002. https://www.census.gov/prod/2002pubs/c2kprof00-ca.pdf; http://web.archive.org/web/20200502174111/https://www.census.gov/prod/2002pubs/c2kprof00-ca.pdf.

———. *California, 2000: Summary Population and Housing Characteristics*. Washington, DC: US Department of Commerce, Economics and Statistics Administration, November 2002. Accessed August 1, 2022. https://www2.census.gov/library/publications/2002/dec/phc-1-6.pdf; http://web.archive.org/web/20230405033940/https://www2.census.gov/library/publications/2002/dec/phc-1-6.pdf.

US Department of Commerce and Bureau of the Census. *1980 Census of Population and Housing Census Tracts: Dayton Ohio*. Washington, DC: Department of Commerce, July 1983. https://www2.census.gov/prod2/decennial/documents/1980/tracts-cities/CensusTracts1980-DaytonOH.pdf.

Valenti, Jessica. "Acting Older Isn't Being Older: How We Fail Young Rape Victims." *The Nation*, September 2, 2013. http://www.thenation.com/blog/175991/acting-older-isnt-being-older-how-we-fail-young-rape-victims#.

van den Dries, Linda, Femmie Juffer, Marinus H. van Ijzendoorn, and Marian J. Bakermans-Kranenburg. "Infants' Physical and Cognitive Development after International Adoption from Foster Care or Institutions in China." *Journal of Developmental & Behavioral Pediatrics* 31, no. 2 (February 2010): 144–50.

Vance, Jeannine Joy. *Twins Found in a Box: Adapting to Adoption*. Bloomington, IN: 1st Books Library, 2003.

Varzally, Allison. *Children of Reunion: Vietnamese Adoptions and the Politics of Family Migrations*. Chapel Hill: University of North Carolina Press, 2017.

Volkman, Toby Alice, ed. *Cultures of Transnational Adoption*. Durham, NC: Duke University Press, 2005.

Walsh, Brad, and Paul Cameron, writers. *Modern Family*. Season 1, Episode 6. "Run for Your Wife." Directed by Jason Winer. Aired October 28, 2009, on ABC.

Wang, Leslie K. *Outsourced Children: Orphanage Care and Adoption in Globalizing China*. Palo Alto, CA: Stanford University Press, 2016.

Wang, Lulu, dir. *The Farewell*. A24, 2019.

Wang, Wayne, dir. *The Joy Luck Club*. Walt Disney Studios Motion Pictures, 1993.

Washington, Myra S. *Blasian Invasion: Racial Mixing in the Celebrity Industrial Complex*. Jackson: University Press of Mississippi, 2017.

Weide, Robert B. "The Woody Allen Allegations: Not So Fast." *Daily Beast,* January 4, 2016. https://www.thedailybeast.com/the-woody-allen-allegations-not-so-fast.

Weitzman, Carol, and Lisa Albers. "Long-Term Developmental, Behavioral, and Attachment Outcomes after International Adoption." *Pediatric Clinics of North America* 52, no. 5 (October 2005): 1395–419.

Westerman, Ashley. "'Am I Asian Enough?' Adoptees Struggle to Make Sense of Spike in Anti-Asian Violence." *NPR,* March 27, 2021. https://www.npr.org/2021/03/27/981269559/am-i-asian-enough-adoptees-struggle-to-make-sense-of-spike-in-anti-asian-violenc.

Wexler, Jade H., Jieyi Cai, Kimberly D. McKee, Amelia Blankenau, Heewon Lee, Oh Myo Kim, Adam Y. J. Kim, and Richard M. Lee. "Understanding Adoption as a Reproductive Justice Issue." Special issue, "Reproductive Justice," edited by Laurel B. Watson, Candice Hargons, and Debra Mollen, *Psychology of Women Quarterly* (April 19, 2023). DOI: 10.1177/03616843231166376.

White, Michele. "Gaze." In *Keywords for Media Studies,* edited by Laurie Ouellette and Jonathan Gray, 75–77. New York: New York University Press, 2017.

Wilkinson, Hei Sook Park, and Nancy Fox, eds. *After the Morning Calm: Reflections of Korean Adoptees.* Bloomfield Hills, MI: Sunrise Ventures, 2002.

Williams, Mary Elizabeth. "Mia Farrow's Sex Abuse Silence." *Salon,* February 4, 2014. https://www.salon.com/2014/02/04/mia_farrows_sex_abuse_silence/.

Willing, Indigo, Anh Đào Kolbe, Dominic Golding, Tim Holtan, Cara Wolfgang, Kev Minh Allen, Adam Chau, Landa Sharp, and Michael Nhat, eds. *Vietnamese.Adopted: A Collection of Voices.* Minneapolis: CQT Media & Publishing and LGA Inc., 2015.

Wills, Jenny Heijun. "Formulating Kinship: Asian Adoption Narratives and Crime Literature." *Adoption & Culture* 5, no. 1 (2017): 64–88. https://doi.org/10.1353/ado.2017.0006.

———. "Sexy." In *When We Become Ours: A YA Adoptee Anthology,* edited by Shannon Gibney and Nicole Chung, 145–59. New York: HarperCollins, 2023.

Wills, Jenny Heijun, Tobias Hübinette, and Indigo Willing, eds. *Adoption and Multiculturalism: Europe, the Americas, and the Pacific.* Ann Arbor: University of Michigan Press, 2020.

"The Winding Career of Sandra Oh." *Fresh Air.* National Public Radio, November 23, 2004. https://www.npr.org/2004/11/23/4183846/the-winding-career-of-sandra-oh.

Windom, Saundrea Henderson. *Orchestration.* New York: Wordee, 2021.

Womendez, Chris, and Karen Schneiderman. "Escaping from Abuse: Unique Issues for Women with Disabilities." *Sexuality and Disability* 9, no. 3 (1991): 273–79.

Wong, Kristina. "A Big Bad Prank: Broadening the Definition of Asian American Feminist Activist." In *YELL-Oh Girls! Emerging Voices Explore Culture, Identity, and Growing Up Asian American,* edited by Vickie Nam, 278–83. New York: HarperCollins, 2001.

Woo, Susie. *Framed by War: Korean Children and Women at the Crossroads of US Empire.* New York: New York University Press, 2019.

Wright, Kristin. "Md. Father Charged with Adopted Son's Death." *NBC Washington,* February 19, 2014. https://www.nbcwashington.com/news/local/father-charged-with-adopted-sons-death/64189/.

Wright, Nazera Sadiq. *Black Girlhood in the Nineteenth Century.* Champaign: University of Illinois Press, 2016.

Wyver, Richey. "'More Beautiful than Something We Could Create Ourselves': Exploring Swedish International Transracial Adoption Desire." PhD diss., University of Auckland, 2020.

Yang, Jeff, and Phil Yu. "They Call Us Very Asian." *They Call Us Bruce*. Accessed January 21, 2022. https://podcasts.apple.com/ca/podcast/144-they-call-us-very-asian/id1217719299?i=1000547760628.

Yano, Christine Reiko. *Pink Globalization: Hello Kitty's Trek across the Pacific*. Durham, NC: Duke University Press, 2013.

Yi, Joanne. "Memoirs or Myths? Storying Asian American Adoption in Picturebooks." *Journal of Children's Literature* 47, no. 2 (Fall 2021): 22–34.

Yngvesson, Barbara. *Belonging in an Adopted World: Race, Identity, and Transnational Adoption*. Chicago: University of Chicago Press, 2010.

Yu, Phil. "How to Hit On an Asian Girl." *Angry Asian Man* (blog), September 8, 2011. http://blog.angryasianman.com/2011/09/how-to-hit-on-asian-girl.html.

Zelizer, Viviana A. *Pricing the Priceless Child: The Changing Social Value of Children*. Princeton, NJ: Princeton University Press, 1994.

INDEX

Adopted (film), 18

adoptees: activism, 107–8; affect and, 17, 24, 112, 114–15, 119, 120–22, 124, 134n30; affective labor of, 134n30; commodification of, 15, 24, 27, 30–32, 114, 126; counterstories of, 108, 122–23; as cute objects, 113; erasure of, 26, 125, 134n28; genetic testing of, 115–16, 144n24; interchangeability of, 21–22, 120, 133n2; mixed-race, 105; objectification of, 2–3, 26–27, 65; pathologizing of, 16–18, 79, 85, 86, 87; as perpetual children, 26–27, 62, 125. _See also_ adult adoptees

adoptees, Asian: adoptee-authored narratives, 87, 145n45 (ch. 5), 145n4 (coda); affect of, 24, 112, 124; as assimilable, 22; authenticity and, 5, 86–88, 127; belonging and, 10, 14, 34–35, 86; commodification of, 15, 24, 27; documentaries on, 43, 136n23; erasure of, 6, 134n28; fetishization of, 1–2, 4–5, 10, 12, 15, 24, 47, 62–64, 114, 127; gratitude and, 7, 64, 69, 109–10, 111–12, 114, 134n41; hypersexualization of, 8, 19, 65, 67; invisibility of, 47–48; melancholia and, 5, 7, 87–88, 127; microaggressions against, 127; model minority myth and, 22, 61–62; objectification of, 40, 81, 125; online communities, 2, 126; racial dif-

ference, erasure of, 7–8, 130n23; racialization of, 47, 60, 63; racialized sexual harassment and, 63; representation and, 3, 91–92, 110; representations in popular culture, 3, 85, 133n2; as rescued orphans, 65; seductive daughter trope, 65; sexualization of, 2, 13–16, 136n8; stereotypes of, 56; as trespassers, 65. _See also_ adoptees; adult adoptees

adoptees, Korean, 47–48, 88; adult adoptee organizations for, 97, 143n42; artists and playwrights, 132n77; as Asian American, 86–87; authenticity and, 86–87; belonging and, 86, 90, 99; community building, 25–26; culture camps, 25, 97; as diaspora, 17, 104; erasure and, 86, 98, 100–101; films directed by, 132n77; identity development of, 6, 98, 100–101, 112; isolation of, 1–2, 129n3; memoirs written by, 132n77; organizations, 2, 25, 41, 62–63; return narratives, 96–98, 104–5, 116, 143nn36–37, 143n39; sexualization of, 3, 13–14. _See also_ adoptees, Asian; adoption, Korean

adoptees, transnational, 7–9; commodification of, 6–7, 20–21, 35–36, 132n66; erasure of racial difference, 9–11, 43–44; erasure of racism and, 63–64; fetishizing

FORMATIONS: ADOPTION, KINSHIP, AND CULTURE
EMILY HIPCHEN AND JOHN MCLEOD, SERIES EDITORS

This interdisciplinary series encourages critical engagement with all aspects of nonnormative kinship—such as adoption, foster care, IVF, surrogacy, and gamete transfers—especially as they intersect with race, identity, heritage, nationality, sexuality, and gender. Books in the series explore how these constructions affect not only those personally involved but also public understandings of identity, personhood, migration, kinship, and the politics of family.

Adoption Fantasies: The Fetishization of Asian Adoptees from Girlhood to Womanhood
     KIMBERLY D. MCKEE

Adoption across Race and Nation: US Histories and Legacies
     EDITED BY SILKE HACKENESCH

The Politics of Reproduction: Adoption, Abortion, and Surrogacy in the Age of Neoliberalism
     EDITED BY MODHUMITA ROY AND MARY THOMPSON